Praise for *Magical Thinking*

"One of the most compelling and screamingly funny voices of the new century belongs to Augusten Burroughs. . . . [He] is blessed with an offbeat perspective and a viciously uncensored wit. . . . Perhaps it is Burroughs's versatility—he can write about love without being cloying, he can describe being an alcoholic without being boring, he can write about his demented family without self-pity—that makes him such a delight to read."
—*USA Today*

"Here's what happens when you read an Augusten Burroughs memoir: You smirk, you laugh, your jaw drops in disbelief, and then you go hug your parents if they were even remotely nice to you." —*Boston Herald*

"Contains riveting descriptions, wise commentary, and touching observations about the nature of family and love. . . . These are tales of domesticity and dogs, tiffs and tenderness, to which anyone who's ever coupled up will relate. Here is the sweetness that perfectly offsets the cynical in Burroughs's thinking, and it truly is magical."
—*The Hartford Courant*

"*Magical Thinking* spans Burroughs's life—he tells us more stories from his weird childhood, and more from the neurotic adulthood that followed. As before, the writing is funny and grotesque. . . . He is very cruel, and also very soft. . . . For the third time, then, Burroughs wins you over."
—*Evening Standard* (London)

"Burroughs's latest collection of true stories are funny, outrageous, revealing. . . . It is hard to believe that one man has had so many strange things happen to him but oddities seek Burroughs out. . . . He is damn funny and, for that, you just can't help but like the man."
—*The Observer*

"Augusten Burroughs's new collection speaks to the devil in us all. . . . As with fellow essayist David Sedaris, Burroughs writes about anything that his wonderfully warped mind desires."
—*Time Out* New York

"Differently delightful is *Magical Thinking* by delightfully different Augusten Burroughs. The autobiographical admixture that made his *Running with Scissors* such an international bestseller—the personal,

P9-DCD-330

the persuasively perverse, and the perceptive—is here in abundance, as is astute observation."

—*The Weekend Australian*

"Burroughs possesses a mind-set best described as superlatively disturbed. . . . Brimming with bawdy language and bodily fluids, this volume by a man 'made entirely of flaws, stitched together with good intentions,' offers an irresistible display of sanity hanging by a thread."

—*Booklist* (starred review)

"This collection showcases Burroughs's sharp, funny, and sometimes brilliant writing. . . . Burroughs's smooth prose, peppered with charming and awkward moments, is occasionally reminiscent of David Sedaris and David Rakoff. But he's no imitator of those essayists. Rather, Burroughs ambles toward insight in a continual state of self-examination and just happens to have peculiar adventures along the way."

—*Publishers Weekly*

"Taking quotations from a book like this is difficult, because you find it hard to stop. Even choosing stories or essays to highlight is difficult. . . . His is the kind of voice that has a reader wondering how he does it with so little apparent effort. Funny, poignant, sometimes restrained, sometimes loudly vulgar, satire that verges on lampoon, nastiness hidden in an open smile; Burroughs turns introspection into a spectator sport. A book to be read slowly and with envy."

—*The Canberra Times* (Australia)

"The cheerfully self-obsessed Burroughs is a sharp and unabashed monologist, connecting with readers through sizzling humor and the profoundly accurate eye for absurdity. . . . Often giddily profane, Burroughs also is capable of dizzying tenderness, and his writing . . . resonates an appealing hope. . . . The journeys in [this collection] are funny and warm, imaginative and irresistible, and you don't even need a passport to go along."

—*The Miami Herald*

"That is the thing about Burroughs. He may at first appear only to be interested in extracting laughs from the more embarrassing moments in his life, but they often unfurl into something unexpectedly poignant. Each keeps you guessing as to how it will end. . . . A fine and very funny storyteller."

—*The Irish Times*

"Fans of Augusten Burroughs's hilarious and bizarre childhood memoir *Running with Scissors* may have feared he'd used his best material.

Happily, this isn't the case. *Magical Thinking* . . . is no cheap imitation. Burroughs once again comes up with gold. . . . This is wonderfully funny stuff."
—*Australian Family Circle*

"Listen, [Burroughs] seems to be saying, I know I'm an egotistical, self-involved wreck, so let's all enjoy the laugh on me. . . . He's still a funny, sharp writer and *Magical Thinking* reads breezily along."
—*Star Tribune* (Minneapolis, St. Paul)

"[Burroughs] is an outrageously addictive personality in both senses of the term, a disturbed writer who entertains with his inner pain."
—*Chicago Sun-Times*

"This latest book confirms that Burroughs is a hilarious and skilled raconteur—he's so awful, it's hard not to like him."
—*Metro* (London)

"Sit back and get uncomfortable. . . . He's so good with the turn of a phrase or nailing down an entire subculture with one sentence that readers will nod their heads in recognition . . . He can sound so lucid, charming, and self-actualized that by the time things ride off the rails, you're right there in the front seat, laughing with the map open on your lap, when all you intended to do was offer directions to the nearest mental-health professional, then slowly back away."
—*The Oregonian* (Portland)

"Burroughs is as erudite as Sedaris, although more out of left field. Sedaris typically finds his humor in mundane reality. Burroughs mines the fantastic and delusional."
—*The Sun-Herald*

"Raise your hand if you've ever been cast in elementary school for a Tang commercial only to be left on the cutting-room floor, drowned a rat in your bathtub, had the roof of your mouth splayed open by a dentist on a routine visit, or had a gay fling with an undertaker in the same viewing room where Rose Kennedy's wake took place. . . . What keeps us laughing and turning the pages even as we shudder at the thought of these experiences is Burroughs's unflagging humor, relentless optimism, and endearingly self-deprecating style."
—*BookPage*

"I'm an Augusten Burroughs addict so the publication of his 'secret notebooks' fills me with glee. *Magical Thinking* is a collection of his wicked and warped observations."
—*The Independent Weekly* (Australia)

"His hilarious take on the banal is the book's driving force, but it's his unflinching honesty—openly fantasizing about his enemies' horrific deaths—that makes it unforgettable."   —*City Weekly*

"Augusten Burroughs is the sort of writer who likes to tell embarrassing stories about himself, but he's not begging for a group hug. . . . [He] sinks to a queasy greatness."   —*Boston Magazine*

"*Magical Thinking* explodes like a Chinese rocket in the face of the unsuspecting reader. . . . Open the book anywhere, and chances are good you'll be hooting, if not grinning, by the end of a chapter. . . . Brimming with brio and outrageous fun . . . Burroughs is a national treasure whose ideas are delightful to read."   —*The Denver Post*

"Burroughs's touch is light and his self-deprecating humor handled with consummate skill."   —*The Newcastle Herald*

"Augusten Burroughs confirms his reputation as one of the funniest, sharpest, and most poignant writers in America today with this, his third volume of autobiographical vignettes. . . . It's a superbly funny, touching, and surprisingly personal book that swings between uproarious humor and devastating pathos. His is almost an unique voice: it's not quite a collection of short, biographical stories, not quite a collection of musings, not quite a novel, and not quite autobiography. It is, however, brilliantly engaging. Read it in one sitting."   —*Gay Times*

"More zany Americana is on offer in Augusten Burroughs's *Magical Thinking,* a set of hilarious autobiographical vignettes."   —*Condé Nast Traveller*

"Augusten Burroughs is a natural storyteller . . . as brilliantly witty, waspish, and self-deprecating as ever."   —*Daily Mail* (U.K.)

"The stories are more like essays: mad, sad, funny meditations on life."   —*Brisbane News*

"Burroughs getting fuzzy-kitten cute? Well, withhold your collective 'awwws' because Burroughs still exists in a screwy world, and he's not about to lose his edgy view of it. . . . Even wallowing in happiness, Burroughs keeps his scissors sharpened."   —*San Francisco Chronicle*

"Dementedly original and unstoppable, Burroughs deserves a shelf all to himself."   —*Kirkus Reviews*

ALSO BY AUGUSTEN BURROUGHS

SELLEVISION

RUNNING WITH SCISSORS

DRY

POSSIBLE SIDE EFFECTS

MAGICAL THINKING

◆

TRUE STORIES

AUGUSTEN BURROUGHS

PICADOR

ST. MARTIN'S PRESS

NEW YORK

MAGICAL THINKING: TRUE STORIES. Copyright © 2004, 2005 by Island Road, L.L.C. All rights reserved. Printed in the United States of America. For information, address Picador, 175 Fifth Avenue, New York, N.Y. 10010.

www.picadorusa.com

Picador® is a U.S. registered trademark and is used by St. Martin's Press under license from Pan Books Limited.

For information on Picador Reading Group Guides, as well as ordering, please contact Picador.
Phone: 646-307-5626
Fax: 212-253-9627
Email: readinggroupguides@picadorusa.com.

Design by Phil Mazzone

Library of Congress Cataloging-in-Publication Data

Burroughs, Augusten.
  Magical thinking / Augusten Burroughs.
    p. cm.
  ISBN 0-312-31595-3
  EAN 978-0-312-31595-5
  1. Burroughs, Augusten.   2. Novelists, American—20th century—
Biography.   I. Title.

PS3552.U745Z472   2004
813'.6—dc22

                                                              2004046785

First published in the United States by St. Martin's Press

10   9   8   7   6   5

SOME NAMES HAVE BEEN CHANGED.

FOR ROBISONSERVICE.COM

Contents

ACKNOWLEDGMENTS

It takes an awful lot of work by a large number of people to turn what I write into a book. My deepest gratitude and thanks to: Jennifer Enderlin, Christopher Schelling, Sally Richardson, John Sargent, John Murphy, Gregg Sullivan, Frances Coady, John Cunningham, Matthew Shear, Matt Baldacci, George Witte, Carrie Hamilton Jones, Nancy Trypuc, Darin Keesler, Kim Cardascia, Edward Allen, Nicole Liebowitz, James Sinclair, Steve Snider, Steve Cohen, Christina Harcar, Kerry Nordling, Alison Lazarus, Jeff Capshew, Ken Holland, Merrill Bergenfeld, Andy LeCount, Tom Siino, Mark Kohut, Rob Renzler, and the entire Broadway sales force. Much appreciation to Dan Peres at *Details* magazine. And the folks at NPR's *Morning Edition*. A few pieces in this collection originally ran on Salon.com in an earlier form, and I thank them for letting me publish them here. Thank you, Ryan Murphy and Mark Bozek. And thank you, Chip Kidd, for your beautiful covers. And K, what can I even say? I'd beat up anybody for you. With love for: John, Judy, Bob and Relda Robison, Haven Kimmel, Lawrence David, Suzanne Finnamore, Lynda Pearson, Millie Olson, Russell Nuce, Jon Pepoon, John DePretis, and Lori Greenberg. I am so happy to be in contact with David Machowski and Greg Fanslow again. Gratitude to Dr. Janet Zayas for suggesting the title of this book. And very special thanks to Norm Vexler for building us a beautiful, beautiful home, perfect to within 1/100th of an inch. Most of all, I want to thank Dennis Pilsits for just everything.

MAGICAL THINKING: A schizotypal personality disorder attributing to one's own actions something that had nothing to do with him or her and thus assuming that one has a greater influence over events than is actually the case.

COMMERCIAL BREAK

When I was seven, I was plucked from my uneventful life deep in darkest Massachusetts and dropped into a Tang Instant Breakfast Drink commercial. It was exactly like being abducted by aliens except without the anal probe. I was a lonely kid with entirely imaginary friends. I played with trees.

Then, one day during penmanship class, a white van pulled up in front of our little gray schoolhouse, and the men from Tang climbed out.

My elementary school sat atop a low grassy hill in the center of Shutesbury, a small New England town that was so "small New England town" one had the sensation of existing within a snow globe at a souvenir shop. The mailboxes at the local post office had ornate brass doors with etched-glass windows. There was a white church with solid mahogany pews and a pipe organ. A small red library was tucked on the edge of the town square and carried books about local birds and field mice. It was retchingly quaint.

Of course, in this wholesome idyllic community, my school was the anchor. It was a gray clapboard building, two stories tall, with shutters. There was a steeple on top and inside a bell that worked. The door was bright red. There were two apple trees on either side. The playground consisted of a sandbox, two swing sets, and an area of blacktop on which was painted a hopscotch outline.

Now that I am an adult and have wasted much of my life as an advertising executive, I can easily imagine the conversation that must have taken place among the occupants of that van, upon their seeing my schoolhouse.

"So Cronkite was grilling the guy, you know? Just really asking the tough questions. Then they cut away to Nixon, and boy oh boy, you should have seen his face. It was li—"

"Jesus fucking Christ, Mitch. Get a load of that."

"Huh? Oh, mother of fucking God. STOP THE VAN."

"Christ, there's even a bell on top."

"Love those trees. But are those actually apples? Christ, yes, those are apples. The client's gonna hate that. Apples clash with the orange flavor."

"So we'll cut 'em down and throw up a couple of maple trees. What's the fucking difference?"

"You know, you couldn't build a set this perfect in Burbank, you really couldn't. This is so New England schoolhouse. We have hit pay dirt, gents. I think we've got a few triple martinis ahead of us tonight."

I was sitting in Mrs. Ames's tedious penmanship class looking out the window when the white van pulled into the circular drive-way. I watched as a window was rolled halfway down and two lit cigarettes were tossed out. Then the doors opened, and the men stepped out.

Mrs. Ames noticed, too, because she paused in the middle of looping a *D*. When she turned her ancient neck to the window, my mind added the sound effect of a branch creaking under the weight of snow before it snaps. I was quite sure that Mrs. Ames was one of the original settlers of the town. She once said that television was "nonsense, just a fad like radio."

Visitors were uncommon at our school. Especially visitors dressed in dark suits, wearing sunglasses, and carrying black brief-cases. These were like the men who followed President Nixon around and whispered things in his ear.

"Remain seated and do not talk," Mrs. Ames said, glaring at us down the point of her nose. "I shall return in a moment." She quickly brushed her hands down the front of her heavy gray wool skirt to remove any wrinkles. She straightened the dainty single pearl that hung around her neck, centering it perfectly between her breasts, which were certainly bound with ace bandages beneath her crisp white shirt.

The group of men removed their sunglasses in unison, raised their chins in the air, and inhaled. I could tell they were inhaling because they slapped at their chests and flared their nostrils. It was a familiar gesture. Many of my mother's friends from New York City or Boston did the same thing when they came to Shutesbury. Personally, I could never understand why, because the air was thick with pollen and insects. If one wanted fresh air, why not just open the door to the clothes drier and stick your face in there?

One of the men approached the school, came right up to the window, and knocked on the wood next to the glass. "It's real, all right," he called back to his associates.

A moment later, Mrs. Ames joined the men outside and, to my horror, smiled. I'd never seen Mrs. Ames smile before, and the thought had never occurred to me that such an act was even possible for her. But there it was, her mouth open in the white daylight, her teeth exposed. One of the men stepped forward, removed his sunglasses, and said something to her. She touched her hair with her hand and *laughed*. Kimberly Plumme, who liked to insert marbles into her vagina at recess, said, "Gross." Her lips frowned in disgust. I myself was horrified to see Mrs. Ames laugh. And then blush. To see her in such a state of obvious bliss was unbearable. I had to look away.

Eventually, Mrs. Ames walked back into the room, and I watched her legs, all plump and plastic-looking through her support hose. She wore high heels of an unfashionable style that made a sharp, angry *sklack* against the tile floor when she walked. She was kind only to the girls. And by "kind," I mean she was not mean. She was punishing to the boys, even the prissy, girly boys like me. But for once, she had something to say that interested me.

"Children, children, may I have your attention please?" She clapped her hands together quickly. *Smacksmacksmacksmacksmack.*

But this was unnecessary because she already had our full attention. We'd been sitting there waiting for her, not daring to breathe lest we disturb the balance of the universe, causing her to fall and die and then not be able to tell us why the men had come to our school. Or worse: somehow cause the men to simply drive away.

"We have some very special surprise guests here today." She looked to the door and nodded, and the men entered the room. "Hi kids," they said. "Hi there, everyone."

It was thrilling to hear them speak in their deep, baritone voices and to see, up close, the dark razor stubble that shadowed their chins. At the same time, an exotic aroma entered the room, one that made me feel light-headed and flushed, like I'd been on a pogo stick. Only as an adult would I be able to name this intoxicating scent: English Leather.

Mrs. Ames continued. "These men are from New York City. And I hope you all know where New York City is. Because we have studied our geography quite a bit this year. Does everyone here know where New York City is?"

We nodded yes, but we all thought, *What's the matter with you, crazy old witch? Why is your face so red?*

Although it alarmed me to recognize that my own face was red, as well. Something about the presence of the men made both Mrs. Ames and me turn red and become hot. The fact that we had this in common made me wonder what was wrong with me.

"Good. Well, then. These men are here to make a television commercial."

Here, I almost peed. She might as well have told me that as of today, I never had to come to school ever again and for that matter was free to hit anybody I wanted to, without being punished. I *lived* for television commercials. The only reason I watched TV was so that I could see the commercials. Faberge Organics Shampoo: "I told two friends. And they told two friends. And so on . . . and so on . . . and so on." Or my current favorite: "Gee, your hair smells terrific!" I was also fond of the commercial with the dog chasing the chuck wagon underneath the kitchen sink: "It makes its own rich gravy."

I watched one of the men scan the faces in the room. Occasionally he would jab his friend on the shoulder and nod in the direction of one of the students. As I was watching him he caught my eye and smiled. I thought he was a very friendly man, very nice. I admired his crisp dark suit, white shirt, and black tie. His hair was thick and glossy, combed back. I smiled at him. He nudged his friend and nodded in my direction, and then the other man looked at me. He smiled, too.

I wanted to jump up out of my seat and run to the men, hugging them around the legs. I wanted to lick the hair on their wrists.

Mrs. Ames announced to the class, "These men would like to use our schoolhouse in a commercial for their special beverage. It's called Tang. Do any of you know Tang?"

There were gasps in the room. *Of course* we knew Tang, the orange crystalline powder that the astronauts brought with them to outer space. I loved Tang and would sometimes eat it by the teaspoon, straight from the jar. I loved the green label, the orange lid. The way the lid was extra wide and easy to unscrew. I even liked the paper eardrum that was over the mouth of the lid when you first opened the jar. You had to puncture the eardrum with a spoon, and printed on top was "Tang, Tang, Tang."

My mother despised Tang. "I've just made this fresh tangerine juice and put it into this nice clay pitcher I bought at the Leverette Arts Center, and you want that god-awful artificial junk." She did like cinnamon DYNAMINTS, though.

Mrs. Ames told us that the men from the van wanted to use some of *us* in their commercial. "Not all of you, now. Only some of you. They're going to have to choose."

Instantly, the students began raising their hands. Except for me. Some voice inside me said, "Don't do it. It's beneath you." Instead, I sat politely at my desk with my hands clasped firmly together. I was very pleased that I'd thought to wear my fourteen-karat-gold electroplated ID bracelet that day. One thing was certain: I would be in their Tang commercial. And if any of the other children tried to get in my way, I would use my pencil to blind them.

"So these men would like to separate everybody into groups and then ask each group a few questions."

Chaos erupted as the kids began to screech with excitement. Desks were shoved back, chairs knocked over. Mrs. Ames tried to gain control of her students by slapping her ruler against the edge of her globe. "Now, now, now, silence! Stop this! Children, come to attention at once!"

Reluctantly, the class came to attention, facing the flag and placing their hands over their hearts, ready to recite the Pledge of Allegiance.

"No, not that," she said. "Just stand still and be silent."

Eventually, we were split up into groups of three. Then group by group the men met with the kids.

I stared hatefully at the back of Lisa Tucker's fat head. I was trying to determine where the odor she emitted was coming from. A hole? Some sort of vent for her brain? I hated Lisa, and so did everyone else. She smelled like feet and something worse, something spoiled and eggy. And she was mean. She was a strong girl who pushed the boys around. Her older brother, Tommy, was one of the big kids who went to the new school down the street. Once he hit me so hard he knocked the wind out of me. I wished that Lisa and Tommy would go swimming in the ocean and be eaten by Jaws. Surely the men would know not to cast her in their commercial.

When it was finally my turn, the men were tired, as evidenced by their loosened ties and the large wet spots that spread from under their arms. They'd spoken to all thirty kids and had notes splayed out on the table in front of them. They looked funny sitting in our small chairs, which had never seemed small before.

The man who had first smiled at me said, "Hi guys. So do any of you want to be in a commercial?" He looked at me when he said this, and I got the feeling that he had already chosen me. His eyes said, *You are special and better than all the other children, and I would like you to come live with me and my blue eyes in a city far away from here.* His eyes said, *I will save you.*

We all nodded our heads yes.

"Good then. Good. So what I want to do is, I want to see if you can laugh. I'm gonna tell you a joke, and I just want to see what you sound like when you laugh. Ready?"

The other children nodded, I thought, like puppets. I smiled and winked at him, like I'd seen people do on TV.

He winked back and nudged the man on his left.

"Okay," he said. Then he raised his voice and made a comical face. "Your mother wears army boots!"

Neither of the other kids laughed.

I tossed my head back in an explosion of delight and laughed so hard I was able to bring tears to my eyes. My face was flushed, my hands dripping with sweat from the pressure.

"Wow," said the man. "You really liked that joke, did you?"

His friend turned to him. "Yeah, Phil, you're a real laugh-riot."

I quickly looked back and forth between the two men, but I wasn't sure what was going on between them. Had I laughed *before* the punch line? Or was it a trick joke? Had I just blown my chance?

"Do you kids like Tang?" he asked.

The other two kids nodded grimly.

"I love Tang!" I gushed. "Only I like to make it with an extra scoop. Plus, you can put it in ice cube trays and then freeze it! That's *really* good."

Where had that come from? I'd never in my life frozen Tang.

"That's great!" said the man with the blue eyes who was going to take me away to live with him in a penthouse apartment.

All of the men exchanged a look. Then my man said, "Thanks a lot, kids."

Disgusting Evan and retarded Ellen immediately pushed their chairs back from the table and fled. But I was crushed, stunned, so I moved in slow motion, carefully rising from my chair. *They might as well run over me with their white Tang van now,* I thought.

"Uh, no. Not you. What's your name?"

"Augusten?" I said.

"Yes, you, Augusten. You were great. We want you." It was the man with the blue eyes speaking, and now I had my confirmation: he adores me, too. Instantly, my mood reversed, and I began to grind my teeth in joy.

I can now trace my manic adult tendencies to this moment. It was the first time I felt deeply thrilled about something just a fraction of an instant after being completely crushed. I believe those three words "We want you" were enough to cause my brain to rewire itself, and from then on, I would require MORE than other people. At the same time, my tolerance for alcohol was instantly increased, and a new neural pathway was created for the future appreciation of crack cocaine and prescription painkillers.

"You want me?" I said, containing my enthusiasm so completely that I probably appeared disinterested.

"Well, yeah. Don't you want to be in the commercial?"

"Well, yeah. A lot." I tried to imitate an excited boy. I was excited but somehow unable to express the actual emotion of excitement. My electrical system was all off now.

"Good," he said clapping his hands. Then he slid a stack of papers across the table. "Then you need to take these home and have your parents read them over very carefully. We're going to be back Monday."

The ride home on the school bus was excruciatingly long. Only ten of us had been chosen to be in the commercial, so the rest of the kids were sullen. Chad, who hadn't been chosen, sat with his head pressed against the window, crying.

Piggy Lisa hadn't been chosen either, and this had made her nasty. She blew spit balls through a straw until she accidentally hit the school bus driver, Mr. Ed. Mr. Ed hit the brakes and glared into his rearview mirror, scanning our faces to see if he could tell which kid was guilty. He was missing one of his front teeth. This made us (or was it just me?) think of him not as a man but as an animal, capable of inflicting great pain and possibly death. "Little girl," he growled at Piggy Lisa, "you spit one more of them thingies at me and I'll come right on over there and milk them little titties a yours like you was a cow."

That shut her up. Piggy Lisa sank into her seat and folded her arms across her fatty chest.

Wendy was the prettiest girl in school, so of course she had been chosen. But Wendy was mentally lazy, relying on her looks alone to see her through life. She was what we called "a dip."

"What does it mean? What does it mean?" she kept asking over and over. She was entirely ecstatic, rising from her seat frequently and twirling around to ask the other kids, "But what does it mean?" Constantly, she tucked her long blonde hair behind her ears.

"It means, you dip, that you're gonna be in some dumb TV commercial for dumb old Tang." This was spoken by Gary, who, because of my powerful mental powers, also hadn't been chosen.

I sat quietly on the middle hump seat over the wheel and tried to contain my insane excitement by staring out the window, and thinking of television cameras.

But as soon as I got home, I sprinted up our gravel driveway and threw open the front door, screaming "I'm gonna be in a Tang commercial! I'm gonna be in a Tang commercial!"

My mother was talking on the phone and smoking a cigarette.

I screamed into her other ear, "I'm gonna be in a Tang commercial! They want me!"

She winced and pulled away, then spoke into the phone. "I have to go, Dee. Augusten's home, and he's hysterical."

As soon as she hung up, I pounced on her again, shrieking about how I was going to *be on TV!!!* I told her that she had to sign the papers right now so I could bring them back to school.

Unfazed, my mother set her cigarette in the clamshell ashtray and uncapped her Flair pen. She signed the papers without reading them and passed them back to me. "Just don't bring home any animals," she said. Then she took a long drag from her cigarette and added, "Who knows? Maybe now you'll become a famous television star like you've always wanted. Then you can move away from your father and me and go live in a mansion in Hollywood."

I inhaled sharply, as if slapped. *YES*, I thought. With an electric gate in front and a tiki lounge by the pool.

Obsessions with television talk shows, movie stars, mirrors, and anything gold-plated had defined my personality from an early age. This trait baffled my highly educated and bookish parents. Whereas my mother loved teak, I favored simulated wood grain. My father's appreciation for old farm tractors was an interesting counterpoint to my fixation on white stretch limousines and Rolls Royce grills.

Although my parents couldn't stand each other day to day, the one thing they did agree on was that I was very different from them. "Where did you come from?" my mother asked me one afternoon as I used a Q-Tip to clean between the links on my gold-tone Twist-O-Flex watchband. Or "Where on earth did you ever hear of such a thing?" my father wanted to know when I told him that even the plumbing in the toilets was made of solid gold at the Vanderbilt's Breakers mansion.

At Christmas, my mother decorated our tree with strands of cranberries and popcorn that she strung together herself, Danish Santas, and antique clear light bulbs. I, on the other hand, saved up my allowance for a good five months for my own artificial Christmas tree, which I kept in my bedroom, festooned with silver tinsel, thick ropes of gold garland, and lights that flashed spastically and constantly. I bought spray snow, which I applied in artful, yet natural windswept patterns, to my windows. I illuminated my tree with my desk lamp, as though it were on a set.

In preparation for my television acting debut, I watched commercials incessantly, committing them to memory and reciting key phrases endlessly to my parents.

"Can I help you fry the chicken?" I mimicked in a high-pitched southern girl's voice.

"I wanna help," I countered in a different high-pitched southern girl's voice.

Then, imitating their mother, I said, "I don't fry chicken anymore. I use new Shake 'N Bake."

I loved to sing jingles. "That great Pepsi taste. Diet Pepsi won't go to your waist. Now you see it. Now you don't. Oh, Diet Pepsi one small calorie. Now you see it. Now you don't."

Sometimes I got the words wrong, but my intentions were true.

"Let's get Mikey to try it. He won't eat it; he hates everything!"

My father, a professor at the University of Massachusetts, couldn't bear my constant performing. "Jesus, son. What's the matter with you? If you don't stop that noise, you won't be in any commercial at all. You'll be right back in your room practicing penmanship."

This muted me, briefly. Long enough to contemplate his sudden death and wonder how I would ever be able to produce convincing tears. Onions, I'd heard, could do the trick if you applied just a small bit of the juice right under your eye. I went into the kitchen and tried this myself, thrilled with the weepy, sincere results. *Oh Dad! Boo-hoo-hoo.*

My mother was slightly more understanding. "He's amazing the way he can just memorize every commercial on the air. You have to admit, he does seem to be made for acting."

And with those words, my mother had cursed me.

The director was a very round man, of face and of fist. His hands were clenched into tight little red balls as he stomped over to me yet again and asked, "Why is this so hard for you?"

Again, I'd missed my mark and spoken my one line too early, out of sight of the camera. I knew my line so well; I'd practiced it in every room of my home, under every lighting condition. Yet now, on the day of the shoot and with the camera trained on me, I couldn't get it right.

"All you have to do is say 'Hey, Mark, where are you going?'

That's all you have to say. Why are you having so much trouble with this?" he asked me, unable to hide his obvious hatred of attractive, brilliant children.

"I don't know," I said, again. "Something is throwing me out of character."

This infuriated him. "What are you talking about, *character*? You're a kid in a school . . . playing a kid in a school! This is not *On the Waterfront*."

We'd been shooting for over an hour. It was a simple setup: I'm walking behind a group of other kids in the hall when I suddenly see my friend, Mark. I pause, turn toward the camera—though without looking at it—and say, "Hey, Mark, where are you going?"

But I just couldn't do it.

The thing is, I'd known since the men first uttered the words "Tang commercial" that I was perfect for this role. All I had to do was be my natural, born-for-it self. But something had gone catastrophically wrong. In my obsession to be a perfectly natural boy for the camera, I was unable to be even vaguely natural, let alone perfect.

And each time I spoke my line, my voice sounded forced, pretentious, dishonest. These were concepts I'd gleaned from a copy of *Acting: A Handbook of the Stanislavski Method*, which I'd found in my mother's bookshelf.

The other problem was that I didn't feel I had found my character's own space within the context of the scene. Why was I walking down the hall? Was I going *to* a class? Or coming *from* a class? These were essential questions, and the director refused to give me answers.

"Will you shut up and just walk!" was what he said.

"But when I walk, do you want me to be walking with urgency or relief?" was my reply.

"Oh Jesus Christ, can we get another kid?" he shouted over his shoulder.

It was my full intention to be so convincing as a normal school child that when these advertising executives got back to New York City they wouldn't be able to forget me. Or else someone important—like Carol Burnett—would see me in the Tang commercial and then call my parents and request that I be flown out to Hollywood immediately.

"Let's try this one more time," the director shouted as he walked back to his position behind the camera. He shook his head from side to side, as the light drained from the sky.

He shouted *action*, and I began my walk down the hallway, fully aware of the camera trained on my every move. I concentrated hard on being normal, on making ordinary footsteps. But I could feel it happening. Like being the passenger in a car speeding out of control, I was unable to stop myself. In a high-pitched and overly rehearsed tone of voice, I recited my line and again peeked at the camera to make sure I'd reached my mark correctly.

I winced as I waited for the director to again scream "Cut!" but instead there was silence. And then I felt a rush. Had I done it? Had I accidentally done it exactly right? I had done it right, hadn't I? I bit my lip to repress the smile that was about to break the surface.

"Forget it. We'll fix it in the edit. This is a wrap!"

And that was it.

I saw the men in the suits standing in a huddle near the director, smoking cigarettes. The man who loved me, the man with the blue eyes, now glanced at me once sharply, then looked away.

Had I failed him?

The men packed up, leaving behind a piece of paper with the dates and times that the commercial was supposed to run on the air.

At home my mother marked the calendar and counted down the days.

I wondered what I would look like on TV. Would the part in my hair be straight? Would it be shiny? I'd used conditioner every night for a week. I wondered if I'd said my lines naturally, after all. Had I given them enough to work with in the edit? I'd been reading quite a bit about filmmaking, and it was amazing how much could be "saved" by a gifted editor.

Then the day arrived. My mother turned on the *Today Show*, and we watched for nearly an hour before it came on.

I saw myself for a split second, in back of Wendy and a bunch of other kids. Wendy said, "Hey, let's go get some!" and the scene changed to Mrs. Ames at home serving Tang to her grandchildren for the rest of the commercial.

My line had been cut. "Where were you?" my mother asked at the end. "Are you sure that's the right one?"

Mrs. Ames had hijacked the commercial. Mrs. Ames and Wendy, who, it seemed, was playing the role of Mrs. Ames's grand-daughter. Wendy, so pretty and noncurious lazy, had been the only child in the commercial to speak.

"Where were you?" my mother cried again at the end. "Are you really sure that's the right commercial?"

"I'm sure," I mumbled, crushed by my own failure.

My grandmother called from Georgia. My mother answered the phone. "No, Momma, we saw it, too. But I didn't see Augusten. He says that's the commercial."

Depressed, I walked out of the kitchen and down the hall to my bedroom.

"Hey, Mark, where are you going?" I said to my mirror, in a tone of voice so natural and plain I realized at once that this is what the director had wanted all along. He didn't want passion, interpretation, meaning, and nuance. He wanted an ordinary kid who could say six words.

Fine, I decided, right there on my bed. I won't be a child actor in television commercials. Instead, I will be the one who thinks up the commercials in the first place. And then I will hire the director myself, and when he can't make the kid give me a passionate, meaningful, and nuanced performance, I'll fire him.

I got up from my bed and went into the bathroom to retrieve a tube of Crest. I brought it back into my bedroom. And studied the tube.

What could I ever think of that would make a person want to buy this stuff?

VANDERBILT GENES

When I was ten years old, I realized I'd been kid-napped as a toddler. Of course, I would have to have been a fairly dim child to miss the clues. Great big pink-elephant clues, trumpeting and lumbering and shitting through the house, ignored by everyone except me. Both of my parents spoke with thick Georgia accents and I did not. Both had a fondness for canned green beans and I did not. Both of them *and* my older brother had straight brown hair, whereas I had a mane of blond curls that my mother's friends always commented on. "Like an angel," they cooed. "Like a girl," the man who installed our new septic system said. Yet there was something else: a primal knowledge. I just *had a feeling about it*. But it was on a family trip to Newport,

Rhode Island, when I learned that I had, in fact, been not merely kidnapped but stolen from the finest family in American history.

My father had decided on a weekend touring the mansions: colossal palaces built on the sea cliffs in the eighteen-hundreds, summer homes for the Rockefellers, the man who invented the paper clip, and yes, the Vanderbilts.

The Vanderbilt estate was called The Breakers. It was the most popular tourist attraction because it was the most astonishingly lavish, a structure that made the White House seem more like a double-wide. The moment I stepped inside the grand foyer, I knew I belonged there. The feeling was similar to what it must be like to be a twin, separated at birth, and then reunited years later on television. I seemed to recognize the lavishly carved ceiling, the gilt mirror, the absence of white shag carpeting, like we had "at home."

The tour guide was very strict: we had to stay in a neat pack, like crayons. We were not to finger the tapestries, sit on the chairs, or lick the paintings. We were to follow, listen, and be awed by our own smallness.

My first instinct was to inform the appalling tourists and my so-called parents that they must all leave immediately. I wanted to point back to the entrance and announce: "I'm sorry, people. But there has been a mistake. You must now leave my home and return to your busses. The rottweilers are being brought up from the wine cellar."

An overpowering sixth sense engaged, and I knew what each room would look like without even needing to explore.

How, I wondered, had I been kidnapped by a southern couple with Del Monte green bean breath? How could it have happened that I would end up being raised by common academic trash? My father, a professor, and my mother, a graduate student earning her M.F.A.—these people had no business with me.

Of course, my "parents" were suitably impressed with the majesty of the house, but I felt possessive and sullen. They walked enthusiastically through the rooms, commenting on the splendor, while I lagged behind them, just at the edge of another family.

When the tour guide pointed to a gold faucet fixture in one of the gargantuan master bathrooms and remarked, "These faucets feature hot and cold running seawater," I glared at my parents. *See what I used to enjoy?* I tried to recall if I'd ever sat in that tub. A dim memory floated to the surface, but a memory without any images, only a taste on the tip of my tongue: sea salt.

Our own faucets had hot and cold running *tap* water, the same plain water that everyone in town had, even the Latts, with their Down's syndrome girl, who lived in a shack near the dump. Our own bathtub featured a permanent dark ring of grime compliments of my older brother, who was seventeen and learning to repair car engines. A common grease monkey, someone who would hit me on the shoulder with the serrated edge of the aluminum foil box and then laugh as pinpricks of blood bloomed through the starched white dress shirt that I always wore. My brother was a farm animal, a grunting primitive. *Not* a Vanderbilt. Certainly not suitable for this vacation to Newport. He had thankfully stayed home with his pet car.

I saw my self, my other self—the one who lived in a parallel universe and had not been stolen—hiding behind the heavy velvet drapes in the formal living room, while my mother searched for me, silk and gold-thread slippers on her feet, martini glass poised in her hand, pinkie extended. "Amadeus?" she was calling out through the vast home, peering behind tufted sofas, under four-poster beds. "Come out, come out wherever you are." In the vision, I am smiling behind a large Ming vase, thinking about dashing outside and scratching the ears of my pet camel.

I also knew with certainty that I was an only child. I had learned about only children at school, and everything those only children felt, I felt. The feeling hit me, too, in the Vanderbilt mansion. Why else would it be unoccupied, a museum? My real parents had been hopelessly distraught when I was taken, neither of them able to bear such extravagance in the face of such unthinkable loss. "Amadeus," my mother would have wept. "Every tassel reminds me of him. All these marble columns he used to dance around." My father would have wiped a tear from his own eye, the memory of me being placed in his arms by my Scandinavian wet nurse while he sat in the library too much for him to contain. Of course they would have sold the estate, at a loss. Unloaded it to the state. "Do whatever vulgar thing you want to with it; I don't care. Sell tickets, print postcards—it just doesn't matter," my mother would have told the governor.

The tour guide pointed to a painting of Cornelius Vanderbilt hanging above a fireplace that was larger than our car. I studied him closely, and it was like looking into a mirror.

How did they do it, I wondered? My parents, how did they snatch me? Was I playing outside alone, perhaps chasing one of our peacocks, while my mother was taking a bath in the marble tub? Had she told me never to leave the house, but at the young age of three or four I simply didn't understand? Or had they done it sooner, when I was a baby? I had no way of knowing, as I could remember nothing of my life until the age of five.

My first memory is of the pyramid of the moon in Mexico City. I was there with my mother, who had taken me on a *trip*. Thinking back, it makes such polished sense. Steal the Vanderbilt child, leave the country, hide out in a motel in Mexico, and eat Vienna sausages stashed in a blue, hard plastic American Tourister. The Dippity-Do also clicked into place. She needed that green hair gel to glue temporary curls into her flat hair. Curls like I had *genetically*.

All criminals leave behind evidence, and my evidence is my pedigree. That, they couldn't remove. My instinctive appreciation for all things shiny. My fondness for gold. The fact that I am not intimidated by fine works of art but instead want to place my tongue on them and taste them. And, of course, my belief that everything I see is mine or was designed with me in mind.

"No," I spat at my father when he insisted it was time to leave The Breakers. "I'm staying," I said, arms folded across my chest.

He lowered his voice. "We are leaving now son, and I don't want to hear another word about it."

I scanned the room for a butler. "Don't call me that: I'm not your son." I wanted to call out for someone to take him away. Perhaps my aging aunt, who lived upstairs in the attic and watched the tourists on a secret surveillance camera, perhaps she would recognize me. I angled my face up to catch the light from the thousand-foot-high windows that adorned the wall of The Great Room, a room formally known as The Amadeus Play Room.

My father—clearly not for the first time in my life—grabbed my arm and pulled. *Oh no you don't,* I thought. *Not again.* I yanked my arm away from his grip and concentrated hard on making my feet extremely heavy. I would not make this easy for him. I felt certain an alarm would sound at any moment. Somehow, this time, an alarm would sound, and people in authority would appear from unseen rooms and they would tackle my father, while I would be quickly whisked away for a de-brainwashing.

He grabbed my arm again and pulled. Stiffly, I slid across the marble floor, the rubber soles of my Kmart sneakers making a screeching noise, a sort of sneaker scream. My mother vice-gripped my other arm, and together they yanked me from the house, as they had done so many years before.

"What's gotten into you?" my father asked when we were back in the station wagon. "If you can't behave, we're going to turn around and go straight home."

Why had no alarm gone off? How could they have done this to me a second time? I felt stunned that these people were not this very moment being shackled together in the back of a blue police car.

"Why did you do it?" I demanded of them, my new grown-up teeth clenched tight, ten years of displacement oozing out of me.

"Do what? What are you talking about? What did we do to you?" my mother asked, turning to look at me.

"You're not my real parents," I told them. "You took me when I was little. I'm a Vanderbilt. You stole me, and I want to go back."

At first they laughed. They laughed until I screamed, "It's not funny! It's criminal. I hate you both. You're monsters." I kicked the rear of their bench seat with my feet. "I hate you I hate you I hate you."

My mother lit a cigarette and sighed. "I can't deal with this hysterics." She turned to my father. "Why don't you let me out, and I'll take the bus home and you can deal with him?"

My father glared at her. "No, you're not going to take a damn bus home."

"Don't you try and control me you son of a bitch."

My father's fists tightened on the steering wheel, and he looked at me in the rearview mirror. "Where did you get this from, hmmm? We didn't raise you to behave like this, concocting these wild fantasies. What's the matter with you? Are you mad because you didn't get your apple pie at McDonald's?"

I sat as close to the door as possible, not caring if it flew open and I fell out onto the highway. Better to be a paralyzed ward of the state than live with these people.

My mother tossed her cigarette out the window and immediately lit another. She reached into her bag and pulled out a stack of papers—a portion of a manuscript she was working on—and began reading silently to herself, her lips moving.

My father settled in and drove, wordlessly. For the remainder of the drive home, nobody said anything, not even the radio. The only sound was the occasional small intake of air from my mother as she read her own work.

By the time we got home, it was dark. My parents went into the kitchen, and they both sat at the table. My father had mixed himself a tall glass of vodka, and my mother sat making marks on her manuscript with her pen.

I went into the bathroom and ran a bath. Then I marched into the kitchen, glared at them, and pulled a container of Morton's salt from the cabinet. They were too numb to say anything; they just watched me without the slightest hint of curiosity. I took the salt with me into the bathroom and poured all of it into the tub before climbing in.

As I sat in the hot, salty water, I thought, *No wonder Mr. Bubble always gives me a urinary tract infection and hives*. Mr. Bubble was for common people. Mr. Bubble was for my so-called brother, their true child. I was a Vanderbilt. I should bathe in condiments and seasonings. It was in my Vanderbilt genes.

Transfixed
by Transsexuals

When I was in the fourth grade all the girls wore Calvin Klein corduroy jeans and wanted to be psychologists. All the boys wore Levis and wanted to play pro football. I wore polyester stretch pants with bell-bottoms and wanted to be Christine Jorgensen, the world's first famous transsexual.

At my school in western Massachusetts the students had their own cubicles. This was the late seventies, when everything was about personal space and emotional growth. We were allowed to decorate our cubicles any way we wanted. Most of the boys taped pictures of race cars or football stars to their walls. The girls favored snapshots of their cats, taken with their moms' Kodak 110 Instamatic cameras.

My cubicle was a shrine to Christine. I had newspaper clippings, photographs, and an article from a magazine that had before-and-after anatomical line drawings.

"Who is this?" asked Mrs. Rayburn, fingering a clipping of an extremely tall woman in sunglasses climbing down the steps of an airplane, parked dramatically on the center of the tarmac.

"That's Christine Jorgensen," I told her, feeling very superior. "Isn't she incredible?"

Mrs. Rayburn leaned in for a closer look. "I'm not sure I know who she is," she said, smiling and intrigued. She must have wondered if this was some new folk singer or perhaps the author of a popular series of children's books.

"She's not *the* first, but she's *one of the first* and definitely the most *famous* male-to-female transsexual," I explained. "She was born George Jorgensen, and then in 1953 she flew to Denmark to have her surgery." I could have talked about her all day.

Mrs. Rayburn appeared alarmed. "Do you identify with Ms. Jorgensen?" she asked.

"Oh yes," I replied enthusiastically. "If I could be anything in the world, I would be her."

Which pretty much ended *that* conversation.

It wasn't so much that I wanted to be a girl. It was that I wanted to make a dramatic change in my life. My parents hated each other, and I hated them. I longed for them to die in an auto accident so that I could be whisked away by uniformed social workers and sent to live in a compound near a major city.

I was in the midst of an unhappy childhood, ripe for transformation. The idea that a person could make such a profound change in life gave me hope. In my world there were boys and there were girls and that was it. And here's this girl who used to be a boy. My whole idea of what was possible in life expanded.

Besides, I already had more in common with the girls.

Boys only seemed to care about trading baseball cards or riding their dirt bikes. And my feeling about baseball cards was,

Give me the gum, and you can have the stupid cards. As for riding a dirt bike, dirt made me anxious, so I preferred my mother's station wagon. And the girls were always much more fun. They read books and talked about what they wanted to be when they grew up. All the boys ever did was snort and then swallow it.

Eventually, I took down my articles about Christine Jorgensen and replaced them with pictures of Jesus on the cross, though I wasn't religious. I had asked my parents "Is there a God?" And when I couldn't get a definite answer from them, when they offered no actual proof, I decided that God was like Santa Claus for adults. But I did like the image of a naked man with his arms outstretched, as though thanking his audience after a performance.

I didn't think much about transsexuals again until I was nineteen and working in San Francisco as a junior advertising copywriter. The receptionist's name was Amber. She was six-foot-four, black, and had Diana Ross hair . . . except that she had been born a man, so her hairline was receding, and she looked like Diana Ross after a particularly brutal round of chemo.

My transsexual obsession was rekindled. Occasionally, Amber wore brightly colored stretch pants, and I couldn't help but stare at her crotch because the fabric dented at the hole between her legs. It didn't make any sense to me. Surely the surgeons could have closed up the hole better than this? Her vagina seemed so large, I could easily have stuck my fist in it. Maybe she needed to go back for a revision but couldn't afford it? This was probably the case. She'd probably saved all her money for the big operation and couldn't afford the finishing touches. In this way it was like buying a Jeep, stripped down until there wasn't even carpeting or an AM radio.

Amber used to eat her lunch alone, downstairs in the vending-machine room. Her lunch was always the same thing: a gigantic plastic tub of spaghetti with meat sauce that she brought from home and an entire bag of Orville Redenbacher's Gourmet Popcorn, which she microwaved and ate one kernel at a time with her long, slim fingers.

I couldn't help but watch her gigantic Adam's apple slide up and down as she swallowed. This seemed to me to be a dead giveaway. This, and the fact that she was six-four and balding.

I started reading every book I could find on the subject. I spent hours at night scrutinizing graphic photographs of post-surgical vaginas. I compared the clitorises created by the various doctors in America, Asia, and Europe. I learned that Amber could have a tracheal shave, where her Adam's apple would be trimmed and made to appear more feminine. I learned that, indeed, many new women have to go back and have their new vaginas revised. And even if you have to finance it, every clitoris needs a hood.

I wanted to show Amber the articles I found but felt I better not do this, in case it upset her that she hadn't "passed." This is something else I learned about, *passing*. And it's the goal of every transsexual.

A transsexual that doesn't "pass" alarms people. I think this is because as a culture, we are uncomfortable with sex to begin with. So when we see someone who is toying with their own sex, it makes us want to grab our penises and cross our arms in front of our breasts. It threatens us in a deep, primal place in our brain stems.

One of my favorite transsexuals was named Caroline Cossey, also known as Tula. Unlike many male-to-female transsexuals, Tula didn't look like a super-tall depressed guy in a matronly floral dress. She looked like Cindy Crawford. With a better body.

In fact, Tula was a Bond girl and a Seagram's model before a British tabloid revealed the fact that Tula was once a guy. This horrified people, probably men who had previously engaged in erotic fantasies of the lovely Tula only to learn she had recently been some bloke named Hal or Martin.

When I turned thirty, I briefly flirted with the notion of undergoing sexual reassignment surgery. Once again, I was ready for a big change in my life. Plus, I was having a really difficult time meeting gay guys who didn't seem gay yet were still caustic. So I figured, as a woman I would have a whole new pool of men from which to fish.

I decided that I would probably opt for the self-lubricating vagioplasty option. This was a more expensive vagina, because it was partially constructed from a one-inch band of mucous-secreting small intestine. The plus side of this vagina was that it was, like the name implies, self-lubricating. So I wouldn't need to give myself away and reach for the K-Y. On the downside, it was always self-lubricating, so you had to wear a maxipad at all times, even at funerals.

I wouldn't make the same mistake that Amber had made: I would absolutely have the tracheal shave. I would also have the "facial feminization" option that was offered by a surgeon in San Francisco.

And even if the hormones made my breasts grow, I would still get saline implants. Because if I was going to be a woman, I was going to be *stacked*.

The problem was my feet. I wore a size-thirteen shoe, and while I could possibly find a surgeon who would be willing to remove my toes and bring my feet down to a more reasonable ten, I might have trouble walking and would have to sit in a wheelchair.

And then, of course, there was the fact that in the end, Rogaine really hadn't worked for me. So I'd be forced to wear wigs. And while there were excellent-quality wigs made from the finest Japanese hair, each wig cost thousands of dollars and New York can be extremely windy in the winter.

It all seemed like so much unnecessary trouble, and it wasn't like I was unhappy being a guy. I really liked being a guy. It's just I was bored with my life and wanted a change.

So here's what I did: I went to the AKC Puppy Center on Lexington Avenue and I bought a purebred shiba inu puppy. He was frisky, smart, and adorable. I called him Becky.

MODEL BEHAVIOR

The most mortifying fact of my life is something that happened when I was fourteen and I have never admitted to anyone: not to friends nor therapists; not even in rehab when we were detailing our own personal spirals of shame did I confess. It is this: I am a graduate of the Barbizon School of Modeling.

And if you asked me, I could—even today—glide down a runway while my jacket slid from my shoulders and down my arms. I could then catch it by the collar at the very instant I reached the end of the runway, pause, and sling it over my opposite shoulder while completing a full-Dior turn and then head back up the runway to exit the stage correctly.

You see, I didn't *just go to modeling school*; I approached Barbizon with the same focus and dedication as any student at M.I.T. or Harvard.

"That's it, yes!" Phillip shouted as I kicked a leg in the air. He touched his short, somewhat plump fingers to the scoop of his neck. His thick black hair was perfectly sprayed into the style of a fifties crooner, and his almost handsome but fatally doughy face was overmoisturized. He looked to be about thirty, but it was a very real possibility that he was closer to fifty. "But when you bring that leg back down, remember to park it at a forty-five-degree angle from your other foot." Then Phillip clapped his hands like an impatient dog trainer and addressed the entire room, men and women.

"People, remember, please. Ladies, when you stand, your right foot is *always* at a ninety-degree angle to your left foot. Gentlemen, *your* right foot is always at a forty-five-degree angle. I can't stress the importance of this enough. Forty-five degrees for the men, ninety degrees for the ladies."

There were about twenty of us, and we were in posing class, first semester.

The previous Saturday Phillip had given us an assignment. "I want you people to *pore* through the magazines—*GQ*, *Elle*, *Vogue*. And gentlemen? I want you to look through *Vogue* and *Elle*, too, because you can use a lot of the same poses the girls use, with very minor modifications. So I want you all to go through your magazines and tear out ten, fifteen pages that feature models in poses you like, that you think you could master. And then I want you to spend *at least* an hour each day falling into these poses. Then, next Saturday, you're all going to go through your poses in front of the entire class. So, really, you'd better practice."

And now my groin hurt from kicking my leg so high in the air. I'd selected my dozen poses from the magazines, but my favorite, the only one I'd spent any real time practicing, was from an ad for Calvin Klein jeans, featuring Brooke Shields.

Goose bumps ran up my arms as soon as I had turned the page in *Vogue*. Brooke was leaning back on her hands, butt off the floor, chest turned toward the camera. Her huge right foot was flat on the floor, and her left leg was extended up and out. Her off-white silk shirt was buttoned only in the middle. Her long chestnut hair and the fabric of the blouse were gently blown back by an unseen fan. Although we hadn't worked with fans yet, we knew it was only a matter of time, and we were all excited. "Fan work" was something you tackled in the second semester, once you had your poses down. That I would even *consider* a fan-assisted pose now, I thought, would telegraph my ambition to the instructor.

At the next class where we were all to demonstrate our poses, I intentionally saved myself for last. I wanted to watch the other students, so that I could modify, if need be, my pose. I was going to be the star of the class, this much I had decided. But to my surprise, the poses were very ordinary. The men chose standing poses, mostly from the Sears catalogue. They stood, and they looked off into the distance, and they pointed. This, I knew, was a pose that only worked if you were standing next to another person. Other people chose to lean against the wall, legs crossed in front, face turned to the side. And while I thought this was a legitimate pose for a bathrobe or perhaps a scoop-neck sweater, I felt it was a limiting pose and not one I would have selected. Amazingly, nobody chose the Brooke Shields Calvin Klein pose. I had felt certain that I wouldn't be the only student to bring this electrifying pose to class. But apparently the other students had naturally gravitated toward a certain comfort zone, a safety area without risks: mediocrity.

Finally, it was my turn, and I assumed my position on the floor. Even with my short hair and no fan, I could feel myself resemble Brooke. I glanced quickly at Phillip's eyes, to see if I could gauge his reaction. And for one brief instant, I felt I saw awe in his eyes. But I wasn't sure. It may have merely been the hair-spray fumes, which had replaced the oxygen in the room. The entire building smelled like hair spray and nail-polish remover. The men's restroom smelled like face powder.

Phillip cornered me as everyone was collecting their notebooks, magazine clippings, and towels after class. He spoke in a low voice that seemed to suggest wisdom and authority. "You have real potential as a floor model. I mean, you *work* that floor."

Had I heard him correctly? "Floor, um, floor model?? What, you know, exactly is that?" It sounded exotic, like a cosmologist who scans the sky for only collapsing stars.

He nodded. Phillip didn't have the looks or the height to be a model, but he had the polish, and he certainly had the passion. Although the curious thing about him was that he was clearly a straight man. He was like some variant breed of straight man that seemed like a fag. "There are catalogue models, runway models, hand models, crotch models, and there are floor models. These are, you know, models who just really do well in a horizontal position. Some people? They just look wrong on a floor. Take Cheryl Tiegs. You never see her lying down, no way. Cheryl just doesn't work when she's horizontal because she's actually got saddlebags. Neither does Christy Brinkley, although she's very thin. She just doesn't work when she's flat because she looks slutty. But you know, there's a lot of work for a model who can work a floor. There's bedding, nightwear, and then the more avant garde. The eighties are going to change everything. With 'new wave' and everything, it's just real exciting."

So there were *specialties*. I hadn't realized that modeling was such a parallel career to medicine. The decision between runway model and floor model was easily as difficult as the one between infectious disease and proctology.

But I still wasn't convinced that I had the looks to be a top male model. I worried that my eyes were too deep-set and that my nose, while Roman, was too long. If I were going to be a top male model, I would have to be ruthlessly honest with myself. "Truly, do you think I have any chance? Or is this just a waste of time?"

Phillip bit his lower lip and touched his fingers to his intensely hair-sprayed hair. "I think you need to grow into your looks. I think you're going to really bloom in four, five years."

"Thanks," I said. Maybe he was right. Maybe I would bloom. This gave me hope. I'd forgotten I was only a teenager and that I would change. Perhaps my eyes would begin to push out from my head. Maybe my face would grow in around my nose. And while this did comfort me somewhat, it also alarmed me. There were too many variables. If my biology decided to screw with my looks, it wouldn't matter how ambitious I was; I'd never be a top male model. The Barbizon instructors would surely understand this. For they were people who had enormous ambitions to make it to the top of the modeling profession but whose genetics had other plans. Their genetics said, *"Oh no. You can't be a top model. But you can teach modeling at a franchise school!"*

Phillip patted me on the shoulder, like a coach. "Now I want you to tape that picture of Brooke Shields up on your wall, and I want you to study it night and day. When I see you again next Saturday, I want to see your leg at the exact same angle as Brooke's. Remember your butt. And really take a close look at how she's got her fingers splayed behind her and the way her eyebrow is cocked just so." He cocked his eyebrow just so. "If you spend a good couple of hours a day, I don't see any reason why you can't master that pose. I really think you can do it."

"Okay, I will," I said, trying to sound optimistic, trying to hide my doubts.

Phillip playfully socked me on the shoulder. "You can do it, sport."

And for the first time in my life, I knew how it must feel to be a valued member of the football team.

In my own defense, modeling school hadn't been my idea. It was my mother's friend Suzette's. "Jesus, just look at him! He's gorgeous! He's so tall . . . and that hair! What magazine wouldn't snatch him right up!"

I was tall, skinny, and had thick, wavy blond hair: all the qualities that ninety-nine-point-nine percent of the female population equate with beauty. To Suzette, modeling school made perfect sense. Especially considering I had dropped completely out of normal school and had seen Brooke Shields in *The Blue Lagoon* six times.

But my mother wasn't as enthusiastic. "I'm just not sure, Suzette. I mean, that sounds awfully expensive. And we just don't have the money. Augusten's son-of-a-bitch father has really cut us off financially."

Suzette said, "I'll pay!" Which was the only argument my mother ever needed on any topic in order to be swayed.

"Oh, Suzette," my mother dripped with polished gratitude. "That would be such a wonderful, supportive act of love." I'd heard her say the exact same thing to people who had offered to pay her car insurance, rub her feet, or sneak a Frida Kahlo print into whatever mental hospital she was occupying at the time.

The next month, I was enrolled in my first class.

Of course, I'd seen the famous Barbizon ads in the backs of magazines for years. They were small black-and-white ads, featuring a handsome square-faced man with the headline "TRAIN TO BE A MODEL . . . OR JUST LOOK LIKE ONE!"

And while it's true that I was obsessed with my hair, with all things vapid or flashy, and with celebrity in general, I'd never considered a career in modeling.

That all changed the moment I saw the glamorous offices of the Barbizon School. I was convinced. *This is me. I was born to be a top male model.*

The Barbizon School was located in a strip mall in Springfield, Massachusetts, tucked between a Radio Shack and a clothing store for plus-size women. When you stepped through those doors, you left the world of weak chins and superfluous hair behind. Smoky mirrors covered the walls, and a mauve sectional sofa created an intimate conversation pit. Framed photographs of Barbizon success stories lined the walls: a woman in a newspaper ad for JC Penney, a Sears print ad featuring a man in a kelly green Izod. In one ad for a tampon, an attractive teenage girl addressed her mother with the headline "Will I still be a virgin?"

Junior high school, with its drab cinderblock walls and flat black chalkboards, simply couldn't compare. Suddenly, it made perfect cosmic sense that I had dropped out. This was my destiny. This was my calling.

"This is a cuticle pusher," Sharon explained to the class. "Never, never, never cut your cuticles. Moisten them first, really get the skin soft. And then push them back with this little stick."

We were in manicure and makeup class, a required course even for the men.

At first I thought this was silly. Makeup for men?

"I'm telling you," Sharon said. "Nine times out of ten when you go on a black-and-white shoot, you'll be doing your own makeup." She turned to the men. "You'll be darkening your razor stubble, bringing out your bone structure. You'll be hiding those dark circles under your eyes. Makeup for black-and-white photography is very different from makeup for color. Color means a print ad, not just a newspaper ad. And if you get magazine work, you're doing really, really well."

Sharon hadn't done "really, really" well as a model. She had been a flight attendant for Pan Am for ten years, but only domestic and not the more coveted international. Then she'd been a hand model in Miami. This surprised me because her hands were absolutely enormous and surely would have dwarfed anything they held, with the exception of a Big Gulp from 7-Eleven. But realistically, Sharon didn't have the face to be even a catalogue model. She had a horse face: long and boxy, with large ears and a nose with a bulbous tip. And although I understood her face for what it was the instant I saw her, it took Sharon years to accept her own lack of traditional beauty. "I'm just not that pretty," she said. "I have nice hands, and I have nice legs. But my face is just so-so. But I make the most of it. And that's what you're going to learn to do here."

I liked Sharon more than the other modeling instructors because she didn't seem resentful that she was teaching as opposed to modeling.

Phillip, for example, always seemed slightly hostile that he still had not achieved a magazine cover. It seemed obvious to me that Phillip would always be a modeling teacher and not a model. But he, himself, had not come to this conclusion. Phillip apparently still had ambitions of one day leaving this teaching crap and ending up with his face on a Times Square billboard in an advertisement for Salem cigarettes or perhaps a Norelco shaver. "It's a tough-as-nails business," he would say on cigarette break.

But Sharon really liked teaching. Maybe if I'd had her for Greek mythology at Amherst Regional Junior High School, I might not have left in the first place.

"Nice shadow," she said to me after I applied dark mascara to the line of my cheekbone. "Looks pretty funny here under the lights, but in a black-and-white photo, that would be incredible. You really have excellent bones."

Coming from Sharon, who had certainly spent years studying her own sad bones in the mirror, this compliment thrilled me. If anybody knew about good bones, it would be the woman who didn't have them.

My favorite class was called "Expressions." Here, we gathered in a conference room and sat around a large oval table holding hand mirrors. Phillip led the class.

"We all look at our faces every day in the mirror. When we shave, when we brush our teeth, and if we're ladies, when we apply our makeup." Then Phillip's voice lowered to nearly a whisper as he became philosophical. "But how well do we really know our faces?"

I knew that my nose was too big and my ears were uneven, the right one slightly higher than the left. I also knew how I looked when I gave a blow job because I'd done it with a banana in front of a mirror.

"You need to know exactly how your face looks when you make any facial expression."

All my years of staring at myself in the mirror had, at this moment, paid off. All along, I'd been doing my homework for this moment.

Then he instructed us. "Look into your mirrors."

First we all glanced at each other nervously. There was some soft laughter. It was weird to be sitting in a room full of people and then stare into a hand mirror. But that's what I did.

"Okay, smile," Phillip said. "And as you do, watch the different stages of the smile. As your lips begin to move up at the corners and then a little higher and then a little higher. When you're in front of the camera, the photographer is going to expect you to be in complete control of your facial expressions. He's going to say 'a little less smile,' and you're going to know what 'a little less' means."

For an hour and a half we smiled.

When I began raising my eyebrows, first my right then my left, Phillip stopped me. "Augusten, don't get ahead of yourself. Today we're working below the nose. We're focused on the mouth."

I felt scolded. And I was surprised that he wasn't thrilled that I already had independent control over my eyebrows.

"You need to perfect a half smile, a full smile, and everything in between; every smirk and almost smirk."

He was right, I knew. I needed to memorize every single facial expression I was capable of making. If it meant staring into a mirror for twelve hours a day, I would do it. Which, it turned out, is exactly what I did.

For hours a day, I gazed into the mirror laughing, frowning, flirting. I imagined a camera pointed at my face, a shutter clicking. In my mind, Francesco Scavullo was shouting "Beautiful, wonderful, now just give me eighty percent less smile. Lower on the right side. No, not that much. Yes, just like that!"

I spent so much time making facial expressions in the mirror that to this day, more than two decades later, when I laugh people say it looks fake.

Which it is.

I am now wholly incapable of making a normal, natural facial expression. All my reactions seem studied and rehearsed because they are.

Nobody ever warned me there would be delayed, long-term effects from modeling school. This wasn't in their gate-fold brochure or in mouse-type on the retail sales agreement. Nobody ever told me that if I went to Barbizon, I'd be fake for the rest of my life.

Graduation wasn't a black-cape affair with speeches from the dean of students and the class president. It was a fashion show at JC Penney in Agawam. We rehearsed for a month leading up to the event. And during this time we also had classes in assembling our professional portfolios, interview skills, business essentials, and half an hour of ethics.

Sharon pulled me aside after one class and said, "I think you're going to do really well. You're the most ambitious student I've ever seen in my life." She was wearing glitter eye shadow, and this touched me because a pretty woman probably would have been too vain to wear glitter. Sharon was able to have some fun with her face, not take it too seriously.

Phillip was cooler. "Good luck out there," he said, and he gave my hand a firm pump. Because we were standing so close, I detected the slightest hint of alcohol on his breath. So, clearly, graduation was a difficult time for him.

On graduation night, I led my female partner down the runway.

The theme of the show was "Romance Is in the Air" because it was late January. I wore a rented pale blue polyester tuxedo, and she wore a beaded fuchsia ball gown and a tiara with glittery pink stones. At the end of the runway, we kissed and then executed flawless pivots before walking back.

And after eight long months, I was a Barbizon model. My whole future as a top male model lay before me, and I was excruciatingly aware of this fact. It seemed predestined. Therefore, all the pressure was suddenly off. I thought, I'm going to be a top male model someday, so for now I'm just gonna hang around the house and smoke.

I Dated an Undertaker

The most distracting thing about getting a blow job at a funeral home wasn't the fact that there were three fresh bodies downstairs in the cooler or one dead body twenty feet away from me in a casket across the room. The most distracting thing was that I was getting this blow job from an undertaker at a prestigious funeral home, in the exact same viewing room where the wake for Rose Kennedy took place.

"Right over there," he said, after I shot my wad.

We were naked, sitting on the thick carpet, with our backs against the sofa. I was smoking a Marlboro Light. He was smoking a menthol. I reached for a tissue and didn't have to reach far; there were boxes of tissues everywhere. It was very convenient for this.

"Wow," I said. "Can you imagine what the Kennedy family would do if they knew what happened here thirty seconds ago?"

He chuckled and took a deep drag from his cigarette. "The Kennedys? Are you kidding? Shit, they wouldn't care. They've seen worse. They've done worse."

I liked the undertaker, but it wasn't love.

Let me just get this out of the way right off the bat: I am not now, nor have I ever been, *into* dead bodies. Nor into the people who make it their lives to work with them.

We met in the twenty-first-century gay guy way: online. He placed a funny ad and I answered it. We exchanged e-mails. One of them made me laugh and spit café mocha on my keyboard.

He was also mysterious because he wouldn't tell me what he did for a living. "I'm in packaging," he wrote. I suspected he was just being a coy fashion designer.

We graduated to speaking on the phone. He was more contemplative than I imagined. A little more serious. His mellow, masculine voice brought to mind images of a methodical patent attorney or perhaps an oceanographer, in other words, a career that did not involve a dark suit and pinkie ring.

"I won't meet you unless you tell me what you do," I joked.

"Okay," he said finally. "I'm an undertaker."

I laughed. "No, I'm serious. What do you do?"

"I'm not kidding," he said pleasantly. "I manage a funeral home. I deal in prearrangements. I don't actually do the *embalming* anymore. Haven't for years."

Dead silence.

"So," he said. "Want to go to the zoo?"

I did sort of want to go to the zoo with an undertaker. But I had to clear the air first. "How do I know you're not some kind of freak? That you're not gonna stab my eyes out with an ice pick when I get in the car?"

"Hey, I'm a nice guy. We always leave the eyes in."

Hmmm. "Okay, Pick." And he was instantly nicknamed.

He came for me the next Saturday in his wine-colored minivan. "Twenty-five cubic feet of storage," he said with a wink. A small placard sat in the window, facing out. It read: FUNERAL DIRECTOR ATTENDING FUNERAL—DO NOT TICKET. I appreciated the implied threat. What police officer would dare ticket Death's minivan?

As I sat, the power locks on the doors engaged. I looked to make sure the knobs were still there, that the door could still be unlocked manually. One does not want to encounter customized door locks on a blind date with an undertaker.

"The name Pogo mean anything to you?" I asked, sliding my eyes toward him.

"Huh? Who?"

Pogo the Killer Clown aka John Wayne Gacy. Serial killers often admired each other's work. Though seldom did they wear Hawaiian shirts. "Never mind. Nice shirt," I commented.

He looked pleased. "Thanks. It'll look great on the boat."

"Boat?" I asked as he pulled away from the curb.

"Uh huh," he mumbled as he made a left down a side street. "I got a little mail-order business on the side. Small-space ads in *The National Enquirer,* that kind of thing. Last Christmas I sold twenty thousand units of Trixie the Christmas Pixie. She had illuminating wings and a glow wand."

I noticed he wore boat shoes and no socks.

"Yup. One more hit like Trixie, and I'll be behind the wheel of a thirty-foot Sea Ray with twin MerCruiser diesel inboards."

I fingered the red, green, and white tassel that hung from his dashboard.

He didn't need to see my face; the disdain emanated from my fingers. "I'm an Italian from the Bronx," he said. "Gimme a friggin' break."

"No, I like it. I like that your people have such pride."

He stopped at the light and shot me a dirty look and a *hmpf.*

"Here, I brought you a present." He pulled a plastic bag out from under his seat and dropped it on my lap. He smiled like a cat with fresh chipmunk blood on his whiskers.

I reached into the bag and pulled out an ice pick. The price was still stuck on it: $2.99.

"Wow," I said. "This is cool. Pick, *ice pick*. You're very clever."

"There's something else," he said.

I peered into the bag, but it was empty.

"Oh, I forgot." He reached under his seat again and brought out two brochures. They were for Batesville caskets: *Committed to the Dignity of Life.*"

I flipped through the stiff, glossy pages. There were bronze caskets, wood caskets, caskets with glass tops like coffee tables. The latter seemed ideal for the dignified ambassador who finds himself accidentally and fatally sideswiped by a UPS truck.

He made a left and headed uptown. "Hypothetically," he began, "which would you choose?"

I'd already mentally selected my model. "The posted-cornered Hanover in cherry."

This surprised him. "Really? I would have pegged you as a stainless steel sort of guy." He spoke this out of the corner of his mouth, leading-man style.

I was charmed.

When I was with him, he was an eccentric entrepreneur. But as soon as we parted, he became an undertaker again.

I couldn't help but dwell on the fact that I was dating somebody who had held somebody else's decapitated head in his hands. Who regularly tied string tight around the end of a dead man's penis so that fluids didn't leak out and stain the tuxedo pants. I was dating somebody who had stitched a suicide's wrists shut after the fact. All with the same two hands that rubbed my back between the shoulder blades, in exactly the right spot.

The only other people who have had experiences similar to those of this man were locked inside institutions for the criminally insane. The difference is, this guy gets business cards.

In honor of our eleventh date, he gave me a Mexican death puppet. A little paper-maché skeleton that he sat on top of the television. Silly, not scary. Innocent. Or so I thought.

A week later, Princess Diana and Mother Teresa were dead. I moved the death puppet off the television, afraid that in another week's time, Katie Couric, Jerry Seinfeld, Oprah—whoever appeared on TV that week—would be claimed by the puppet. I set it on the floor, in an area I figured to be just above my nasty downstairs neighbor's head.

In some ways, it was comforting to date an undertaker. He had this whole mortality thing out of his system. He didn't brood like a tortured artist with a subconscious death wish. He didn't taunt death by driving sports cars around sharp corners with his eyes closed. Death wasn't a mysterious notion that he romanticized. Death didn't rule his life; life ruled his life.

He lived remarkably in the moment, laughed easily. Being with him was like putting your mouth on the lip of a juicer dish while the oranges were being mashed. As he would say, "This is real-time, baby." In a way, he seemed more alive than other people. Maybe this is why I dated him. Or maybe I thought he would protect me from Death since they shared an office. Maybe I felt that if he liked me enough, he could talk his buddy the Reaper out of taking me, pull some strings. Or perhaps I was just testing my own limits, like when you're a kid and you stand in the dark in front of the bathroom mirror and shine a flashlight under your face to try and scare yourself: *I'm dating an undertaker. . . . Ahhhhh!* Then again, I might have just liked him for him, and this undertaker thing was just what he did for a living. That's simple enough, right?

Except why would somebody do this for a living? Why would

a *gay* somebody do this for a living? Had he not seen enough death already?

Why not run a coffee bar, design fabrics, program computers, or install alarm systems? What kind of a person has as a goal in life the desire to delay the decomposition of human bodies, dress them in formal wear, and display them in anticorrosive boxes? Did he attend a funeral as a child and say longingly to himself, "Someday . . ."

And, more important, why would I date this kind of person?

At first, my friends reveled in the novelty of the concept. "Does he make you take cold showers before sex and tell you to lie very still?" Ha-ha-ha, all around. Eventually that became "Are you *still* seeing that undertaker?" As if I were still laughing uncontrollably at a joke to which the punch line had been delivered twenty minutes ago. "But isn't it . . . depressing?" I told them about the T-shirt with the garish hula girl emblazoned across the front. I told them about his smile, one of his best features. They nodded suspiciously.

One night, I went to his office to fool around. We'd never done it there before. His "office" was a large brownstone. He was wearing red boxer shorts when he answered the door. "Got the whole place to myself, all five floors."

I hesitated briefly before stepping inside. "Are you . . . alone?"

He gave me a puzzled look, like *What do you think, dickwad?*

"No. I mean *alone,* alone."

He pulled me inside and closed the door behind me. "Oh, that. No, we got a full house tonight."

I cringed slightly and took a peppermint from the bowl near the door. The idea that we were not alone was one thing. The idea that we were not alone yet were the only ones alive was quite another.

We went at it on a sofa in a viewing room on the third floor.

Afterward he said, "I think this is the room where we held one of the Kennedys' funerals. I forget which one."

Rose Kennedy instantly appeared above my head shrieking and brandishing her rosary, attorneys on either side of her.

"Wanna go downstairs to the refrigerator?" he asked.

Normally, two boyfriends might "go downstairs to the refrigerator" and grab a beer after sex. This refrigerator was not that kind of refrigerator.

"Ready?" he asked as we stood in front of the large steel door.

I nodded.

He opened the door and turned on the light. Four bodies lay on steel gurneys, covered by sheets. I stepped inside the room.

He walked to one of the gurneys and lifted the sheet to peer at the face. "This fella was in the prime of his life. Thirty-two. Drug overdose," he said. There was pity in his voice but not real sadness. It was almost like he was looking at a beautiful sports car that had been totaled on the interstate. And I thought, *Maybe that's just how all these dead bodies become after a while, like so many wrecked cars*.

I, however, had not had the numbing luxury of seeing a career's worth of dead bodies, and I felt queasy at the thought of starting now. "I don't want to see him," I said, folding my arms across my chest. Instantly, the novelty of dating an undertaker vanished in the frigid air.

"You should," he said. The undertaker does not drink or do drugs, and I have a long history of doing both. The undertaker does not want me to become one of his clients.

I approached the body.

"It's okay," he said as he pulled down the sheet.

He was a very handsome, athletic man. He looked to be sleeping. I followed the contours of his face with my eyes. It felt wrong for me to see him like that. It felt like theft.

"Maybe he thought he'd do just a line or two," the undertaker said. "Or maybe he did so much that it seemed normal. But see how his muscles are? This guy worked out. He was probably at the gym the day before yesterday."

All I could say was "That's amazing," because it was. It was somehow almost holy, seeing the man like that, naked and gone.

"That's just life. Only this one ended too soon."

"Great," I said. "A profound undertaker."

"Who gives great head," he added.

"This is so twisted."

"Welcome to the world. Ain't it a pisser?" We left the room. And we kissed for a long, hungry time.

AND NOW A WORD
FROM OUR SPONSOR

After work today I went to Daphnia, my usual barber at the Astor Place barbershop. Astor Place is the geographical region in New York City where the West Village intersects with the East Village. Somehow in the late eighties, Astor Place became trapped in time. As a result these few blocks are filled with people who still consider safety pins to be a fashion accessory. The people who live around here tend to favor black leather, studs, and Mohawks. While people from Omaha may come to Astor Place and think, *Gosh, now these must be what you call the 'hip' people,* Manhattanites view the residents of this area more correctly as heroin addicts who have aged poorly and are stuck in the past. The Astor Place barbershop itself was here long before Astor Place was cool, in any decade. And Daphnia was probably here for opening day. Jacob Astor himself likely pinched her ass after she trimmed his mustache.

Daphnia looks like Sophia Loren after some decades of terrible luck. The same raven-colored hair, teased high into a dome. But Daphnia's hair is dented at the top, as though she banged her head on the shelf where she keeps her combs and clippers. Daphnia has a similar beauty but ignores it. Although this time her eyeliner wasn't smeared, so maybe she was having an okay day. I sat down in her chair and took off my baseball cap, and she said, "Same thing?" and I said, "Yeah, same thing." *Same thing* being short on the sides, flat on top, natural in the back. I hate that line they give you in the back, the one that goes straight across, dumbing down the haircut. It's so technical college.

She zooms the clippers over my hair as usual. But then she does something she's never done before: she buzzes all over my ears, even the lobes, and way, *way* down my neck.

And I'm thinking, *This is really bad. It's starting. The hair where you don't want it.* That's when I noticed how shiny my head looked, like a baby crowning. My balding skull saying *"Here I come"* through the ever-thinning hairs on top.

And this, despite the fact that I drench my scalp with Rogaine every time I stand in front of a mirror (about two dozen times a day). The Rogaine makes my scalp itch madly, which is probably my genetic material mutating. So when I'm forty-six, I'll have to have my cancerous scalp removed and replaced with hip tissue.

Women just smirk at baldness, as if it's cute. How adorable would they find it if they began to lose their breasts in their late twenties? If both tits just shrunk up—unevenly I might add—and eventually turned into wine-cork nubs. Then it would be a different story. Then men would get the pity they deserve from women, as opposed to the smirks. There would be little ribbons you could wear on your jacket for Baldness Awareness Month. There would be marathons where people wept openly as bald men crossed the finish line, smiling and wiping sweat from their fleshy heads.

As far as I'm concerned, baldness is the male breast cancer, only much worse because almost everyone gets it. True, it's not life-threatening. Just social-life threatening. But in New York City, there is no difference.

Now if I had thick Italian hair, as opposed to this crappy, vague Nordic hair, I would probably just buzz it off like the rest of the fags. And I wouldn't care, because then it would be by choice. So I'm thinking maybe I should just get my head tattooed to look like very short stubble. Nobody would know unless they got very close to me. And my intimacy issues prevent that.

"You okay?" Daphnia asked while she was brushing my neck and ears with her whisk broom.

"Yeah, I'm just annoyed by how fast I'm losing my hair."

She laughed. "Is fact of life for the man."

I scowled and looked at her breasts.

Then I went home to write terrible ad scripts for an awful new product. I was recently teamed up with an art director whom I privately refer to as Dim, as in "Look, Dim forgot to wear shoes today!" He's the sweetest guy, and he has absolutely no annoying attitude. On the other hand, he's difficult to work with because things like space distract him. The other day I caught him sitting in his chair looking up, then all around, as though for a fly. Then he fixed his gaze on the wall, cocking his head slightly to the right, a puzzled look on his face. I stood in the doorway to his office and stared hard at him, thinking he'd sense my attention and snap out of it. Finally I said, "Everything okay?" And he said, "Isn't it weird how you can't see air? But it's there."

So I'm working with him on a butterlike product called, beautifully, BenCol. It prevents your body from absorbing eighty percent of dietary cholesterol. Thus the name, a shortening of "beneficial to cholesterol." Despite the fact that it sounds like an allergy medicine or a laxative, I must make it sound like a miraculous breakthrough, accidentally discovered on a farm in Denmark. Not a trick of science but a gift from Nature.

The strategy reads: "So pure, it's odorless. Natural, because it's derived from trees."

So I'm trying to write something that's spare and elegant and slightly magical. But really, I'm wasting my time. Because they don't want elegant and magical. They want shit, in their own proprietary color. They want this, I'm sure of it:

VIDEO:
Amy Irving, star of *Yentl*, stands in a sun-drenched gourmet kitchen (brushed-steel appliances, cherry cabinets, an island with a granite countertop), waving her hand over dishes of prepared food items: eggs, steaks, lobster, fried chicken.

VOICE-OVER:
Hi. I'm Academy Award nominee Amy Irving. And I've got incredible news! Now, all the foods you know and love can actually lower your cholesterol by fifteen percent—guaranteed! Introducing BenCol. A revolutionary breakthrough, discovered in Nature. BenCol is a rich, creamy spread that's sweet and delicious. Use it just like butter, and it lowers your cholesterol throughout the day. In two weeks, your cholesterol will be fifteen percent lower—or your money back.

We called it BenCol because it's beneficial to cholesterol. But you'll just call it delicious.

VIDEO:
Amy bites into a drumstick, eyes wide with pleasure.

SOUND EFFECT:
Crunching chicken skin.

SILENT SUPER:
BenCol—for deliciously lower cholesterol.

So that's exactly what they want. In the old days—the eighties—this kind of advertising was referred to as "Two Cs in a K." Which translates to: two cunts in a kitchen. Although this spot uses only one cunt, the formula is the same.

I can't believe this is my career: mad-scientist fake butter. And I just wonder whether in five years the FDA will discover (oops!!!) that it causes some sort of untreatable cancer or additional limb growth.

I really wouldn't have such a problem with it if a normal food company were the manufacturer. I could almost buy into the whole idea if it came from Kraft or General Foods. Except this stuff comes not from the kitchens of Sara Lee but from the labs of a leading drug manufacturer. It doesn't take quantitative focus groups in shopping malls to know that people do not want an artificial butter from the makers of America's favorite synthetic broad-spectrum antibiotic agent.

After Olestra (may cause anal leakage), people are a tad suspicious of products that do things that are too good to be true in the natural world.

I tell this to the account people, and they say, "But it comes from trees!"

To which I reply, "Yes, and so does napalm and rubber cement. But that doesn't mean I'm going to spread them on my English muffin."

And poor Dim doesn't understand my resistance. He lumbers into my office like a child with a few canine chromosomes and says, "Hey. Wanna brainstorm? Maybe we can make it rain, he he."

I tell him, "After my nose stops bleeding."

This causes his face to fall. "Oh, wow, man. Sorry. Yeah, sure." And he backs away.

Is it me? Have I finally rotted to the core? It's like my passion for advertising is directly related to my hair. The more hair I lose, the more I detest my job. My life is going bald.

Last weekend, I spent Sunday in a Starbucks writing Amtrak

TV spots. I was drinking double espressos and really trying to be positive instead of enraged and spoiled. One of my problems is that I have completely disconnected those blue envelopes my paycheck arrives in with doing any actual work.

So I wrote all about the *experience* of Amtrak. About how you can drink chardonnay ten feet from an alligator or cross the desert in your pajamas. The whole thing turned out to be very Zen, because I really got lost in the writing. When I read the scripts to my boss, who has a habit of shoving his fist through walls, he said, "That's fucking great shit, man. Cowboy poetry."

I liked this comment because it made me feel sensitive yet masculine, like a professional bodybuilder who collects porcelain figurines.

The client, however, didn't agree. She was furious. "It's not about the chardonnay or the crocodiles; it's about the fare. It's about $158.00 round-trip to Boston."

And she was really bitchy about it, too. We had served excellent cookies and espresso in the meeting, and I wanted to reach across the table and take her cookie away. "Give that Mint Milano back, you bitch. If you can't at least be polite, you don't get a treat."

Here is a woman who is solely responsible for the brand image of Amtrak, our nation's flagship railroad, and she's wearing a tacky pantsuit from QVC and twelve-dollar shoes. She sat back in her chair like a trucker and complained, "Why the hell don't you talk about the new engines we got? We got all new engines on most of our trains. Why can't you say, 'Come aboard and experience our new engines.' Why can't you talk about that if you don't wanna talk about the price?"

I smiled and very calmly said, "Because people don't ride in the engine. They don't care. All they care about is what they see out the window and will they get where they're going on time."

She glared at me and said, "I don't want you working on my business."

Likewise, bitch.

And from now on I fly everywhere.

I wasn't always this bitter and gangrenous. I got my first job as an advertising copywriter when I was nineteen, four months after I moved to San Francisco. I had long, curly hair and wore sunglasses at all times, which in the mid-eighties felt totally rad. I was so thrilled to not be pumping gas at a Getty station that I arrived in the office at four-thirty in the morning and left at midnight.

One of my first projects was to write a print ad for a potato.

The National Potato Board needed to replace its current ad, which featured a potato covered in thick, green latex paint and the headline "What must we do to make you realize we're a vegetable?" This was when they were trying to reverse the perception that potatoes were just junk food.

The new strategy was all about speed. Microwave ovens were relatively new, so speed was exciting news. And potatoes were known to be slow. So I did an ad that featured a potato in a wind tunnel, like a car. The headline was "Aerodynamically designed for speed."

The potato people were very happy. They bought the ad, and then they needed me to write the actual body copy.

For this, I would need a recipe. So I contacted the woman at the ad agency who was in charge of getting me a very fast recipe for a potato, and she kept telling me, "I'll get it to you tomorrow."

She was a very busy woman who lived on a houseboat in Sausalito, and understandably, my potato recipe was just not a top priority. So in place of a real recipe, I wrote my own temporary place-holder recipe. It read: "Just slice a potato, broil for ten minutes, then sprinkle liberally with parmesan or blue." Which is exactly how the ad ran in magazines.

It was one of those things that just slipped through the cracks. And nobody even noticed until *Adweek* magazine did a small article about my clever potato ad. They liked the visual. They liked the headline. They questioned the recipe. "We'll have to try this curious recipe in our *Adweek* test kitchens," they snidely remarked.

I was thrilled to see my ad in *Redbook*. And I was especially proud of my fast and simple recipe. I liked to imagine extremely busy moms in Tennessee reading my recipe and thinking, *Wow, I never realized you could make a potato so quick,* and then serving it to guests. I liked to imagine the guests crunching into the raw-ish potato, gluey with melted cheese. The potato slices would surely have been scalding hot in some places, cool in others. They would have been starchy and caused cramps. "Gosh Phyllis, these potatoes are so . . . fresh."

This was great advertising.

Maybe what I need to do is diversify. Perhaps I've spent too many years in traditional consumer advertising and now need to write commercials for prescription yeast-infection medications or make infomercials.

As cheesy and downscale as infomercials are, they can be curiously persuasive. Last Saturday I spent the afternoon sitting on the curb in front of Dean & Deluca drinking one double espresso after another, like the alcoholic that I am. As a result, I was still charged at three in the morning. So I turned on the TV and started cycling through the channels, hoping to find either an incest movie or a conjoined-twin separation documentary. Instead, I found something equally compelling: an extreme close-up of a man's forehead, with his fingers sliding back through the hair. And then, instantly, another image of another man, doing the same thing. Then a man rising up out of a pool, shaking the water from his head and smiling. The camera then zoomed in really tight so I could see a pimple just above his eyebrow and, yes, his hairline.

I continued watching, and this compelling montage of mens' foreheads turned out to be an infomercial for a doctor specializing in "hairline-rejuvenation surgery." This phrase was repeated over and over, in every possible context. "Many of our patients resume their active lifestyles just two days after hairline-rejuvenation surgery," and "even during intimate moments, Dr. Sisal's hairline-rejuvenation surgery is completely undetectable." I figured the reason they kept using this phrase was to distance this procedure from the dreaded "hair transplant," which everybody knows results in a head that looks as though it belongs on a doll.

Just as I was about to change the channel, having satiated my unexpected need to gorge on men's foreheads, they showed a series of before-and-after images.

These were truly remarkable. I put the remote control down, fluffed the pillows, and leaned back on the bed. Men who were once balder than me were now standing before a mirror and running a comb through their thick hair, smiling confidently at their own reflections. One man was shown blow-drying his hair and using a round vent brush.

I nearly wept. I used to own a vent brush! I owned three different-sized vent brushes!

This was the "get on all fours and get banged like a bitch!" porn equivalent for bald guys.

The perfectly named Dr. Sisal explained that he used a magnifying glass during the procedure. I could relate to this. I used a magnifying glass myself at least once a month to monitor my Rogaine progress. The doctor then explained that the patient is given a local anesthetic, and "donor" hair is taken from the back of the head and placed in "micro grafts" to the front of the head. These micro grafts were the secret, Dr. Sisal said. Instead of transplanting clumps of hair to the front, creating an obvious rug, by implanting hairs individually he was able to achieve a "natural appearance that gives you the confidence to participate in any activity you wish."

The idea was thrilling, because the activity I wished to participate in was standing in front of the mirror and applying large gobs of hair gel.

While I'd wasted my life writing misleading ads for potatoes and engineered butter substitutes, people with graduate degrees had cured baldness!

I ordered the video: $9.95 plus shipping and handling. When it arrived a week later, I watched it immediately. And I was crushed. Unlike the infomercial, which featured upbeat, synthesized music and lots of shots of hairy-chested men leaping out of pools, the video had a more somber, homemade feel. It was an assembly of interviews between Dr. Sisal and some of his former "clients."

Here, there was no fancy, professional lighting, no music track, no busty blonde eager to run her fingers through any man's hair.

These men sat at their own kitchen tables, beneath overhead fluorescent lights. On the wall behind one guy was a red plastic clock shaped like a cat. The eyes moved from side to side with the seconds. The men spoke in monotone of their experience at Dr. Sisal's clinic and how "happy, yeah, really positive" they felt now, with full heads of hair.

But the persuasion was gone.

In this video, all the clients looked like what they were: middle-aged bald guys who had chunks of hair cut out from the back of their head and sewn onto the front. They all shared the same uniform, half-circle hairline. And while their mouths said words like "happy," "success," and "thick," their eyes were all flat with disappointment.

These were the first men who'd been fooled by the infomercial, just like me. Only, they hadn't had the chance to order the video for $9.95 plus shipping and handling because there was no video. Now these first men, they *were* the video. They probably got their hairline-rejuvenation surgery for free in exchange for appearing in this video. And they probably had to sign legal forms stating that even if they had regrets, they would publicly say they were happy, thrilled, *overjoyed* with the results of Dr. Sisal's procedure. I knew how this shit worked. I did it all the time.

So while my brief fantasy of ever being able to gel my hair into cool, sitcom spikes in the front was over, my interest in my career was suddenly rejuvenated. Maybe I could write these infomercials. And maybe I could write them better and more manipulative than anyone. Surely there was some manufacturer with a toxic facial mask, overheating electric blanket, or recycled aluminum life preserver who could use my services?

THE RAT/THING

This morning at four-thirty I woke up and walked into the bathroom to take a leak. I am one of those people who must wake up at least six times during the night to either pee or eat refrigerated M&Ms. I am probably prediabetic as a result of my constant M&M consumption, thus the need to pee frequently at night.

So I was standing there in the dark, half-asleep, trying to keep my burn-victim dream afloat, when I heard a vague, dry scratching noise coming from the bathtub.

Definitely not a drip.

I paused midstream to listen, but there was no sound. So I played the alcoholic's wild card and pretended I never heard anything in the first place. But then as I was getting ready to flush, I heard it again. I turned on the light and peered into the tub, where I saw an actual rat/thing trying desperately to scratch/shuffle up and outside. It would make a run for the slanted rear of the tub, get halfway up, and then slide back down the smooth, white porcelain.

I was struck with a bolt of distilled horror like I have never known before. Far worse than suddenly finding yourself walking through a prison cafeteria wearing Daisy Duke shorts and a Jane Fonda headband.

And like a campy cartoon housewife, I climbed on top of the sink, crouching under the ceiling and scorching my balding head on the light bulb of the vanity. I am over six feet tall, so this was a very sad sight.

Knowing I couldn't remain on top of the sink, I climbed down and made my way to my desk, where I sat at my computer. I lifted my feet off the floor and folded my legs up underneath me to think.

Where did the rat/thing come from? Where? And of course, the answer came to me in the same way Jesus comes to those who drink in trailers: as an epiphany.

The rat/thing came from the faucet.

How else? It certainly couldn't have come from the floor and climbed straight up the side of the tub. Nor could it have come from mere air. It had to have come from the faucet. Which is really, when you think about it, nothing but a steel foyer for rodents to enter your home.

The fact was: if a rat/thing managed to claw its way out of my tub and enter the main area of the studio apartment, I would never be able to locate it. Everywhere there were mounds of foreign magazines, month-old newspapers, a thousand or more empty sixteen-ounce beer cans. I happened to live in squalor that was more than four-feet deep throughout the apartment. If the rat/thing made it into my debris field, it could easily make a nest for itself under the bed in an old aluminum beef vindaloo container or it could simply die beneath an old copy of Italian *Vogue*. It could die and it could rot.

Quite simply, if the rat/thing did manage to make it out of the tub, I would need to move. I would need to simply abandon the apartment. And because this would place me in default on a lease, I would also need to leave the state.

A rat/thing with sinister red eyes and sharp little talons would be quite at home here in my little hovel.

I had to kill it.

I looked around my apartment, scanning for a vehicle of death. *The Secret History* by Donna Tartt? It was on the floor next to my bed. Surely, this would flatten it. But the problem was, there was no way I could flatten the rat with a hardcover book, especially not a first edition. Like strangulation, flattening-by-book was too intimate an act. If I were a serial killer, I would not be the kind that stabs and then eats the victim. I would be the kind that hides in a tree and shoots at the aerobics class.

Again, I heard the scratching. I got out of the chair and turned on every light in the apartment, making it as bright as an operating room. Somehow, the apartment needed to be extremely bright in order for me to think clearly.

Then I saw the red can, Raid ant killer, on the floor next to the toilet bowl. I read the back about how contact with skin can cause damage: "If inhaled, remove victim to a source of fresh air or, if necessary, provide artificial respiration."

Very slightly, my mouth watered. It was worth a try.

I stepped up to the tub. The rat/thing was cowering near the drain. But cowering? Perhaps planning, perhaps conserving strength. I could see the muscles beneath its dirty white fur. It absolutely looked at me, making eye contact. Its little whiskers twitched. Its tiny claws and feet tensed, ready to charge.

I aimed the can at the rat/thing and pushed the button. Right away, it began to scurry toward the opposite end of the tub, and I followed, still pressing. A moist cloud of toxic, ozone-burning, nature killer filled the tub, and the air became slick with the scent.

I sprayed the rat/thing until it was dripping.

But instead of killing it, the Raid had only emboldened the rodent. Now, instead of merely trying to scamper up the impossible incline, it was charging furiously from the drain to the other end and making it higher up the incline. Because the tub was slick with Raid, it fell back. But had the tub not been slick with Raid, the rat/thing would have certainly escaped. Peering closer, I saw that its eyes were now clouded, the corneas burned away by the chemicals. Blindness had obviously empowered the rat/thing, made it bold and angry and determined.

I held the button down until the brand-new can of Raid was sputtering a drizzle.

And yet, there it was. The rat/thing, running an angry circle in the center of the tub, shaking its coat like a dog, and sending little Raid droplets flying everywhere.

I tossed the empty can on the floor and looked at the beast for signs of impending death. I watched its little chest contract and expand with encouraging speed. Imminent respiratory failure? Tachycardia?

And then I realized it did have a *little* chest, not a large chest. This wasn't technically a rat/thing. It was, more specifically, a small white mouse.

Still. Now was not the time to ponder semantics. I no more wanted a mouse under my bed than a rat. Both were heinous as far as I and any reasonable New Yorker were concerned.

I was horrified. But also? A little thrilled. Because it was terribly exhilarating to find myself in a primal battle against another animal. It was me, at the top of the food chain, versus It. I was defending my territory. So in this way, the battle was slightly fun. It was slightly fucking fantastic!

But the fumes had become overpowering, and my head was beginning to hurt in a way that suggested toxicity and a future lawsuit. So I left the bathroom and went over to the patio door. I opened this and peered outside at the trees. Then I lit a cigarette.

I returned to the bathroom, waving the fumes away from my face as I walked through the doorway. The rat/thing was still alive. I had to close my eyes and then reopen them again to make sure what I was seeing was fact. The rat/thing was not dead, not injured or impaired. I'd felt certain that once the Raid soaked through its coat and into its skin, the creature would be dead. But no. It was charging from the front of the tub to the back, furious and crazed.

The little fucker.

Then with hideous, calm precision, I locked the drain and turned the water on full blast and scalding hot. I did this automatically, dutifully, without a trace of emotion. I was simply a nurse administering pain medication to my comatose patient, an electrician changing a fuse. I was somebody from PETA handing out a brochure on the street.

I was going to drown the rat/thing. And while I was at it, I would boil it, too.

I watched as the tub filled with steaming water. "Calgon, take me away!" I joked. This was at approximately eight-thirty in the morning. At nine, it was *still swimming.* The Raid had made an oil slick on top of the water, and the rat/thing paddled through it like a furry little ice breaker. Even more alarming, the water level had brought the rat/thing closer to the top edge of the bathtub. Eventually, the rat/thing would be able to flip itself out onto the floor.

It was simply unkillable.

I needed to think fast.

My Maglite flashlight was by the front door. I could see it if I learned forward and peered around the open bathroom door.

Instinctively, I ran out and grabbed it, then came back into the bathroom and turned off the light. It was a crazy idea that came to me out of thin atmosphere. I didn't question it; I only complied.

I turned on the flashlight and made a dancing pattern on the water, disco tub. I turned the light on and off, on and off. I made the light zigzag across the water, and the rat/thing began to tremble. It began to seize.

I choked a laugh out, surprised, thrilled. "Oh my God," I said. "The light is doing something to it."

I began making vigorous, complex patterns on the water. I drew crosshatches made of light. I made figure eights. I shined the light into the rat/thing's eyes, then flicked it off and on again like a strobe.

Miraculously, beautifully, the rat/thing became confused or epileptic. It had what I can only assume was a heart attack. Twitch, twitch, twitch, the little body shaking while the skinny whiskers tapped the air.

And then it died.

Automatically, it rolled over on its back and floated in the oil slick on the surface. I watched, mesmerized. And very gently, it bumped against the side of the tub and then drifted back out to the center.

I said out loud, "Mom? Are you okay?"

Then suddenly mortified by my inhumanity, my seemingly instinctive knowledge of how to kill, I left the bathroom and went back to the porch to breathe fresh, cold air. How had I known that would work?

What was wrong with me that I couldn't have simply placed one of those humane, nonkilling traps in the tub and then freed the thing outside, in a patch of grass, like a human being instead of a killing machine?

I was filled with sickness, as though I'd just killed somebody and had their body in my tub, limbs waiting to be removed with my mother's good carving knife. I truly was Jeffrey Dahmer's long lost twin brother.

I decided to throw on some clothes and go downstairs and have an espresso. I needed to get out of the apartment.

Only in Manhattan can a person go downstairs and find a

market that serves espresso twenty-four hours a day, along with bags of freeze-dried peas and squid, for snacking.

After I got my coffee, I leaned against a STOP sign and sipped, pretending it was a normal day and I was only up this early so that I could go running and not because I'd just been on a killing spree.

Across the street was a hardware store, and it occurred to me that I would need to go to this hardware store as soon as it opened. I needed a pair of industrial rubber gloves so that I could remove the rat/thing from the tub. I also needed steel wool to clean the tub.

I returned to my apartment and checked on the rat/thing. It was still dead, the air in the bathroom now warm and moist and toxic.

I turned on the television and watched a little QVC.

As I watched the host demonstrate the George Foreman grill (which actually does seem incredibly easy to clean), I thought about how I would remove the rat/thing from the tub. I wouldn't be able to touch it, not even with industrial rubber gloves. I figured that what I could do was remove all the paper towels from the roll and then flatten the tube and use this to lift the rodent. Of course, I would wear the rubber gloves while I held the tube.

This turned out to be an excellent system of removal. Although feeling the unexpected weight of the creature at the end of the tube made me queasy. But I was able to hoist it out of the water, dripping, and then place it into a paper-sack–lined shopping bag.

It made a heavy, wet "smack" sound as it hit the bottom of the sack. I willed myself not to focus on the sound, because I knew if I did, I would pass out, then throw up and choke. So I steeled my brain and thought instead of very happy thoughts: the luscious glass of a Leica fifty-millimeter lens, the clean smell of a new air conditioner, green M&Ms.

As I learned forward to depress the drain switch, my seven-hundred-dollar Armani glasses slipped off my face and into the water. No splash, just a plunk.

I paused, looking at their distorted form on the bottom of the tub.

Then I reached into the water with my gloved hand and removed the glasses, placing them into the sack along with the rat/thing. There would be no possible way I could ever wear them again. Not after they'd made contact with the infected water.

I peeled off the gloves and placed these as well in the trash bag, which I then secured at the top and brought downstairs to the curb.

After a quick trip to the store, I returned to the bathroom and filled the tub with four gallons of bleach and hot water and let it sit while I called in sick to work and watched daytime television for the next five hours.

Then I used an abrasive cleanser and a sponge to scour the entire tub as well as any of the tiles that would have been within visual range of the rat/thing. I wore normal yellow kitchen gloves for this, as my biohazard level was lower. Next, I used an S.O.S pad, which stripped some of the porcelain away. I wished I could have scrubbed ALL the porcelain off, as it was all rat/thing infected now. Forever. The rat/thing's soul was in my bathtub, and I'd just signed my lease for another year.

I wanted to cry, and I wanted to move. I wanted to move into a thirty-story Upper West Side apartment building even if it cost me my entire paycheck. I did not belong in the East Village with the "live-and-let-live" animal-loving NYU students. I belonged uptown with the surgically youthful moms who paid two thousand dollars each year to an exterminator to insure they didn't have so much as an ant in their kitchen.

I called a friend who dates a plumber, and the plumber called me back (I paged him) and told me the most horrifying thing I had ever heard in my life: "Vermin sometimes climb up into the plumbing and get *trapped in the shower head.*" Which meant that I may have been showering, may still be showering, may someday be showering with piping-hot water filtered through a dead rat, without even knowing it.

This meant, naturally, that I would be unable to take a shower again for the rest of my life. Only sponge baths with Evian.

I now associated my entire bathroom, all cleaning products, and my eyeglasses and the distinctive smell of Raid with the rat/thing. Worse, I would think of it every time I showered for the rest of my life. I would be standing under the stream of hot water, and I would be checking my skin for hairs and whiskers. I could never take a bath again, either. Not with the very real danger of seeing a rat slip out the faucet into the tub of bubbles. These things happen to people "all the time," the plumber said.

Also, I would now probably become sick with hantavirus.

I knew that one of the identifying traits of serial killers is that many of them tortured animals as children. The difference, I needed to believe, was that I was no longer a child. This had to count for something.

After a horribly long day, I needed a mental break. I threw on my parka, with the raccoon fur around the hood, and I went to see a movie.

But what to see? Something sweet and stupid and harmless. At the movie theater on Second Avenue and Twelfth, a title caught my eye. I thought, *That seems good. Jodie Foster and a puffy, friendly farm animal, a butterfly.*

I unzipped my jacket and headed inside to see a movie I'd heard the name of but knew nothing about. It was called *The Silence of the Lambs*.

DEBBY'S REQUIREMENTS

The year I snuck an interracial lesbian couple into the background of an American Airlines commercial, I was feeling particularly flush. (The dykes had been a real coup, considering the client told me, "No white, white bathing suits; no black, black people.") I'd just been promoted from senior copywriter to associate creative director. With this promotion came a fat raise and the loss of the measly four hours a week I had to myself. Now, I would be expected to live at the office. I knew some copywriters who actually slept there several nights a week, talking full advantage of the shower in the men's room. Now I would never have time to clean my apartment. As it was, I was reduced to taking one Sunday a month and just scooping everything into trash bags. But even this Sunday would be taken from me.

So I decided I would treat myself to a cleaning lady.

In Manhattan, the idea of hiring a cleaning lady is not as bourgeois as it might be in Harrisburg. New Yorkers regularly drop off their laundry to be washed and folded. So why wouldn't they have somebody else scrub the inside of their toilet bowl?

I approached my friend and former blind date Brad, the heir to a fortune made from Saturday morning cartoons. His grandfather had created a character that got its own show, then its own lunch box, then its own studio. So having been raised with house-keepers, Brad was very experienced in these "domestic matters." And because he was agoraphobic and never left his apartment, he would know firsthand how good the cleaning lady really was because he'd follow her from room to room, watching her clean while he ate sunflower seeds. In the two years I'd known him, he'd already gone through eight different cleaning ladies.

"Call Debby," he said. "She seems pretty good so far."

"Pretty good, huh?" I said. "I want *really* good."

Brad said, "Well, she's a grandmother, and she doesn't stink or anything."

I liked the idea of a grandmother cleaning my apartment, especially one who didn't trail a nasty vapor. Perhaps she even smelled like lilacs or, better yet, spray starch. I decided to take Brad's referral. It beat looking through the Yellow Pages under "Cleaning Lady," which would undoubtedly bring a transvestite in a French maid's uniform to my door.

"I'm not like Brad," I told Debby over the phone. "I won't need you to come every day. Just once a week. Is that too little for you to even be interested in?" For all I knew, she was a three-day-minimum housecleaner.

"Oh no," she laughed. "That's normal. I don't have any other client like Brad. He wants me there seven days a week including holidays. Believe me, you could serve clams casino off Brad's bathroom floor."

She had a pleasant, friendly voice without an accent. This was a relief, because I knew from experience that I wouldn't be able to learn even "hello" in another language.

Oddly, I found myself lowering my voice on the phone, trying to sound mature and calm, like I was talking to a blind date.

She was uncomfortable giving me even an estimate over the phone. "You say it's a studio with a little bedroom attached," she said. "But I've seen some studio apartments that are as large as houses. Everybody's idea of size is different." Tell me about it, Debby.

We agreed that she would stop by my apartment the following Saturday to see how large it was and how many hours it would take to clean, in order for her to set a fair price.

That morning, she buzzed my intercom promptly at ten. Because I lived on the third floor of a walk-up building, I always had a little time to prepare myself for visitors after they buzzed. But nothing could have prepared me for Debby. While not technically a dwarf, the top of her head was level with my nipples. I'm six-one, so this would have made her about four and a half feet tall. And she was awfully young to be a grandmother. Was it even possible to be a grandmother and still be in your thirties? She had a powerful build, like a compact pit bull. And despite her limited height, there was something intimidating about her. One might expect a woman like this to have a scrub of short, spiky hair, but Debby had a long brown ponytail that hung down her back.

"So . . . may I come in?" she asked, smiling up at me.

"Oh, of course," I said, snapping out of it. "It's not very big." I immediately regretted saying this, but Debby didn't seem to notice. Instead, she scuttled into the main room of my two-room apartment and surveyed it with the steady, calculating eye of a professional. "How often do you need to change the filters on those things?" she asked, pointing to the two air conditioners that were stuck in the wall under the windows.

Silence. "I'm supposed to change them?" I asked.

She said, "Don't worry, sweetie. I can take care of that. Let's see the kitchen area."

"Well, I don't really cook much," I said, pointing to the L-shaped area of the room that contained counters, a stove, and a refrigerator.

She smiled at me, like I was a child. "Yes, but dust doesn't know that you don't cook, does it?" She was at a height where the light slanted ideally across the surface of the counter, revealing a thin layer of dust on top of three years' worth of filth, which had bonded permanently to the laminate surface.

I was horrified, as though I'd been walking around in underwear I only *thought* were clean. And now had to take them off for inspection.

"And the rest?" she asked.

I led her into the bathroom, where she tucked her ponytail inside and down the back of her shirt, then leaned forward over the tub, silently appraising. "See this ring?" she said, pointing to a ring of filth that circled the inside of the tub.

I nodded, ashamed.

"This is a combination of dirt and minerals from the water. It's not easy to get off. But don't worry. I can make this tub look new again."

She was incredibly positive, I thought.

Next, she fingered the caulking between the tiles on the wall near the sink. "Mold," she said sharply. Her eyes narrowed, and she suddenly looked angry. "I hate mold." She leaned in even closer so she could get a really good look. Then she looked up at me, while her head was over the sink. "People can get very sick from mold. If they're allergic, mold can even kill a person."

Here, she frightened me. Her eyes seemed to display a sort of madness, but I thought perhaps it was because I was looking down at her, and she was at such an unusual angle, with her head over the sink and her neck craned so she could face up at me.

Then she straightened and I saw her smile had been replaced with a clean, straight line. She shook her head, as though to clear an ugly thought. "Anyway, let's see where you sleep."

I thought it was odd that she said "where you sleep" instead of the more common phrase "bed."

Checking to make sure her ponytail was still secured under her shirt, she bent forward and checked under the bed. "Can't see much," she said, rising back up. "But I have a pretty good idea," she added, looking at me with something akin to disapproval.

She'd become chilly. On the phone and for the first few minutes, she was very friendly, perky, and optimistic even. But now she seemed darker and almost angry, as though my sloppiness was a personal affront.

She opened my closet door and asked if there were "any off-limits areas in the apartment: a box of porn, toys, anything you don't want me to stumble across."

I was almost unable to recover from hearing the tiny, young grandmother say the words "porn" and "toys," but I was able to mumble, "No, you can look anywhere."

She continued, as though reciting from a memorized list. "Any pets? Cats? Dogs? Birds?"

"No, not even a plant," I said.

She scratched above her ear, then examined her hand, like she was looking for fleas or some sort of debris. Seeing nothing, she freed her ponytail. "Well, this is a very manageable apartment, I'd say. I would estimate that we're talking six hours. Plus, an initial cleaning that would probably last for about twelve hours. So that's ninety dollars a week plus one-eighty for the first week."

I was surprised by the price because I somehow had expected it to be less. Forty dollars? Fifty? Ninety seemed very close to a hundred, and a hundred seemed extravagant. Plus, six hours each week seemed like a lot. I could understand a big, up-front cleaning, but after that, couldn't she clean my little studio in half that time?

But she was a *little person*, so I felt tall-person guilt. Plus, her moods scared me, and now she was staring up at me, waiting for my answer, wondering what was taking me so long to agree. And I needed a cleaning lady, so I said, "That's fine."

"Terrific, sweetie. I'll be back tomorrow," she said. Her mood had warmed once again, and she was smiling.

Mood changes and passive-aggressive behavior—hallmarks of my own character. I couldn't let her win at these mind games. I had to play, too. And win. I adopted a sunny, positive, and confident attitude. "Great, Debby! So Sunday will be our day. Can't wait."

"Yes. It'll be great," she said. Then added, "And before tomorrow, I'll need you to get a few things. I have a list here. I'll need everything on it. If you forget something, I'll have to go out and buy it myself, and then you'll be charged for my time in addition to the price of the item."

She passed me a photocopied list. At the top was a title: "Debby's Requirements." I slipped the list into my shirt pocket and followed her to the door. "Well, Brad said you're great, and I'm really happy you have time to fit me in," I said. "Thanks a lot."

She said, "Not a problem." And then she trudged down the stairs.

After she was gone, I couldn't shake the feeling that something was wrong. Why was I so intimidated by her? Was that even it? Or was it the feeling of foreboding that I couldn't shake, like something bad was happening. Like I was about to step onto the electrified third rail of the subway tracks. Maybe I was being paranoid.

I decided to go get the items on Debby's list right away, before

I forgot and she charged me eighty dollars for walking down-stairs to the Korean market for a can of Ajax.

And here, on this list, is where I found my first piece of evidence that something was, if not exactly wrong, not exactly right, either.

The first item on the list: "I will require at least a dozen boxes of Arm & Hammer Baking Soda because I am allergic to harsh chemicals and prefer to make my own cleaning agents."

Right there, I wanted to call her up and say the deal was off. If there's one thing I am *not* allergic to, it's harsh chemicals. I want to know that the blue stuff that cleans the inside of my toilet was tested—and tested again—on rabbits, monkeys, and anything else they can cram into a laboratory cage. I want the most industrial-strength cleaners, the most abrasive agents, the most corrosive solvents.

It got worse. The next item: "Because I have contact dermatitis, typical Playtex gloves are unacceptable. Gracious Home carries the one-hundred-percent cotton gloves I prefer."

Gracious Home was the fabulously expensive housewares store uptown. It was the place to go if you wanted a seventy-five-dollar box of Italian mothballs or a three-hundred-dollar pair of cotton gloves because somebody you knew had *contact dermatitis*.

Item three read: "One bottle each: apple cider vinegar, Evian, inexpensive white wine (dry)."

Was she going to have a party or clean my apartment? There was a note in parentheses following this entry that read: "The vinegar is for cleaning purposes; the Evian and the white wine are for my refreshment."

I wasn't even halfway finished reading her list and already I wanted to fire her. "Natural-fiber broom (no nylon bristles), Handi-Wipe brand reusable wipes (no paper towels . . . think of the waste!!!!), save all your newspapers (I use them to clean the windows), lemon juice, salt, white chalk, plain steel-wool pads (no S.O.S.), olive oil (for the care of your fine wood furniture)."

I'm willing to cut people a lot of slack, but I draw the line at a greasy coffee table. It was bad enough that she was going to be cleaning my apartment with condiments. I did not want my furniture slathered in salad dressing.

Still. With my jaw clenched, I bought almost everything on the list, including the cheapest white wine I could find. I even took the subway uptown and bought her a pair of cotton gloves for twelve dollars.

When I got home, I checked the paper to see what movies were playing the next day. Unlike Brad, I didn't want to hang out in my apartment while my cleaning lady prepared lunch on my floor.

On Sunday at eleven, Debby arrived red-faced, and whether this was from climbing the stairs or from a morning Bloody Mary, it gave her a healthy glow. "You're so on time," I said with a fake smile, irritated that she had insisted on getting to my place before noon. On Sunday.

"Time is money," she said.

Never would a cliché prove to be more prophetic.

"Well, I'm just gonna take off for the day. I figure I'll see a movie and then go to the office and do some stuff there."

She smiled. "Did you get the items on my list?" But her eyes were narrow, not the eyes that belonged with a smile.

I smiled back at her, but in a way that suggested I might be withholding something. "I sure did."

"Everything?" she asked.

"Yes," I said, nodding my head.

She looked surprised. Apparently, she was accustomed to experiencing a certain percentage of rejection.

"Well, except the olive oil," I said. "I just can't, you know, have everything all sticky."

She looked horrified. "Oh, no! But that's the most important thing on the list! It's wonderful. It's not greasy or sticky or anything. You'll love the way everything comes out, I promise."

"Well," I said, now with a little shrug and apologetic smile. "It sounds nice. But I didn't pick it up."

"That's okay," she said. "I saw a little food store downstairs. I'll just get some in there."

I smiled. "That sounds fine."

"But I'll have to charge you for the time."

"But it's just downstairs," I said, my smile frozen, now just the memory of a smile.

"*I know that*," she said in the weary tone one might use with a telemarketer. "But it takes away from the cleaning. I have to stop everything I'm doing, then go downstairs, then select a brand of oil, then pay for it, then put my money away and come back upstairs. It's not like *Bewitched*, where I can just wrinkle my nose."

She wrinkled her nose, and it made her look like one of the singing Lollypop Guild munchkins from *The Wizard of Oz*.

I didn't want to argue with her over fifty cents' worth of her time. "Whatever you need is fine."

"Great," she said, suddenly, incredibly happy. It was unnerving the way she could go from cool efficiency to sarcastic to sweet within the space of thirty seconds. I found it very manipulative and controlling. It put the other person constantly on-guard. And it was extremely intimidating, because you never knew when she was going to snap.

I made a mental note to refine these skills within myself.

Six hours later, when I returned, I was greeted at the door—and this before it was even opened—by the overpowering smell of vinegar. What were my neighbors thinking? That a douche-obsessed woman with a gigantic, three-foot vagina lived next door?

I unlocked my apartment and stepped inside and was nearly knocked over by the stink. But when I turned on the light, I was pleasantly stunned. There was an actual luminosity to the room. I could tell, even from the distance of the doorway, that everything was utterly spotless. The floor, which was a standard-issue Manhattan-apartment parquet wood, glowed exotically. It was so generic, I'd never even noticed it before. And suddenly the grain of the wood seemed somehow illuminated.

It must have been her olive oil.

I walked through my small apartment and was impressed over and over by how immaculate everything was. Up to a certain point. Because as my eye traveled up from the lustrous floor and past the height of the doorknobs, I noticed that things didn't seem quite so spotless. For example, the window ledges were clean even inside the corners, where nobody can ever get at the grime. And the window glass itself was as clear as air. But not the top window. It had been swiped but not polished clear, like below. There were streaks. And the mirror, too, that hung above the sofa. Here it was more obvious, a line dividing the top half from the bottom. Spotless on the bottom, filthy with fingerprints above.

I checked the bathroom. Toilet? Yes, you could proudly offer it to your guest's dog to drink from. But not the shower head.

And when I looked very close—in between the tiles, packed into the edge between the medicine cabinet mirror and frame—there was white powder. Which could only be baking soda.

And then there was that smell. While the apartment—at least from the waist down—was clean, the vinegar was making my eyes water.

Still, I decided, it was probably worth it. Surely by tomorrow when I got home from work, the fumes would be gone. And what did it matter that the apartment wasn't so clean up top? Most of the dirt was down low, anyway. Dirt fell, it didn't rise.

So, I decided, Debby had done a pretty good job *considering*. Considering, of course, meaning considering she only cleaned as high as she could reach. Maybe I'd bring this up to her next time I saw her.

Then I saw her bill, handwritten and placed in the center of my kitchen counter. "Hello Augusten. I hope you find the apartment to your liking. The floors were very dry and absorbed two bottles of extra-, extra-virgin olive oil. Because of the added time applying the oil to the floor and the damage to my already bad knees, I've had to charge you an additional forty dollars, in addition to the twenty-three dollars for the oil and shopping time. See you next Sunday! Debby."

Two hundred and fifty-three dollars for an apartment that was exactly half clean?

Was she insane? Grandmother or not, she was a thief.

All week long, I found myself trapped in a paradox. While I was tempted to be extra-sloppy and leave globs of toothpaste in the sink, clothes hanging everywhere, and empty food cartons all over, I knew that I would be punished for this. Debby would charge me extra. On the other hand, if I didn't do anything, she wouldn't know how upset I was over her bill.

I was distracted at work, obsessing over it. And in the end, I decided that at least I would bring up the issue of the half-clean mirror.

So the next Sunday, I made sure I was there, waiting for her.

Debby arrived at ten and was startled to see me standing in the doorway. She had obviously expected to find me gone for the day, so she was munching comfortably on red licorice twists. "Oh!" she said. "Hi there."

"Hi Debby," I said, cheerful. "I just have one little thing to ask." I figured "ask" was the right way to put it. Make her a part of the process. Make her feel involved. I walked over to the mirror and pointed at the glass. "I noticed?" Again, raising my voice in a question, my smile firm on my face. "I noticed that the mirror looks really beautiful."

She smiled, but then as I continued it reversed into a frown.

"But only from the center down. The top of the mirror is dirty,

Debby. And it's the same with the windows. It's like you only cleaned half of everything. The lower half."

She looked at me and asked, "Are you criticizing me for being a short person?"

Instantly, a vision of myself on Court TV flashed in my mind. "No, of course not," I said. "I'm just saying that I'd prefer it if you could clean the entire mirror, and not only the lower portion. If you have to use a chair to stand on, that would be fine."

"Use a chair? To stand on? What exactly are you saying?" She shoved the package of Twizzlers into her jacket pocket. She clenched her teeth, and I saw the muscles in her jaw work, like she was chewing cud.

"I just mean that if you're not tall enough to reach the tops of things, please use a chair."

Suddenly, she smiled. "You know what? That's a great solution. Thanks. I'll do that." She removed her jacket and hung it over the arm of the sofa. "Thanks for the tip," she said, but without any trace of sarcasm.

Two could play at her devious little game. "You're welcome. I'm glad I could help."

And I left.

That evening, I decided to call Brad. I told him about the list and then about the bill and how she added on all this money we didn't agree to. I told him about the weird thing with the chair. He was silent for a moment, and then he made this little spitting sound.

"What was that?" I asked.

"Nothing, I was just eating a grape while you were talking, and I spit the seed into an ashtray."

"Watch out, Debby's going to charge you twenty bucks for that."

"You know," Brad began, "I believe she's eating things."

I waited for him to continue, but he didn't say anything else so I prodded him. "What do you mean? What's she eating?"

He exhaled into the phone, like it was extremely difficult for him to hold the receiver to his ear and operate his mouth at the same time. Brad was very handsome, with dark hair and strong features. He even looked privileged. "What I mean is that I think she's stealing food. Last night, I had some leftover Chinese food in a box in the refrigerator that I was going to eat tonight. And when I opened the container, there was only a tiny bit left."

"Maybe you ate more than you thought," I said.

"No," he said. "Impossible. I portion control very carefully. I had precisely half a container left and then tonight just a smear across the bottom: a noodle or two and a tiny shrimp."

"So what are you going to do?" I asked, curious to know if he was going to fire her over this. He was accustomed to firing the help. He might even be at a stage where he enjoyed it.

"I'm going to try an experiment," he said. "To see for sure."

A week later he called me back with the results. "Well, I got confirmation. Debby's stealing food. I know for sure now."

"What do you mean? How?"

"I ordered a container of shrimp chow fun because at least I know she likes shrimp. Then I left it unrefrigerated for two days, I hid it in the closet. Then I put it back in the refrigerator, full, and that night when I checked, it was almost empty. She called in sick the next day."

What a brilliant idea. If I did the same thing, would she become suspicious? And would it be wrong to do it just for fun?

"So are you going to fire her?" I asked him.

"Oh, no. I'm enjoying her too much. She's become my hobby."

As the weeks passed, I became consumed with work. They handed me an additional account, on top of the three I already had. Now, I truly had no time for myself. I couldn't even pick up my dry cleaning because they were always closed when I came home at ten. And I was working every weekend, too.

I became more and more dependent on Debby. An extra day here. A new errand there. Gradually, cunningly, she had wormed her way from "housecleaner" to "personal assistant" all the way to "psychological crutch."

It started with the closet. One Sunday when I came home from work expecting her to be gone, she was still there. "If you gave me some money, I could really transform this closet. I could super-organize it, and you'd have so much more room. I could install a storage system where you could keep your shoes, your socks, your bills, and paperwork." She outlined a dazzling wire shelving plan that was sure to simplify my life.

"How much?" I asked. I was quite familiar with her ways by now. We'd worked out a very specific cleaning routine, and if it deviated by so much as one extra glass, I would pay. With Debby, everything came at a price. Tighten up those annoying doorknobs? Thirty dollars. Have that slip-covered sofa repaired? Two hundred twenty. You know, freezers need to be defrosted: fifty dollars, please. And I was buying enough *salt* each month ("Works wonders on mold!") to seize the heart of every retired snowbird in Florida.

Debby looked at the closet, then back at me. "I checked. The system I have in mind is four hundred and change. I figure it'll take me two days to install it and then get all your belongings put away. Let's call it an even six hundred."

"Fine."

"Done."

And she was gone.

A week later, I was out six hundred dollars, but I knew where my shoes were.

By this time, I was using Debby to take care of all the day-to-day tasks that a person normally takes care of himself, with the exception of wiping my ass. But how long before I was paying her for that, too? And what would she charge?

All the extra money from my raise was going to her and then some. And what did I have to show for it? A very small, half-clean apartment, minus one chair, which Debby said broke when she tried to stand on it. And which I suspect she smashed intentionally.

"I could help you find a larger apartment," Debby told me one Sunday. "You've outgrown this space. Face it: you're gonna need more suits, and with all the travel you do, you're gonna need more luggage."

My apartment *was* too small, and in the back of my mind, I'd been toying with the idea of looking for something larger. The trouble was, I didn't even have time to check the paper for listings, so there's no way I could actually look for an apartment. Where would I find the time?

If nothing else, Debby had time. And for a little extra money, Debby's time could be mine, split with Brad of course.

So in two weeks, she was twelve hundred dollars richer, and I had the lease for a one-bedroom apartment on a tree-lined street in the West Village.

"But Debby, I really don't want to live in the West Village," I told her.

"Of course you do," she said. "It's a beautiful area, and it's on your subway line. No, you should absolutely be in the West Village. Besides, it's a done deal. There's no backing out now. Sign the lease, Augusten."

I wanted to tell her to find me a place in the East Village or uptown somewhere. But I was afraid of her. I felt kidnapped. I signed the lease.

Then there was the problem of moving and packing and unpacking. "The moving company packs everything," I told Debby. She'd offered to pack my apartment herself for a thousand dollars to make sure nothing got broken. "Moving companies are notorious," she warned. "They break everything, especially the Jews, who are really sloppy. You should really have me do it." But

I couldn't afford to have her do it. As it was, I was living paycheck to paycheck.

But she did talk me into letting her *unpack* the new apartment. I was going to fly to L.A. in a week to shoot a contact lens commercial, and we decided she would use this week to put my life back together. Although I wondered, how will she know how to arrange the furniture? Where to put everything?

Ours had become a complicated relationship. I was dependent on her, and she knew it. She was a swindler, and knew that I knew.

"How much?"

"Nine hundred, and I'll have everything unpacked and put away."

We decided that I would simply leave nine hundred dollars in cash on top of a box in the living room. When I got home, I'd be able to relax in my new apartment on a tree-lined street in the West Village, where I never wanted to live.

By now, Debby had her own set of keys to my old apartment, so before I left for L.A., she needed a set to the new place. I was tempted to deny her and take my first step toward freedom. Only I didn't have the chance. When I handed her the set of keys I had made she said, "Oh, I already got mine. Actually, I kept the originals and gave you the copies I had made. See? I think of everything."

"Yes, Debby. You do."

"That reminds me, actually," she said. "I need twelve dollars for the keys."

Actually, it turned out to be a good thing that Debby had keys. I was running late on the morning I was supposed to leave for L.A. Because all my stuff was still in boxes, I had to tear everything open to find what I needed for the trip. Checking my watch, I saw that if I didn't leave, I was going to miss my flight. So I carefully fanned nine hundred dollars in cash on top of the largest box in the living room. I slung my bag over my shoulder and grabbed the doorknob. It came off in my hand. The knob on the other side of the door fell to the hallway floor outside my apartment.

Surprised, I poked my finger through the hole that remained in the door and tried to pull the door toward me. It didn't budge. I was trapped in my apartment.

This seemed so impossible that I laughed. Surely, I could not be locked inside my apartment.

But the door wouldn't budge.

And I was going to be late.

But there was a fire escape. I'd never used one before, but it had to be easy because even drunk squatters were supposed to be able to save themselves.

So I opened the window and climbed out onto the fire escape, wondering if this was really going to work or if I was going to fall to my death.

But actually, it did work. I was able to climb down to the bottom of the fire escape, where I then had to unhook the ladder extension to make it all the way to the ground. The iron was rusty, and I worried that I might cut myself and then get tetanus. Then I was on the sidewalk. The trouble was, I couldn't get the ladder extension back up in place. And my window was open. Anybody could now just hop up onto the ladder and climb into my apartment. There would be nine hundred dollars fanned out on a box waiting for them.

On the corner was a lesbian bar with a pay phone. I used the pay phone to call Debby and explain the situation.

"I'll be right there. Ten minutes, tops," she said, almost breathless with excitement, like an E.M.T. Then in a calmer, more lyrical voice she added, "What would you do without me?"

Have a beer blast.

When I returned from L.A. my apartment was unpacked, and everything had been arranged according to Debby. She'd even hung my pictures on the wall at waist height. Then on the kitchen counter was a note: "Welcome home Augusten. As you can see, your new home is beautiful. Unfortunately, I greatly underestimated the amount of time it would take to assemble the apartment. In fact, I underestimated by exactly half. Therefore, I will require another nine hundred dollars (in cash) at your earliest convenience. See you Sunday!!!!! Debby."

I was horrified. She'd arranged my furniture only to allow for the wide sweep of her mop and not with any aesthetic eye. The table, the sofa, and the coffee table were all lined up against one wall, creating a large expanse of bare floor in the center of the room. Against the opposite wall were the two other living-room chairs and an end table. It looked something like a reception area. And on top of this, she wanted twice the amount we agreed on.

I was about to sit on the sofa to think when I saw a hair. It was a long, brown Debby hair. And the sofa cushions themselves were dented in such a way that I could almost see the outline of her body. As though she'd been napping.

And suddenly, it seemed clearer to me than any window Debby ever polished: she was taking advantage of me. And I'd been allowing it. She was drinking a bottle of cheap white wine at my apartment every Sunday. She was taking naps on my sofa. She was cleaning only the lower portion of the apartment. And now she wanted more money?

"Brad, what should I do?"

Brad sighed into the phone. "Well, I think you've let her take over your life. And you need to create a boundary."

"How?"

"Fire her sorry ass."

"Yeah, but—" I stopped. Could I fire her? Was it just that simple? Was I actually the one in control? "Can I just do that? Fire her?"

Brad chuckled into the phone. "Sure you can. Tell you what.

I'll fire her, too. We'll both fire her, and that'll make the blow even harder."

In many ways, Brad was such an excellent friend. If I ever needed somebody to drive the getaway car, I knew I could count on him.

"Okay, I'll call her now. And then are you gonna call her?"

"No," Brad said. "No, I think I'll make more of a game of it. Maybe I'll bake some laxative brownies and then fire her when she's home on the toilet, calling in sick."

I didn't have the passion to play any more games with Debby. I just wanted her gone. After I hung up with Brad, I called her. "Listen Debby, we have a problem." I was furious, so my voice was firm and authoritative.

"Yes we do," she countered. "You owe me money and I'd like it."

I was shocked by her own tone of voice, which was angry, demanding. "I just walked in the door five minutes ago, Debby."

"I checked your flight information. You got home last night, plenty of time to call me up so I could get my money."

"I had to take a later flight," I said. And then thought, she checked my flight arrangements?

I said, "You're fired, Debby. I won't be needing you anymore. I'd like my keys back."

"You cocksucking faggot," she shouted. "You can't fire me."

"I sure as shit can, you ugly fucking midget. Send me back my keys, you granny-cunt."

"Go to hell," she screamed and hung up.

Debby had to die.

First, her grandchildren had to be killed in a fiery car crash, and then she must slip under the Eighth Avenue bus.

I called a twenty-four-hour locksmith and had them change my locks. It cost me three hundred dollars but this was three hundred dollars I was happy to spend. Debby was now locked out of my life.

But it didn't take her long to discover what I had done, and she began calling me nonstop and leaving venomous messages on my machine. "You spoiled, lazy, gay cocksucker. You give me my fucking money."

I changed my phone number and had it unlisted.

A week later, a summons appeared. Debby was suing me in small-claims court. I was to appear before a judge in two weeks.

Although I was editing my contact-lens commercial and would be working very late for the next month, there was no way I wouldn't show up for that meeting. Luckily, I'd always paid Debby with checks. Debby always wanted cash, but I never gave it to her. "Sorry, I didn't get a chance to go to the ATM," I always said, which was true. "Next time," I always promised. As a result, I had a record of all the money that I'd paid her, with the exception of the last nine hundred dollars I'd left in cash on top of the box. Hard evidence.

When the date arrived, I saw Debby waiting on a bench outside the judge's chambers. She was dressed in a suit, her hair in a bun. She looked, for the first time, like a possible grandmother.

We didn't speak, but I smiled at her. I smiled because I was carrying a briefcase filled with receipts and check stubs.

When we got in front of the judge, I was relieved to see that he was tall. Even though he was sitting behind his desk, I could tell. He was a handsome, tall grandfather, wise and calm. Surely, he would side with me against the evil troll.

Debby outlined her case against me. She claimed that we agreed on a fee of eighteen hundred dollars to unpack my apartment and that I only paid her half and she was due the other half.

I presented my evidence against her. Checks, signed receipts from Debby herself. The judge examined the receipts and he said, "You've paid this woman twelve thousand dollars? Over the past eight months? Just to clean your apartment?"

Then he looked at Debby. "I don't see what your case is, Ma'am. This man has paid you to clean his apartment, and he's paid you quite a lot of money. Do you have any proof that he owes you money?"

She was furious and defeated. "No," she said.

The judge then said, "Well, you need to prepare yourself a little better. I'll give you a month to pull your case together."

Then to me he said, "And you should get yourself some Windex and a roll of paper towels."

He set a date to appear before him again in one month.

But wait! Hadn't I just won? Why was he giving her a month to prepare her case? It didn't make any sense.

No matter. I'd just come back in a month with my same briefcase filled with documents.

Debby and I were forced to share the elevator going down, and she made a point to stare straight ahead, at the "3" button on the elevator, while I stared at the top of her head and imagined hitting it with a hammer. I'd won, or would win, and wanted her to feel it. No longer would she steal from me or control my mind and life.

Except that on the day I was to once again appear in front of the judge, I was called out to an "emergency" client meeting in New Jersey. Of course, there are no real emergencies in advertising. There is no appendix that must suddenly be removed. There is only a logo to be made larger at the last moment. "But I have to be in court," I said, trying to get out of it.

"We'll get you out of jury duty, don't worry," my boss told me.

"But this isn't jury duty; it's something else." How could I possibly explain Debby to him? "My housekeeper was stealing from me, and I have to go to court."

But because this was advertising, there was no excuse that was more important than the emergency meeting. Thus, I missed my court date.

And a month later, a notice arrived, certified mail. It stated that because I failed to appear before the judge, I was now ordered to pay Debby the sum of nine hundred dollars.

I held the notice in my hand and read it again. Of course, I'd known this would be the result of missing the hearing. And my boss had told me to "just put in an expense report for it." But still. It was the principle of the thing.

I called Brad to complain. "So now I have to pay her nine-fucking-hundred dollars," I said. "I mean, even though I'll get the money back from the agency, still. *Still.*"

But Brad was very clever, and he had a great idea. "Meet me at the Citibank on the corner of Fifth and Fifteenth in an hour," he said. "And bring a friend. I'll bring my car."

It was a big step for agoraphobic Brad to leave his apartment, but when I saw him standing on the corner in front of the bank, he actually looked happy. Excited, even. I introduced him to my friend, Kevin, and we went inside the bank to do our business.

Afterward, when we were in his car, I said, "Brad, this was such a genius idea. You're amazing. You should really leave your apartment more often and spread some of your evil around the world."

"Aw, shucks," he said with pretend modesty. Then, "That's it over there."

He'd stopped the car in front of an apartment building on Ninth Avenue and Fifty-Third Street, an area known as Hell's Kitchen. And where else would the little demon live?

"She's on the second floor, apartment 2B."

"I can't believe you even know where she lives," I said, stepping out of the car and hoisting one of the bags up onto my shoulder.

"I check everybody out. She lives in a one-bedroom. Her grandkids live in California along with her kids. They all hate her. You know, she's fifty-three?"

"No way," I said, breathing heavy, trying to keep the awkward bag balanced on my shoulder. "She doesn't look it at all."

"Well, she will when she gets done counting these," he said.

And we dropped the last of the bags in front of Debby's apartment door. Six bags, all together.

Nine hundred dollars, exactly.

In pennies.

ROOF WORK

For the past week I have had this curious bubble on the roof of my mouth. It's about the size of small lima bean and firm like one, too. I've been flicking at it with the tip of my tongue constantly. This bubble occupies so much of my mental energy, it might as well be a uterus, sprouting outside my body.

On Friday night it began to hurt. Not a stabbing pain but a dull ache. Not an emergency but rather a warning. I wasn't sure if the pain was because I was endlessly tongue-slapping it or if it was getting bigger and more life-threatening. So I decided to go downstairs to the pharmacy and buy a compact so I could have a small mirror to shove in my mouth. But buying the compact turned out to be unexpectedly shameful because of the smirk I received from the young Hispanic girl behind the counter. I think she actually winked at me like *You go, girl*. This brought up all sorts of transsexual issues from childhood, and I wanted to explain myself, tell her about the tumor. But it was just too involved.

I took the compact upstairs to my apartment and went into the bathroom. Here, I opened it and rested the mirror side facing up on my bottom teeth, angling it so that I could see the roof of my mouth in the medicine cabinet mirror in front of me. I was surprised by how small the bubble was. And yet it was causing so much pain. Did cancer cause pain? I thought I remembered that it didn't, until it was too late. I decided to do some research.

After three hours on the Internet and most of a bottle of scotch, I came to the conclusion that the bubble was just some sort of benign cyst that needed to be lanced. Probably, I concluded, I had jabbed the roof of my mouth with my toothbrush and this somehow created the cyst.

So I removed my friend Suzanne's wedding picture off my wall and held the thumbtack over the flame of my Bic to sterilize it. Then I went into the bathroom again and did my compact-mirror trick. Very quickly, I stuck the thumbtack into the center of the bubble, bursting it.

The relief was instantaneous. A clear liquid was able to escape from the bubble. As I wrote once in an American Express newspaper ad: The pressure is off; the weekend is on.

I decided I would call Bob and see if he wanted to have a spontaneous Friday-night date. Bob is this very friendly and short forty-year-old who answered my personal ad on AOL. We've had four dates, sex on the third. And the night before last he invited me over to his apartment on the Upper West Side, where he cooked a rack of lamb. He's an excellent cook. But as I was walking around his apartment looking at pictures, I came across a picture of an extremely handsome man in a bathing suit. I said, "Who is this?" and he said it was him, taken when he was thirty-two.

Immediately, I felt gypped and wanted to date the younger Bob, no matter how good his rack of lamb was.

But he was so funny and charming that I decided eleven years wasn't really that significant an age difference. And the nine-inch height difference between us didn't matter so much when we were lying down.

I phoned Bob and got his machine. This sort of made me feel a little suspicious, because I didn't recall him telling me he had plans for tonight. Maybe he had gone out for milk? A movie with a female friend? Or maybe he was asleep.

Then I figured, Fuck it. I might as well go to sleep, too. So I undressed, climbed into bed, and turned out the light. In the dark, I poked my tongue around the roof of my mouth. The bubble was gone.

The next morning I woke up, and automatically my tongue went to find the bubble. By now it was such an automatic function, I knew it would take weeks to unwire my brain. Except my tongue did come across something. Not a bubble. The opposite: a hole.

Alarmed, I got out of bed and went into the bathroom to inspect my mouth. What I saw was a tiny hole, right in the center of the roof of my mouth. The hole was much larger than a hole created by a thumbtack. It was more like something you'd expect if I'd used a ball point pen.

Hmmmmmmm.

All weekend I obsessed on the hole. I looked at it hourly and gargled with warm saltwater and Listerine constantly, hoping to prevent infection.

On Monday I returned to work and was extremely busy. Thus, I was distracted from my hole until returning home at night to see it still there and gaping.

By the end of the week, the hole was still there.

It was still there by the end of the month. And, I thought, perhaps slightly larger. The edges of the hole did not appear pink and infected. Rather, they were the color of the rest of my mouth. So this meant that the hole was now a part of my body. Except that I was certain the hole was larger than it was originally. And who was to say it wouldn't grow larger, still? Eventually, would I be able to tuck the entire tip of my tongue in there? Perhaps be able to store things in the hole? The possibility of dating a drug addict in Rikers occurred to me. I could stow his heroin bag inside my mouth and nobody would think to even look in the hole because a person isn't supposed to have such a hole in the roof of his mouth.

The hole didn't hurt. Couldn't that be considered a good sign?

But no. I decided that there was no good sign to be had. A hole is a hole, and a person is only supposed to have so many. And this hole was dangerously close to becoming an orifice.

I decided it was time to see my dentist. This is not an action I undertake lightly, as I do not care for my dentist. She believes not in local anesthetic and laughing gas, but in acupuncture and positive imagery. For this reason, I dislike her but have always been too busy to find a good, real, drug-oriented dentist. She was all I had, so I phoned her office. When the receptionist told me there wasn't an opening for four weeks, I told her about the thumbtack.

Moments later, I was in a cab to her Park Avenue office.

Dr. Bridges sat me in her dental chair and forced me to explain my self-surgery to her. She did not approve at all, and she let me know this as she inspected my curiosity. Finally she said, "I think you need to see Mac. He's the oral surgeon next door. I think he should take a look at this. Let me give him a call."

Five minutes later she returned. "Guess what. It's your lucky day. Mac can see you right now. So you wanna just leave here, then walk two doors toward Park. He's number twenty-seven. Tenth floor, suite twelve."

Mac was a large, hairy beast of a man. He was disheveled and sweating profusely. His shirttails hung out of his pants, and I knew that he used them to wipe the considerably thick lenses of his glasses. He didn't shake my hand but instead said, "What did you do?"

There was something about his facial expression that made

me feel he was either brilliant or insane. My brother is a true genius, so I am familiar with the look.

Mac inspected my mouth. I again repeated my tale of self-surgery, only Mac didn't seem to find this so odd. It was almost as if he felt that there was nothing wrong with self-surgery as long as a person knew what he was doing, which I pretty much felt I did.

I glanced around his office and saw that there were piles of books everywhere. They were so high in places they nearly reached the ceiling.

I decided that Mac was not insane, just brilliant. He probably read science fiction novels and then wrote the author, pointing out flaws, just to demonstrate his superior intelligence.

"Know what this is?" he asked, sliding his chair back on its wheels.

"What?"

"I see this a lot. You've got a cyst there that was caused by the bones in your palate shifting. How old are you?"

The bones in my palate shifting? "Thirty."

He grinned in a self-satisfied fashion. "I knew it. That's when it happens. Thirty, thirty-three. See, what it is, is a congenital abnormality. It's the same thing that would have caused a cleft palate, but for some reason in the womb, that didn't occur. But the bones have shifted, and that's what created the cyst."

All I heard was *cleft palate*.

I could have been born with a harelip? That would have changed my entire life. People with harelips are not often seen in public. Like conjoined twins, they tend to stay indoors and order in. Exactly as I would have done. I came *this* close to living my life like a shy Japanese girl, covering my mouth constantly and blushing, though from harelip shame.

But by some fluke of nature, perhaps because just as it was happening my mother rolled over on her side, thus knocking the genes apart, I was spared a life of deformity. I said, "What do I do?"

"We need to clean it out up there. It won't take but ten minutes. You have the time to do it now?"

I said, "Sure,"

He brightened. "Great."

I sat there and clasped my hands on my lap. While I did feel a sense of betrayal that I was genetically defective, I also felt grateful that I somehow got off the hook. After Mac cleaned out my mouth, whatever that meant, this whole thing would be behind me.

A moment later he reappeared holding a needle that was at least a foot long. Suddenly, he no longer looked brilliant. He looked insane.

Before I could say anything he stuck the needle into my mouth, instantly ending all sensation above the neck.

Then he produced what appeared to be a common art director's X-Acto knife, and the roof of my mouth was opened back like a car hood. I didn't feel anything, but the sound was hideous: like sawing through Styrofoam. Plus, I had the very new and unnatural sensation of feeling the roof of my mouth lying across my tongue.

There was intense pressure as he began pulling at something with pliers. "We're just gonna clean this whole area out," he said.

I was breathless with the shock and violating horror of this sudden mouthal rape. It was a total Central Park Jogger moment, and I was feeling very close to blacking out. I willed myself to stay awake—in exactly the same way that I will the plane to stay aloft while flying—because if I did go unconscious, I had a feeling he might be so focused on his excavation that he wouldn't even notice.

And then just as suddenly as he had begun, he was closing me back up, stitching the roof of my mouth back in place, pulling out the great wads of deeply bloody gauze that had somehow been stuffed in there. Then he was stuffing more fresh gauze back in.

He had me up and out of the chair a few minutes later, and he was tucking a prescription into my hand. "We'll have the results of the biopsy sometime next week," he said, "so call maybe Wednesday, Thursday." Like we had tentative dinner plans, not like I had possible oral cancer. Noticing my alarm, he added, "Don't worry. A biopsy is just standard procedure." And I thought, that's exactly how all horrible things begin: with those words "standard procedure."

An hour later at home, a dull, thrumming sensation began, like an awareness under my nose. Was this the tip of excruciating pain carving a hole into my Novocain cloud?

My mind kept replaying the surgery. I was powerless to stop the movie in my head. Only now, my brain added visuals to what before were only sensations. Where I had felt the roof of my mouth being carved open and pulled forward, now I could see it. I could see inside the bloody hole, too. Over and over, these images played, a loop of gore. Many people have a fear of the dentist. Because they are terrified that *exactly this* will happen to *them*. Everybody knows that dentists are capable of great destruction, but few people actually experience it. At that moment, I would have traded two impacted wisdom teeth and a gingivectomy just to be free of my internal horror movie.

I had gauze pressed firmly against the roof of my mouth, and I kept worrying that when I pulled it out, the skin would stick to it and I'd end up with the roof of my mouth in the palm of my hand.

Looking in the mirror, I saw thick black stitches tied around my front teeth like ropes around a dock. The roof of my mouth was anchored to my teeth; otherwise it would collapse onto my tongue.

I thought, *I am not ever going to get liposuction, a nose job, or pec implants. Nor am I going to get that new dick-enlargement surgery.*

No elective surgery. Ever.

I wished I could fast-forward three weeks into the future. Or at least eight days, when the stitches would be out.

How was I gong to walk around in public with these ropes tied around my teeth? Thick, black ropes. Holding the roof of my mouth in place.

Imagine, I thought to myself, *what a transsexual must go through*.

I stayed home from work the next day because of my "roof work." I couldn't eat anything, but that didn't matter because I discovered that I liked codeine. I looked forward to taking it and wished I had more pills. A year or two's supply. It felt like such a gentle lift. I could easily get addicted. Unless I already was.

Codeine became the highlight of my day, if not my thirties. If the doctor had given me more than twenty pills I most certainly would have taken them all, right down to the cotton in the bottle. And then I would have brewed tea from that.

I took two more pills on top of the previous two that I had taken a few hours before. I wasn't taking them for pain now but for pleasure. If a person has to have parts of his head split open with an X-Acto knife, it only seemed fair that he should then get to have some fun.

I felt like ordering Chinese food, but I was kind of afraid to eat anything until the following day. I didn't want to stretch the sutures or get debris lodged up into the roof of my mouth. The last thing I needed was to live the rest of my life with a small nugget of General Tso's chicken tucked somewhere inside my head.

I decided to take one more codeine to make up for my starvation.

I wondered, too, if I could ask Mac to give me a few more. I looked at the prescription bottle, and it didn't say anything about refills, so I assumed that meant *no*. I realized I could really become hooked on these happy pills. They gave me a glorious feeling of general well-being and didn't make me fat, like alcohol. I wondered if there was any harm in being addicted only to these?

Maybe this is why dentists become dentists in the first place, so they can cop handfuls of these pills anytime they want. What other motivation could there possibly be to open people's mouths and scrape their gums and clean their scummy teeth or fill cavities? But then, didn't dentists have the highest suicide rate? So I guess those few dentists who don't kill themselves spend their lives making their patients wish they were dead.

As I held the amber plastic prescription bottle up to the light to admire it, I thought about my family's unfortunate history with The Mouth.

My mother, a smoker since late childhood, experienced a cancer scare when I was eleven. The dentist had noticed some suspicious white patches in her mouth and told her he was concerned they might be malignant. This caused my mother to bite her fingernails and smoke two cigarettes at a time until her biopsy results came back negative.

The alarming incident had scared her to the point where for many years later, she was unable to light up a cigarette without saying "I hope to God I don't ever get some awful cancer of the mouth."

My father, too, had his own problems. He was seemingly unable to brush his teeth or see a dentist, ever. As a result, his teeth were brown, with deep black spots along the edges. My father's teeth were quite literally rotting in his head. Which wouldn't have been surprising, perhaps, if my father had been somebody who gutted animals for a living or maybe was a careerist woodsman. But my father was a high-ranking professor at the university. So his gory, ghoulish smile was quite a shocking surprise.

Yet, until now, I'd seemingly escaped the mouth issues that ran in my family. I'd never had so much as a cavity my entire life. And while my teeth were not movie-star straight, they weren't crooked, and I didn't have too many of them. I had what my dentist called "excellent teeth."

But then, this wasn't about my teeth. This was about my mouth, my head. This was about being genetically defective and about now paying the price.

I set the prescription bottle back down on the table, and an alarming thought entered my head. What if the biopsy came back positive? What if I had late-stage mouth cancer and had to have large portions of my jaw removed? In this case, I decided, I would go on Valium immediately, along with codeine and something else. I would also make sure I had a flask with me while they removed my mouth and other parts, part by part.

I was lonely now and wished I knew Bob better so he could come over and snuggle up with me and tell me if I should eat anything or not.

I wanted to see a movie. I wondered if popcorn was really bad if it was soaked in enough butter. I tried to imagine.

It might be okay.

Maybe I'd phone the theater.

A week later, my stitches were removed, and I was able to smile. Not that I would, but now I could, without looking so pasted together and temporary. I went back to work at the ad agency and felt immediately sickened by the stack of conference reports, job orders, and messages on my desk. My biopsy had come back negative, and I now realized that I was slightly, oddly, disappointed. Not that I didn't have cancer but that I didn't have *something*. I needed something to distract me from my ordinary life, and at least the "roof work" had done that.

Fuckhead Bob canceled plans with me tonight so he could go upstate and visit his ex-boyfriend. He's blown me off and is hoping that I'll just get the message and go away.

It's the modern, passive, gay way to be direct. I know this

behavior because it's something I would do. This is how compatible we are. Anyway, I think it's because I told him that I smoke. Ever since I mentioned that I smoke ("only when I write") he's mentioned smoking in every single e-mail, and the e-mails have been dwindling in their frequency.

I understood the score very quickly and went ahead and placed another personal ad on AOL last night, after he canceled.

I love placing personal ads on AOL. It's exactly like a combination of ordering from the L. L. Bean catalogue and writing a letter to God, only you get replies. My experience has been good with AOL. I always meet somebody interesting that I wouldn't normally meet in my social circle. Especially considering that my social circle consists almost entirely of faces on a television screen. Placing a personal ad feels proactive, not so much like changing destiny but helping it along.

So I placed this ad, and I asked for an Italian or a Greek because I love that dark swarthiness. And I placed the ages between twenty-nine and thirty-five, which incidentally places Bob entirely out of the category because he is Jewish and forty.

So now that my "roof work" is over and I still have my mouth, I feel ready to bring something new into my life. Screw little Bob, who will eat a small dead lamb but will not date somebody who smokes leaves, I'll find a new person, and this will be my Something. A handsome, hairy-chested Greek man is far better than mouth cancer, and he will occupy just as much of my thoughts.

It then occurs to me that I am mentally unstable.

So I decided to close my office door and go online. Maybe I can do some research and find out what's wrong with my personality and then fix it.

BEATING RAOUL

It's good to mix 'em up," Raoul says of the martial arts. He currently holds a brown belt in karate but hopes to have his black belt by autumn. In the meantime he's taking tae kwon do to supplement his judo. He's also a semiprofessional downhill skier and a former investment banker who retired a multimillionaire last year at the age of thirty-three. He is extremely handsome (a former model) and articulate, and read *Ulysses* when he was thirteen. ("It really shaped me in many ways.") He is fluent in three languages, four if you count Mandarin, which he can only read. He tells me all of this while he plucks a slender, nearly transparent bone from his steamed Chilean sea bass.

I nod. "That's great," I say as I stab a leaf of kale and fork it into my mouth. It tastes nothing like the bacon cheeseburger that

I wish I were having right now. A greasy bacon cheeseburger at home, on the sofa, in front of MTV.

I'm thirty minutes into my first date with Raoul, and I am surprised by the intensity of my hatred for him. Truly, it is stunning.

"I don't watch TV," Raoul says, when I ask him if he likes MTV.

"Never?" I ask.

"Rarely. Sometimes a little PBS or CNN. I used to watch a couple of shows, but not anymore. Not since I stopped drinking."

I try and veil my glee by adopting a mask of compassion. "So you had . . . a drinking problem?" I want to pound the table and cheer. I want neon signs to appear, huge arrows that point at him, flashing FLAW, FLAW, FLAW. I like flaws and feel more comfortable around people who have them. I myself am made entirely of flaws, stitched together with good intentions.

"No, I didn't have a drinking problem. But you know," he shakes his head, "who needs the extra carbs?" Raoul's teeth are so white they look plastic. Though I am certain they are real and that he has never had a cavity, because no doubt he flosses four times a day.

And this is where I notice that all the bread sticks are gone. A trail of crumbs leads from the basket to my side of the table. When Raoul takes a sip of mineral water, closing his eyes, I quickly brush the crumbs off my shirt.

"CNN had a thing about carbs the other night," he says. "You see it?"

I never watch CNN. I hate news and information and anything that threatens to puncture the bubble of oblivion in which I live. "No," I say. "I missed that. But I agree, carbs are just awful. I usually don't eat them. Except, you know, when I eat out in restaurants."

Raoul smiles. "I thought you said you always eat out in restaurants, that you never cook?"

"Well," I backpedal, "I meant restaurants with tablecloths."

I have been on a spree of answering personal ads lately, and Raoul is the tenth date I've had this month. I believe in the concept of personal ads because you get to meet the interior of a person first. As opposed to meeting somebody while standing in line at a movie, falling for them because their looks make you swoon and only discovering much later, after hundreds of dating dollars, that you find their insides as appealing as Alpo. At least theoretically. In practice though, I'm not sure there's much of a difference. After all, I answered Raoul's personal entirely on the basis of his picture, which was incredible. I only skimmed the content of the ad, skipping over words I didn't like ("spiritual," "motivated," and especially "experiential"). Instead I downloaded his photo, enlarged it in Photoshop to scrutinize it, and then replied with a brief, witty note and a picture of me standing in a field, shirtless.

"The soup is really good," I say.

"It's a little salty," he answers.

I immediately agree. "It's good in a salty way. My body must crave salt for some reason. Maybe I didn't drink enough at the gym and I'm dehydrated." Why am I doing this? Why am I shape-shifting in front of this man? And the answer is, of course, because he is handsome and perfect, and I feel I am neither.

Raoul takes a large sip of water. "So tell me about you," he says, smiling.

"Well, I'm in advertising. Like Darren Stevens on *Bewitched*." I have used this line hundreds of times, and sometimes people smile.

He doesn't smile.

I nod and go on. "So that's what I do for work. For fun, I really like going to movies. I see pretty much everything."

Aces align in his eyes, like a winning slot machine. "I love movies," he says. Finally. Something in common.

"Yeah? What's your favorite?"

"*American Beauty*," he says, not having to think. "I saw it ten times. It's the most incredible movie about Buddhism I've ever seen."

I can't stand spiritual gay men. They annoy me more than flavored coffees. A spiritual gay man simply means he has a yin/yang tattoo on his ass, which you can be sure has had electrolysis. "So you're a Buddhist?" I ask, pleasantly.

"Put it this way," he says, clasping his fingers together under his chin, "I'm very interested to know as much as I can and experience as much of the moment as possible." The candle between us flickers when I cough. "What about you? What movie did you really like recently?"

Suddenly my mind goes white, and I cannot remember seeing any movie, ever. This happens to me. Somebody asks me a simple question, and my petulant child of a mind turns away and faces the wall. "I liked *Deliverance*. The pig scene was great."

After dinner Raoul shocks me by asking me out again. "We could take a walk in the woods up in Inwood. It's really beautiful, more untouched than Central Park. And it would be really nice to be together in Nature."

Because I am so surprised by his invitation, as I'd assumed that Raoul didn't like me either, I say, "Okay." Even though I am wary of Nature. After all, where do most manhunts for escaped serial killers begin? Exactly. In the woods. After I agree, I ask myself why. And all I can think is that I'm doing what my friend John once told me to do: dismiss the first date, write it off. You have to give somebody two or three dates before you can really know.

I tell myself how good this is that I am making an effort, giving Raoul a fair shot, not being so judgmental.

The following Sunday I meet Raoul at Inwood Hill Park, at the northern tip of Manhattan. I have never been above

Seventy-Third Street, so this is something of an adventure, and I am carrying two hundred dollars in cash in case of an emergency. When I see Raoul sitting on a bench, I smile automatically. He is wearing shorts and a loose T-shirt and appears very casual and sexy, yet at the same time very wholesome and down-to-earth. I suddenly feel crazy and judgmental, not to mention shallow.

"It's great to see you, Augusten," he says, extending his hand.

We shake, and then Raoul pulls me close in a hug. "And you feel great," he tells me. "Man, you must work out all the time, you're just all muscle."

I am deeply flattered by this, much more flattered than I should be. My feeling is, now I will follow him anywhere.

As we walk, Raoul tells me a little more about himself. He feels that life is an adventure and that if you want something, you just have to go out there and get it. "I wanted to have enough money to retire at thirty-three, and that's what I did," he says. "I'm living proof that you can't fail if you have a plan. You only fail if you don't have a plan." As we walk past bushes, Raoul extends his hand to touch the leaves, often identifying them by their Latin names. He wants to know if I am where I want to be in my life. "Are you on course?" he asks.

I can't help feeling that if he were standing now in front of a jury of my friends and acquaintances, they would all whisper and scribble the word "odious" on their legal pads.

Finally we reach a small clearing. Here in the middle of the woods is green grass, a pool of sunlight, and an old log overturned and perfect to sit on. Raoul walks over to a large ancient oak tree and places his palms on the trunk. Then he leans forward slowly and kisses the bark. "This is Beth," he says. "She's my favorite tree."

Okay, I officially despise Raoul now, so I reach into the flap pocket of my cargo shorts and pull out a box of Marlboro Lights. I light a cigarette and blow a plume of smoke into the air. "Nice to meet you, Beth."

Raoul is horrified. "You smoke?" he asks, with utter disgust.

"I'm trying to quit."

"Well, you either smoke or you don't. You don't 'try' to quit; you either do or you don't."

"Okay," I say, "you're right. I'm thinking about quitting but haven't really tried, so, yes, I smoke."

"Well I wish you wouldn't smoke here in the woods," he says.

I remove the cigarette from between my lips, toss it on the grass, and mash it into the earth with the tip of my hiking boot. "Okay," I say.

The corners of Raoul's mouth curl into a frown of distaste. "Let's head back," he says.

Somehow we end up in bed. It seems clear that we have nothing in common, but Raoul invites me up to his apartment—a two-bedroom on Central Park West—and I accept because his muscular calves seem to have a curious power over me. Once upstairs, he tells me again how sexy I am.

I am ashamed that I am so easily swayed by this compliment. All my life I have felt bad about my skinny body. So I have worked out for years and have grown much larger and stronger, and although my own mirror still reflects back to me the image of a skinny kid, other people see somebody else entirely and sometimes want to sleep with him.

Raoul takes his shirt off, and his chest, muscular, hairy, masculine, engages my interest. And within ten minutes we are undressed and in bed.

It turns out Raoul has a condition known as micropenis. This means his penis is less than three inches long, fully erect. It looks like a large clitoris, sticking out above two balls.

"Suck my big, fat cock," he tells me. "You like that big dick?"

I am dizzy. I am literally dizzy. I was so shocked to encounter the micropenis and now am even more shocked to encounter his apparent lack of knowledge about the micropenis. I grip it in my hand, and it's lost, so I use my thumb and index finger to jerk it.

"Yeah," he says. "Yeah, man, stroke that long, hard cock. Work it."

I am now engaged in what I consider volunteer work. I am jerking him off purely out of pity. This is really no different from donating five percent of my paycheck to the United Way every month, and it occurs to me that maybe now I don't need to give to the United Way and instead can keep the cash for myself for dating, which I am obviously going to have to do quite a bit more of.

He comes. "I need to wash up," I say.

Raoul is distant, cool. "Go ahead," he says, standing and slipping into a pair of briefs. Then he says, "Thanks."

"No problem," I say, drying my hands on his expensive towel. "But I should be going."

"Yeah," Raoul says. "That's cool. I really enjoyed meeting you, Augusten. But, you know. The smoking thing, that's sort of a deal breaker for me."

Later, at home, I wonder if dating in, say, Dayton, is different. Out there, maybe you have a pool of fifty guys from which to choose. So maybe you pick the guy with whom you have the most in common, and you just iron it all out as you go along. But here in Manhattan, if a guy has last year's sideburn length, forget it. If you can't check off every quality you listed in your delusional personal ad, next. There's always another guy.

Am I any better? If Raoul had been okay with my smoking, would I have been okay with his mini dick? After all, he was handsome, smart, successful. Maybe if I got to know him, I'd actually find that I liked him.

The funny thing is, if he'd come right out and told me on the first date that he had a dick the size of a pencil eraser, if he'd made a joke about it ("But I'm so perfect in every other way"), maybe I would have liked him. As it was, he not only didn't admit his flaw, he was entirely oblivious to it. So although Raoul was far from perfect, he seemed to think he was quite close.

And for me, that's a deal breaker.

HOLY BLOW JOB

Lately, you can't pick up a newspaper or click on a website without encountering yet another horrifying story involving a priest, his penis, and a child. Suddenly, inexplicably, we have turned our collective eyes away from terrorists and are now obsessing over men of the cloth. We have stopped asking "But how did little Tabitha get a machine gun in the first place?" and are now asking "Is Griffin spending too much time with Father O'Brian?"

Well, I'm here to defend our Holy Fathers. The fact remains, Catholic priests have given me some of the best blow jobs of my life.

"Do you really think this is okay?" I asked Father Bill in Chicago. We were sitting in his black Crown Victoria, parked on

Mayrose Street. A street, I might add, that is not altogether unpopulated, especially at ten at night. "It's fine," he told me. "We'll just look like a couple of guys waiting for somebody to come out of a store."

But I wasn't so sure. People *looked* at a black Crown Victoria. It was a surveillance vehicle that attracted attention. "Maybe we should just pull around, you know, in back of something."

He smiled, and I was struck by how warm and sincere his smile was. Then I remembered, *Well of course it is*. What else would it be? The pine tree–shaped air freshener that hung from his rearview mirror gave the car a pleasing, artificial scent. Somehow, this aroma suited him. "Would you feel more comfortable if we parked in the alley?" he asked. I told him I would. Father Bill put the car in gear and drove around the block. That's the great thing about Chicago: it has alleys.

I was fascinated by Father Bill. He was a ruggedly handsome man in his mid-forties, and when we met in the bar, I would have never pegged him as a Catholic priest. In fact, he looked suspiciously like a software developer I once dated. "Are you in software?" was my opening line to him, my come-on.

He rested his drink on the bar and turned to me, sliding sideways on the stool. "As a matter of fact . . ." he said in a leading tone of voice, ". . . no. But I could be if you want me to be." I smiled at his charming offer to reinvent himself for me. It showed that he had a playful personality. But I told him no, that was okay; he could just be whatever he was. And because I am from New York City and not Chicago, I pressed the issue. "So what *are* you then?"

He chuckled to himself and glanced down at his hands. The answer was, it seemed, a private joke between him and his fingers. I looked at his thumb for a clue. He didn't look like a construction worker or a typist.

"I'm a Catholic priest," he said.

I thought he was maybe joking, going for shock value. But after I sat down and had a few more drinks, adding to the fifteen or so already coursing through my veins, it did turn out to be the truth. He was an actual Catholic priest, the kind that knows many old ladies by their first name. When I pressed him, he was even able to quote from the Bible. His memory was astonishing, and I realized that his ability to recall a certain verse from a particular passage within a given chapter of the Bible meant he probably could have sailed through medical school. And he still would get to wear a uniform at the end, only he'd also get to drive a sexier car.

He signaled the bartender and ordered us another round. He was drinking something red, which I teased him about. "Is that the blood of Christ?"

He smiled at this but politely, letting me know he'd heard that one before. "Not quite. Just a Cape Codder."

I leaned in. "I thought you guys weren't supposed to go to gay bars. Or be gay, for that matter." *Or drink*, but I didn't say this, because really, anyone's allowed to be an alcoholic.

Here he laughed wickedly. "Oh, we do a lot of things we're not supposed to do. Trust me."

And who wouldn't trust him? A priest!

And that's how I ended up in his car, now parked in neutral behind a restaurant in a scummy alley in Chicago.

"I'm sorry," I told him. I said this after my penis refused to become erect. I was upset by my impotence, at twenty-six, but also didn't want to disappoint Father Bill. He was such a nice guy. "I've had way too much to drink," I told him.

Here, he pulled his face up from my lap and sat back against the seat. He said, "You know, you should really go to rehab."

This was a stunning thing to hear, especially from a man who had, not an hour ago, bought me five drinks. "Really? That's an interesting remark. Do you think so?"

"I think so," he said, closing his eyes.

I tried to size him up. I decided that perhaps he was being passive-aggressive, sort of punishing me in some clever *priest* way for being too drunk to get hard, thus spoiling his free evening. Catholics were the world's foremost experts at applying guilt in subtle but damaging ways. "So why do you think I should go to rehab?"

He turned toward me on the seat, which was an awkward position for him because the steering wheel was in the way. It struck me as a pose he used often in his work, one of accessibility and compassion. Body language that says "Here I am, open to you." Father Bill continued, "Well, now that I get a better look at you outside the bar, there's something in your eyes that makes me think this is not a one-time event, like you told me at the bar? When you apologized for being 'loaded.' I think that's the word you used. Because you had a lousy day at work? Anyway, now something—call it instinct—is telling me you do this a lot. Like every night."

He was right, of course. My drinking was quite out of hand. And the fact that he was now able to see this impressed me. "Well," I said. And then we sat silent in the car, and I noticed he didn't have air-conditioning or a CD player, and this humble fact made me feel tender toward him. I felt strangely connected to him at that moment and became instantly aroused.

He noticed. And this is when I got one of the best blow jobs of my life. Along with, at the end, a piece of paper with the name of a rehab hospital scribbled on it. "It's in Minnesota. It's the best. Lots of celebrities go there."

He seemed to think that this would be something that might impress me, and he was sadly correct. The possibility of seeing Elizabeth Taylor or Robert Downey, Jr., in withdrawal would be enough to make me want to go to rehab whether I was a drunk or not.

I left him then, parked there in the alley. He offered to drive me home, but I told him my apartment was only a few blocks away.

Of course, I never saw him again. I left Chicago and moved back to New York City and went on with my life and my drinking until my drinking was my life. Then one day I opened an old date book and came across Father Bill's scribbled note. I'd apparently tucked it away for later, forgetting. And then *later* came. And I called the number on the paper and checked myself into rehab, which, in fact, did save my life.

So you could say he was a scumbag priest who drank, went to gay bars, and picked up guys to have sex with in cars. On the other hand, he did save a life. True, only the life of a gay, alcoholic, ad guy, but a life nonetheless.

So while I'm sure there are many priests out there who have *helped* many people, I wonder what percentage of them can actually claim to have *saved* a life. Surely God is going to look at his checklist and say "Okay, we've got this series of blow jobs here, which is gay. Which, you know, I technically can't allow. On the other hand, you did save a life. So," clap of the hands, "get into the bus, you're going up."

The other memorable Catholic-priest blow job occurred when I was much younger, just fourteen. I suppose this would be the height of fashion now, to receive a blow job from a priest when you are a teenager. This is now, of course, all the rage.

His name was Father Christopher, and he was a priest at the local Catholic Church in western Massachusetts, where I grew up. My mother wasn't Catholic; my family wasn't particularly religious. But my mother loved Catholic symbolism, and she enjoyed the services. She was a poet and a painter, so perhaps the rituals appealed to her dramatic side.

Father Christopher was the associate of a priest my mother knew, and I sort of had a crush on him because he was young and almost hunky. He looked like he should be out on a grassy field in a pair of shorts kicking a soccer ball and not indoors in the dark, dressed in a black smock dress lighting candles.

My mother attended church most Sundays, and sometimes, out of boredom, I would go with her. I seldom attended the actual service, instead preferring to walk around the hallways, exploring the vacant offices that extended from the church itself. I got to look up close at the naked Jesus attached to the cinder-block walls with eight-inch bolts, the inspirational posters that were so corny they made me laugh, and the various implements and accoutrements of the Catholic religion, all of which I found strange and fascinating. I especially loved the brass tithing tray with the long black broom handle on the other end. I wanted, desperately, to steal it and hang it in my room above my bed.

Often on my explorations, I would pass by Father Christopher, and we would exchange a nod and a glance. The first few times, I thought his glance meant "I'm watching you so don't steal anything." But then I began to detect something else in his eyes. Something that reminded me of my dog, Brutus. It was hunger that I saw. And being a hungry, attention-starved teenager myself, I gave him back the same look he gave me.

It happened when I went into the men's room. I'd passed him in the hallway and then turned left and gone into the bathroom with the sole purpose of peeing. But a moment later, the door opened, and in walked Father Christopher. My first thought was, he thinks I'm going to smoke in here. And while I did, from time to time, steal cigarettes and smoke, that wasn't what was on my mind. But instead of scolding me, he simply walked up to the urinal next to mine and peered over the metal divider.

It was such an unexpected thing. Truly, you really can't say what you'd do in such a situation until you're suddenly there.

I pretended not to notice, and then, when I was finished peeing, I looked at him and said, "Hi."

His eyes were glazed over with some sort of mad glue, and he could not stop staring at my crotch. He was clenching his jaw—I could tell by watching the muscles twitch. And he was sweating, which was odd since the building was always freezing, like a meat locker. His hands were in his pants, and I saw then that he was playing with himself.

Okay, twist my arm. I was fourteen, bored, angry, horny, lonely, and for various reasons my threshold for strangeness was very high, so I simply dropped my pants and stepped away from the urinal, facing him.

And this turned out to be my first excellent blow job from a Catholic priest.

He sobbed after I came, and I felt terrible. I didn't feel terrible for me. I mean, it wasn't like he was somebody I trusted who molested or betrayed me. He was a hunky young guy in the wrong career who got my rocks off. For a straight guy, it would be like being fourteen and having one of the centerfolds from *Playboy* step out of the magazine and hand you a bottle of mineral oil. Like you'd complain? Like you'd go, oh my God, you've damaged me! On the other hand, I was unusual. I was an unsupervised youth, old for my age, not a virgin. I wasn't a good Catholic boy.

But standing there watching, I felt terrible for Father Christopher. He sobbed, and shook and appeared, there on his knees, like he was about to divide into pieces, which in a way I suppose was exactly what was happening. He, the priest, was vulnerable and ruined for that moment. And I, the fourteen-year-old, felt kind of thrilled and kind of like, What do you expect? You worship a naked man; this shit's bound to happen. There seemed to be nothing to do but step around him and leave, and when I tried to do this, he reached up and grabbed my arm. "Please," he said.

"It's okay," I told him. "You're going to be fine. Nothing terrible happened."

When I moved back to Manhattan after my brief stint in Chicago, I thought my priest days were behind me. For somebody who was not a member of the church, it seemed to me that to receive two blow jobs from two different Catholic priests was an extraordinarily rare, nearly miraculous coincidence.

So imagine my shock when it happened a third time.

Only this time, there could have been no way for me to know.

I was in a cab on my way back from J.F.K. I'd been out in L.A. for three weeks shooting a commercial for UPS. As always, I got loaded in the bar at the airport before boarding the plane and then had more drinks on the plane itself. By the time I landed in New York, I was completely wasted.

The cab driver turned out to be really cute. He did not, for once, smell like a farm animal or wear a filthy turban. He was Irish and in his late thirties, and although I don't remember what we talked about, I do remember that we kept checking each other out in his rearview mirror. Funny how even a cab can turn into a gay bar when two gay guys are in it. Anyway, by the time we were in Queens, it seemed inevitable that something was going to happen, and I could finally add "cab driver" to my list of sexual partners.

In fact, he pulled into a deserted area in Long Island City and climbed into the backseat. After we were finished, he got back in the driver's seat, turned on the meter, and continued driving me home.

"You're a funny cab driver," I told him. "A lot friskier than any other cab driver I've ever had. Plus, you speak English."

He laughed. "Well, I wasn't always a cab driver, so that's why."

"Oh, don't tell me. An actor."

"Actually, I was a Catholic priest."

MARK THE SHRINK

Last night, Mark the Shrink invited me to dinner at Zucca, a trendy new restaurant in Chelsea, to celebrate the birthday of someone I don't know. I was wary of crashing the party, but he said it was okay. So I arrived with him, and suddenly we were seven people instead of six. So now we had to wait an hour for a table, on top of the forty-five minutes everybody else had already been waiting before Mark and I got there. But this was not the worst thing. What horrified me most was that they were all shrinks.

A table of shrinks, and me, the alcoholic, high-school dropout, Anne Sexton fan, advertising copywriter who was raised in a cult by a crazy psychiatrist. At first, I just wanted to slide under the table and squat among their legs, unnoticed. I felt profoundly out of place, like I should be wearing a thin cotton teddy with the back open and paper slippers. Or at the very least, some sort of electronic ankle bracelet. When one of the shrink's whole fish arrived, I tried to make an ironic comment about how skillfully she removed its head with her knife and how perfect this was for a shrink. She looked at my forehead, smiled politely, and said, "Don't you like fish?"

I felt like an inpatient who suddenly found himself eating with the doctors. I felt that at any moment, a nurse would come to the table and remove me, apologizing to the others.

Luckily, the shrinks were in a mood to blow off steam or if not to actually blow it off, to smother it with alcohol. So after about half an hour, they were all drunk and telling amusing stories about their very sick patients, all of which made me feel extremely mentally healthy and mature. "I just want to say to her, *If I had your life, I'd want to kill myself, too!*" one of the shrinks said, and the others howled and banged their knives on the table in recognition.

After dinner Mark followed me toward Third Avenue and then invited himself over, making this the second night in a row that we've spent the night together. And the puzzling thing is, we still didn't have sex. And I still don't know why. I do know that he's interested in me, physically. But I'm apparently not interested in him. And yet we never discuss the issue. We're affectionate, but when it starts to become sexual, I shut down. I withdraw. I get my tunnel-vision thing. And I feel like I'm being smothered by wet blankets. And then all thoughts drain from my head, and my face becomes hot, and I shake. This never happened to me when I was drinking, but now that I've been sober for a few months, my internal rot is floating to the surface. Mark must know something is wrong with me. But he acts as though my reaction is the most natural reaction in the world, which then makes me confused. He drifts off to sleep. And I remain flat, looking at the ceiling.

When he left this morning, he said, "Maybe we'll talk before you go to L.A. for your shoot." But I didn't know if he meant talk about last night, about not having sex. Or talk in general. The odd thing is, I have no idea what he's feeling. And he's a shrink, for fuck's sake. But I'm starting to go a little crazy, needing desperately to be in control of the situation and feeling terrified he won't fall in love with me and knowing that I can't even know what my own feelings are until I know that he's safely in love with me so then I can decide.

I don't want to know what my feelings are until I know what his are. Somehow I know this can't be right.

Mark is strange, oddly disconnected. If you didn't know he was a shrink, you would think that there was something wrong with him in a subtle way that you would not be able to put your finger on. Of course, then you would find out he's a shrink, and that would be it.

Since I left the window open, we were both bitten by mosquitoes in the night. But here's where our reactions differed: he said, "I've got bites on my hand, flea bites or something," and I thought that I had created the bites myself, with my mind and my own anxiety. So that's the difference between a neurotic who believes it's all his fault and a trained medical professional who naturally seeks a cause based in the facts of reality.

He does seem to like me. He seems interested in my odd past life, what little I have told him about growing up. But he doesn't yet know of my alcoholism and recovery and constant journal writing. He knows I write every day for hours but has no idea that all I'm writing about is me. It seems wiser to let him think I'm an aspiring novelist instead of just an alcoholic with a year of sobriety who spends eight hours a day writing about the other sixteen. Plus, I've had to "minimize" my past. So while he knows my mother had a psychiatrist and that I was close to his family, he doesn't have any idea just what happened. I wouldn't want him to think I had a thing for shrinks.

I love his hair. He looks like a disheveled Prada model or an indie film actor. He looks nothing like a shrink or any kind of doctor, a fact that now disconcerts instead of comforts me, because it makes him more difficult to read and understand, and thus manipulate and control as I'm compelled to do.

Mark the Shrink doesn't reveal much about himself. Instead, he listens closely, which encourages me to chatter constantly around him like a patient. Then later he says something that shows he listened and took copious mental notes, all of which disturbs me.

Yet, I am obsessed. I think about him constantly, wondering if he thinks about me and listening to the score of *Romeo and Juliet*, the 1996 version, which has expanded in meaning from the one Des'ree song to the entire album, now that I have seen the movie (again) with him.

I've known him for three weeks and look at how swiftly and completely I have fallen for him. Shouldn't he recognize this and be alarmed? Isn't this symptomatic of something?

We met in a way that you wouldn't think would be a possible way to meet a shrink. I was wearing a tank top and shorts, fresh from the gym. I was walking south on University Place, on my way to get an espresso when I passed this handsome and cool guy lurking on the corner. I noticed him, then turned away and walked on. Out of the corner of my eye, I saw his head turn to follow me. Then as I was walking, the person in front of me opened a door, and I was able to see a reflection in the glass that I was now being followed. With a sudden heart-pounding sense of panic at the idea of a possible meeting, I ducked into a magazine store and purposefully began thumbing through a copy of *The New Yorker*. A few seconds later, he came into the same magazine store and began thumbing casually through *The New Republic*. I felt him look at me, so I replaced the magazine on the rack and left the store. He followed. I walked quickly, and then I felt a hand on my arm.

"Hey," he said in a slight Southern accent.

"Hey," I said back to him, surprised that he was Southern and feeling immediately comfortable with him for this fact, because my parents and older brother are all from Georgia. So even though I do associate the accent with people who are either drunk or insane, it's familiar.

Then out of the blue he said, "You wanna get some coffee?"

And like in some thinly plotted porn movie I said, "Sure."

So we went to French Roast on Seventh Avenue and drank coffee and talked, and he told me he was a shrink, and I told him that I was in advertising but wanted to be out of it and be a writer. And then he said, "Are you straight?" And I said no, why? And he said, "As soon as you said hey to me, I thought you were straight and that I made a big mistake, so I've been sitting here the whole time worrying that you were just some really nice and friendly straight guy."

So that's how we met.

I've been indoors all day wondering what he's doing and feeling left out now that I know he's on call tonight. I hate this.

I wish he'd call me this evening and say "Let's go get eggs."

He never eats at McDonald's, which is right near him: a bad sign.

For some reason, I am horrified to be an alcoholic around him and am tempted to never tell him. To simply never have been one. Never drink again and never mention a word. Have it revealed to him in years, as a surprise.

If he were a plumber would I feel the same? No. I would think he was strange, distant, and oddly disconnected. The fact that he's a shrink makes me feel safe. Because if anybody should have a psychiatrist for a boyfriend, that's me. And yet.

Mark the shrink is still in bed, curled up and sleeping with the easy depth that only an exhausted doctor can. For the past five weeks he's been coming over to my apartment after his shift and falling into bed. We never have sex. We only sleep. We never talk about it.

I find it endearing how comfortable he is, able to just *be*.

However, I hate him for having thick hair and being twenty-eight, while I have almost no hair and am thirty-one.

It seems like he has always been here in my bed. He seems to just suddenly belong, like a part of something that was missing and has now been returned without fanfare. Almost like my dog-tail dream. Sometimes I dream that I look down and suddenly see that I have a dog's tail. At first, I'm shocked, but then a second later realize, *Well of course I have a dog's tail*. Like it's the most natural thing in the world, and I've always had it but just not realized it.

Maybe I should tell Mark the Shrink about my dog-tail dream.

It occurs to me that I'm in a different decade than this person. No, not different, *next*. I am in the next decade. He is in the last one. The one that comes right after childhood. And I am in the one that comes just before middle age.

So, basically, he's ten. And I'm forty.

Why does three years seem like an enormous amount when it involves crossing the line of a decade?

Now that I know him, he seems to me to be made out of sensitivity, like it's a substance. Like a snowman. We went to a movie, and halfway through I felt his fingers, cold, on my arm. And I didn't move, because I wasn't sure he had intended to actually hold onto my arm. And then I touched his hand with my finger tips. And then he sank against me, and our hands made out while we watched Al Pacino do Shakespeare. And he has intense hands. There's something going on there with those hands. They know things.

He's probably not a shrink but has confused himself with his own shrink, whom he probably sees four times a week in his inpatient residential home, from which he's gained day privileges.

I wonder what his catch is. He can't just be single and that good looking and a doctor. It doesn't make any sense. It makes sense that I'm single because of my alcoholism and advertising career and entire history. There's always some reason. What's his?

My friend Suzanne says to be honest with him. She says to be myself, that shrinks are wrecks and that that's why they're shrinks.

But I'm afraid to tell him that, inside, I'm a mess. That my confident, outgoing exterior is just a mask that hides the fact that I am damaged at the core, have a cracked trunk. That I drank my twenties away to forget my childhood, which was beyond-belief fucked up. The other day he opened the closet to borrow a sweater, and he saw my box. And he said, "What's this?" And I freaked out and said, "Nothing." But I said it too quickly. And because he's trained, he became suspicious. "It's a big nothing. You almost have no closet left." So I told him it was all my journals from childhood, and when he suggested we open the box and take out a journal, I told him that I've never opened it and that I don't think I ever will. Clearly, this was a fucked-up moment. But he let it slide. I closed the door.

Just for a little while I want to pretend to be normal. I want to fit in among the doctors, to sit at the table and laugh freely without having something to tell.

Always, something to tell.

"I have to tell you something." Always a catch. Not just baggage, but luggage, steamer trunks, moving vans.

I just don't want to snap the shiny spell of Mark the Shrink thinking he's met a normal and successful guy who is well-adjusted and can make jokes about fish at dinner with his friends.

Maybe I could tell him just enough about me to seem interesting, not real.

Should I put this in a letter?

I don't want to go to L.A. with this on my mind. I want to be able to tell him but not force it on him like a bigger deal than it is. Although I guess it is a pretty big deal. And there's a very real possibility that a responsible shrink would know better than to become involved with someone who has a history of alcohol abuse, among other things, and less than one year of sobriety.

I'm in L.A. shooting a UPS commercial. The actual shoot isn't for four days, so basically there's nothing to do but sit around the pool and then hop in the car to go to the production office and look at the wardrobe for ten minutes, then come back to the pool.

I called Mark the Shrink last night and woke him up. He was sleeping at seven-thirty at night because he had worked until four in the afternoon, having worked all night before. I apologized and tried to get off the phone, but he wanted to talk. He said he missed me, which made me gain sudden weight in my chest because of what I was about to tell him.

"I have something to tell you that you're not going to like," I said.

There was a pause, and then he said, "What is it? Are you HIV positive?"

I said no. I said, "I'm an alcoholic. I don't drink anymore, but I did, a lot and for a long time. I quit a year ago. Or, actually, I guess just slightly less than a year ago."

He said, "That's incredible. Congratulations. That takes so much courage and an incredible amount of dedication. I admire you."

Feeling admired and shielded from his sight thanks to the three thousand miles between us, I lit a cigarette, being careful he didn't hear the match. I did confess to him that I smoke sometimes, especially when I write. And he said that he likes to smoke sometimes, too. Since I write constantly, I smoke constantly, but I'm not going to tell him either of these things now. I need to ease him into the facts of me, not just do an information dump.

We talked about our odd sex. I told him how it's really difficult for me to have sex with somebody unless I know them very well and am extremely comfortable with them. This sounded better and more hopeful to me than the truth, which is I can't have sex with somebody unless they are a stranger and I'm drunk.

He said he's not worried about the lack of sex between us and that he understands completely and that I should never feel any pressure and to please let him know if he ever pressures me because he doesn't want to do this.

So he's perfect.

Too perfect?

I can't put my finger on it, but there's something off with him. I asked him, "What is it about being a shrink that is so fascinating, that caused you to go into the profession?"

He said, "Nothing. I never really wanted to be a shrink. It was an accident. I wanted to be a photographer, and that's what I was gonna do. But I had to take a biology class in college, and I turned out to be really good at it and . . ." He trailed off, but I pushed for more. "And, well, I just ended up taking more and more science classes and then my parents were really happy and they said, 'Be a doctor,' so that's sort of what happened."

I couldn't imagine going through four years of undergrad, four years of medical school, and then a residency all by accident.

But this is the thing about him: he doesn't seem to be passionate about anything. He's level-headed and sleepy. And there's something about him that I am so drawn to, like he possesses some unknown force that causes me to cling to him. Is it because I want to figure him out? Is it because he never pressures me about anything? Is it because I can be false with him and hold back my facts or because I can tell him everything and in the end there is no difference?

Nine months later. Mark the Shrink and I are no longer dating, but we are friends. We stopped dating when I returned from L.A. There just didn't seem to be anything to hold on to. We weren't going anywhere, and we weren't pulling away. We were just floating, suspended in liquid. And I guess I want more. And I don't know what he wants.

We talk on the phone once a week and sometimes go to a movie. He tells me about his ex-boyfriend, the one he spent two years with, from twenty-five to twenty-seven. The ex-boyfriend wants to date Mark again but not exclusively. He wants to date others as well. But Mark doesn't want this. Mark wants one person. But maybe "wants" is too strong a word.

Two weeks pass, and we don't talk.

I think of him but do not call because I am busy with work, and if I call him, I'll just have to say "I can't talk now because I'm busy, but I wanted to say hello."

Instead, Mark's friend Gary calls me. He says, "Have you heard from Mark?"

"Heard from him? What do you mean?"

Gary says, "Nobody has seen or heard from Mark for two days. He's missing."

I hear the word "missing," and something inside me is filled with a certain though unnamed knowledge.

An hour later Gary calls back. He is sobbing. "Mark is dead," he says. "He checked into the Chelsea Hotel and overdosed on sleeping pills."

What do I say? How? What? Why?

There is nothing to say.

"He'd worked two shifts in a row. Then he went to the hotel, checked in, and took the pills. He had his little tape recorder with him. He left a message for his parents."

I want to know what he said on the tape but know that I can't ask and will never know.

Half a thousand people attend his funeral on the Upper East Side, including the table of shrinks I had dinner with. The president of

Columbia University School of Medicine is there. He stands at the podium in an extraordinary suit and weeps openly and with utter dignity. "This is a single, catastrophic event."

I am astonished by the people who come to the podium to remember Mark the Shrink. They are doctors, artists, friends from the South, a few patients. I had no idea how large his life was.

He kept this to himself. It was his secret.

TELEMARKETING REVENGE

Lately, I am receiving numerous calls each night from telemarketers. They're calling with the frequent urgency of dumped boyfriends. At this point, I cannot help but wonder, is the entire telemarketing industry one big, jilted, clingy gay guy? They call to offer tremendous discounts on long-distance service, convenient debt consolidation, or simply to inform me that I have won a powerboat.

I can always tell a telemarketer before they even say a word. The phone rings and I answer. Immediately, I hear this pause and commotion in the background, like the person is calling from the cosmetics floor at Saks. Then they stumble through the beginning of their canned greeting: "Good evening, Mr. Burr—" Always, they are unable to pronounce my incredibly esoteric name: Burroughs. Two of the most primitive syllables combined into one word. And yet it always seems to come out as "Bee-rows, Burg-hose, or Burr-ouch."

Singularly, these calls are annoying. But when they happen four, five, and six times a night, my annoyance is transformed into something more nefarious. By law, saying "Please remove me from your calling list" is supposed to stop these people from calling you. There's an actual law in New York that says so. A "go away telemarketer" law. But does it work? Of course not. If anything, it strengthens their resolve. The same banks continue to call me. Not a day goes by that some phone company doesn't harass me. And if I win another fucking speedboat, I will be able to sell the lot of them and build a mansion on the waterfront land in Florida, which I allegedly won a week and a half ago.

So I decided to try an experiment. To seek a sort of curious revenge.

Last Thursday, a call came through, just like every other. I answered the phone, there was that malevolent pause filled with background sounds, then the obligatory mispronunciation of my name. Only instead of hanging up on the guy—it was a man this time; often it is a woman—I said, "Oh, wait. Who is this?"

He repeated the name of the company he was calling for. It was a credit card company.

I said, "Gee. You know what? I am kind of interested to hear this, but the thing is, I have my grandmother on the other line."

"Okay, well then I can try you again—"

He was about to let me off the hook, but I cut him off. "But I really want to hear about this deal. I am interested. The thing is, I need a MasterCard that works harder for me. And I'm just about to hang up with my grandmother, so is there any way, you know, I can call you back?"

There was a pause. And I did not want him to become suspicious. I played Regular Guy. "Like, do you have some weird number or extension or whatever, so if I call you back I can ask for you, and you can just run through the deal real quick?"

I must have concealed my dubious intentions well enough because he said, "Sure. My name's Paul. You can just dial 1-800-555-6575 and ask for extension 14."

I said, "Great. Thanks, Paul. I appreciate it. I'll get right back to you, man."

"Great," he said. "Talk to you soon."

I hung up the phone and smiled. I went to the kitchen and removed an icy Blenheim ginger ale from the refrigerator and brought it back to the dining-room table. I did a quick little excited dance in place, and then I picked up the phone and returned Paul's call.

"This is Paul," he said, this time sounding more like a normal employee at a desk, as opposed to a telemarketer. I realized he was not accustomed to receiving calls from potential telemarketing victims and was thus less feral, more humanistic.

"Hey Paul, this is Augusten Burroughs. You just called me."

"Oh, great," he said. Then he launched into his lengthy speech, which I'm sure he was reading from the computer screen in front of him.

I grinned and paid no attention, waiting only for him to stop talking. When he finally did stop talking, I said, "Hey bud, you have a good voice."

"Excuse me?" he said.

"Your voice," I said. "I like it." I was trying to sound as friendly and casual as possible, not seductive or sexual. I was using a Regular Guy voice, like, "Hey, how 'bout those Mets last night?" I was doing this on purpose, to confuse him.

"Um. Okay," he said, unsure.

I let an awkward silence well up between us. Then I asked, "Do you have a digital camera?"

"What?" he said, sounding very confused by the sudden change in direction the call had taken.

"I said, do you have a digital camera? You, personally, Paul. Do you have a digital camera?"

"Mr. Burr—"

"—*oughs*. Burroughs," I said, helpfully.

"Mr. Burroughs, I just need to know if you're interested in the MasterCard with an introductory interest rate of a low three percent." He was sounding a little brisk, and I didn't want to risk losing him.

"Yes," I said, finally. "Yes, I want it. I want that card. Definitely."

"Okay. Okay, well, good," he said, smiling, I knew, could almost hear his lips curl around his teeth. I heard tapping at the keyboard.

"EXCEPT," I added, "I want you to go home tonight and with your digital camera, Paul, I want you to take a picture of your penis and e-mail it to me." I let that sink in. "I'll give you my e-mail address. It's AugustenB@aol.com"

There was silence. But I did hear him breathing, which was strangely intimate and surprisingly thrilling. He was no longer a telemarketing asshole but suddenly a breathing human animal, and I had momentarily short-circuited his brain.

"It doesn't have to be hard, Paul. Soft is fine. But I want you to take a picture of your penis and e-mail it to me, then I will get this credit card. In fact Paul, if you send me a picture of your penis I will get both a Visa AND a MasterCard."

Here, he hung up.

I thought, no, no, no, no, no. You don't get to do that. When I hang up on a telemarketer, they always call me back. I waited ten minutes, and I called him back.

This time he answered his phone with a slight hesitation, and there was a wariness in his voice. "This is Paul," he said, rather suspiciously.

"Hi Paul," I said. "It's me. How about that penis picture? You gonna send it?"

"Fuck off, you queer," he spat.

"Hey man, I'm not the guy calling other guys at home during

the evening, okay? I'm not the guy making all these weird offers to other men."

This pissed him off. "What the fuck are you talking about? I'm asking if you want a fucking MasterCard."

"Paul, all I know is that this is the *third* time we've talked tonight, you're saying 'fuck' to me, I'm a guy, and your penis has been mentioned numerous times. Jesus, you're acting like you're some teenager. Work through this shit with a shrink, man. I don't care if you're gay."

Here again, I achieved silence. But not for long. The breathing became heavy and then, "What the fuck kind of game are you playing?"

"It's no game, man. You want to close a sale? I want to see your penis. It's a fair exchange if you ask me."

He hung up again, and I reached for my perfectly spicy, scratch-your-throat-like-a-cat-claw-hot Blenheim ginger ale and took a long swallow.

This particular credit card company has not called me again.

And, to my delight, AT&T never called me again after I asked one of their friendly Southern females if by any chance she happened to be a male-to-female transsexual, and if so, what vaginal depth her surgeon had managed to attain for her. "Four inches is pretty common," I told her. "But if you dilate religiously, you can probably achieve five." I even got the phrase "self-lubricating" out before she hung up on me.

My Last First Date

Dennis's superior mental health was obvious from the first date, like a cleft palate. The other thing about him that was obvious was that he had shapely, muscular legs. His calves were so sculpted they looked artificial, like silicone implants. This is a look I'm fond of. In fact, if I had been born a girl there is no doubt in my mind that my chest cavity would have been stuffed with two softball-sized orbs of silicone before my eleventh birthday. In this way my own mental health is somewhat like a cleft palate.

We met at the Starbucks on Astor Place and Third Avenue. I'd answered his personal ad the week before, and we'd had a couple of long conversations on the phone. My first novel was just a week away from being published, and I had decided that it was time for me to date. It had been over a year since I'd dated anybody; I'd never dated anybody as a published author. And since being a published author is all that I ever wanted in life, I felt that I had never actually had a date as the real me. It was the old me that slept with one-third of the men in Manhattan. It was also the old me that drunkenly confessed to my last boyfriend that his famous best friend was the most sexually attractive man I'd ever seen in my life.

When Dennis showed up he was on time and in shorts. At this point, I didn't know that he was so mentally healthy; I only knew that he was extremely sexy and punctual.

I already had a double espresso, so he introduced himself and said, "I'm just going to run inside and grab a coffee." He threw me this smile that told me his first impression wasn't one of repulsion. His teeth were so white I was certain they were all capped. But this, like silicone calf implants, was also just fine with me. I am what's known as an "early adopter." This means I had a laptop computer in 1984, when they were rare and the size of briefcases. I also had a cell phone that was larger than a loaf of bread. So new technologies have never frightened me away, even if these technologies are implanted into the body with the intention of making what's natural look better.

When Dennis returned, he set his tall coffee on the table, then sat down, knocking his leg against the table and causing his coffee to slosh out. "Fuck," he said, shoving the chair back. "Oh shit. Great. What a first impression." He looked at me with a genuinely disappointed and helpless expression on his face. I could tell he felt lousy and clumsy, and I was completely charmed. He frowned, and this made me see that his gray goatee is really a muzzle and he looks exactly like a schnauzer.

I love schnauzers.

Rarely do very handsome men allow their faces to run around without a leash. I am not *very* handsome, but I am above-average handsome, which means I have spent only one-sixteenth of my life in front of a mirror practicing facial expressions, as opposed to the maybe one-fourth that a very handsome guy might have. Yet I can tell you that if I had accidentally spilled coffee on a first date, I would have immediately made facial expression number 69b: Spilled Coffee on First Date face.

And that was my first clue that Dennis was of superior mental health. He had no reason to try and mask his awkwardness with a stoic face, no need to pretend to be blasé.

My stomach was in knots because I was trying to act casual.

Dennis wiped off the table with a couple of napkins and sat down. There was a flirty, smiling back-and-forth thing that went on. I learned that he was half Italian and half Austrian, which to me translates into half sexy and half insane.

When he told me of his hatred for nuns, caused by years of mean-spirited and Gothic Catholic schooling, his voice increased to a shout. He went from looking friendly and smart to furious and unstable. I thought it was hysterical that he was still so enraged about Catholic school, thirty years later. I laughed and said, "You are a ranting crazy person. You're not as normal as you appear."

He smiled, then began to chuckle at himself. He blushed very slightly but enough for me to know I was right, that in some way he was crazy and we both knew it. Here he told me he was in therapy. He backed into this declaration carefully, like steering around a little girl on her Big Wheel. "Well, I, uh . . . I hope I'm not too crazy. But probably I am. You'd think after like, what? I guess, what? Fifteen, sixteen? Yeah, sixteen, anyway. I guess after sixteen years of therapy you'd think I'd be over the Catholic school shit."

He glanced at me, and I knew he was waiting for my reaction to his therapy.

I said, "That's fantastic."

He said, "Yeah? You think?"

With true enthusiasm I said, "It's fucking great. That is just so essential."

"So you're in therapy?"

I said, "No. Not really. But I have been. I mean, sort of. I, when I was twelve, I lived with my crazy mother's psychiatrist. She, you know, gave me to him. He was very odd. Actually, he was pathological. Eventually he lost his medical license. But sometimes he was very good, maybe brilliant. Anyway, my point is I think therapy is great."

He looked alarmed.

I realized my mistake at once. I must ease people into the facts of me, not deposit large, undigested chunks of my history at their feet. Too much of me too fast is toxic. Damn. And I thought I was holding back. "It sounds pretty disturbing, I guess."

"Yes, it does," he said, with concern. He had leaned forward, as if to study me up close.

"But it was actually a lot of fun. Eccentric. Anyway," I clapped my hands together exactly like a talk show host, "I've had a lot of therapy since then. To get over it."

His face relaxed, slightly. But he remained quiet. He wanted evidence that I had, in fact, gotten over it with the help of a trained mental-health professional.

"I had a really intense stint of therapy in rehab, then for six months after I got out." I regretted everything I was saying but was unable to stop. What would be next? *I think it'd be cool to be a transsexual, except I'm too tall. And I wouldn't want to be a woman, you know. But the drastic lifestyle change would be cool.* Dennis was very easy to talk to. He'd have been a good therapist.

"Rehab?"

I explained how I drank my twenties away trying to forget my childhood. This seemed perfectly understandable to me, almost Hollywood.

Dennis seemed worried. But then, as if inspired by angels, his face suggested a change of emotion. It was the benefit of the doubt, flying into his ears and lodging in his brain behind his eyes. He suggested dinner. "Do you eat meat?"

The bells of destiny began to ring. It was like standing in the spire of a church on Christmas morning. Do I eat meat? DO I EAT MEAT? This man—this handsome, silver-haired man with the wicked sense of humor and the excellent legs——he could have no way of knowing that not only do I eat meat, I eat meat exclusively. That "meat" is my favorite word. That meat has been a part of my life since I worked on the "Beef: Real Food for Real People" advertising campaign when I was an eighteen-year-old vegetarian copywriter. It was as if God's hand came out of the sky and slapped me on the ass. *Here's your fella*, God said, throwing his head back in a fit of celestial laughter, smug with knowledge.

I said, "Did I mention my meatacious nature to you?"

"Huh?" he said, puzzled.

"I didn't tell you all I eat is meat, did I?"

He started to laugh because it seemed to be the thing to do, but he got caught up on one of my words. "All you eat is meat? No vegetables?"

"I loathe and detest them," I said, making my words wink as much as a word can.

"I see," he said, playing along. "Well, you'll love this place, then. They come over to your table with a huge chunk of meat, and they carve it onto your plate. Oh, and they give you these little plastic disks. One is red and one is green. And when you want more meat, you put the green one out, and when you've had enough, you put the red one out."

Was this true? Was he serious?

We walked four blocks south to a Brazilian restaurant that I must have walked past a thousand times on my own and yet never noticed. This further proved my own belief that there is only so much any given person can see for themselves in Manhattan. It takes two people, looking in all directions at once, to see everything.

We got a good table for two, right near the front, where we could watch the other carnivores enter. A moment after we were seated, before we'd even placed our white cloth napkins in our laps, the meat man arrived. He was carrying an entire leg of something in one hand and a hatchet in the other. Our plates were already there, were there before we were. And wordlessly, he began carving the meat onto them in thick, steaming slices.

Dennis glanced at my plate and then down at his. There were at least three pounds of meat between our two plates. He smiled in a way that suggested mischief and remarked, "We are at the top of the food chain."

I said, "And we can eat anything we want."

Unlike every other person I've ever shared a meat-based meal with, Dennis did not comment on how clogged his arteries were about to become or how many miles he would have to run to burn off the fat. He tucked into his plate with quiet bliss. This, I thought, was a very good sign.

"So are you close to your family?" I asked.

He stabbed a quarter-inch-thick slab of medium-rare beast. "Not incredibly close. But we all get along and everything." He carefully sliced the beast into a bite-sized piece and steered it into a small pool of sauce at the edge of his plate. "We don't really see each other very often. I don't know, it's weird," he said. "Two of my brothers and my sister all live within like twenty minutes of each other in Pennsylvania. They all have kids around the same age. And yet," he popped the beast into his mouth, causing the fork to clank against his front teeth. "And yet, they never see each other. Maybe once every couple years."

His mother, he explained, died of cancer. It had been a particularly sadistic cancer, and it took a long time for her to die. She suffered, and he spoke gently, kindly, of her. "She raised five kids with no help from anybody. She did the cooking, the cleaning, took care of everything and everyone as best as she could."

He told me that his father lived alone in an efficiency apartment near his siblings. When he spoke of his father, his eyes flashed with complexity. I didn't want to pry, but I wanted to know more. "What's your dad like?"

"He's, oh I don't even know how to describe him. Okay, he's like this. He believes that he put a roof over our heads and made sure we had food on the table and that was enough. That was more than enough. That was his entire responsibility, and as far as he was concerned, he was a good father."

"I think it's a generational thing," I said. "Because my father was pretty much the same way. But it seems like women have pretty much pussy-whipped all the straight men, so they're a lot more expressive and participatory than they used to be."

Dennis said quickly, "You mean, straight guys are the new gay guys."

"That's exactly what I mean. Straight guys are like fags used to be. And the fags *now* are more like straight guys *were*. Fags today are all about body building and pickup trucks, and straight guys are all about feelings and open-toe sandals."

This got us onto the topic of guys and dating. Dennis told me about some of the lousy dates he'd had over the past few years, including the recent date in Central Park where he cried.

"I've never cried on a date," I told him.

"It was more than cried. It was like a complete mental collapse."

He explained how he had met a guy through a personal ad, the old-fashioned kind in the back of a newspaper. He answered an ad this guy had placed. So they spoke on the phone—for hours—over a period of a week. Their chemistry was intense.

But when they met, the man was shaped like a pear, and he had a tiny head.

I said, "That's the catch. That's why his ad was in the newspaper and not online, with a picture."

Dennis said, "Well, I tried to overlook that. I kept thinking, *We were really connecting on the phone; I can overlook his body.*"

"Yeah, but the tiny head," I said.

"Well, yeah. I know. That was hard to overlook. So anyway, we met in the park, and I just was so wound up from our conversations, so let down, I guess, by the way he looked. And so tired of dating and ten years of being single and having really terrible dates that it just hit me."

Selfishly, I thought to myself what a good sign it was that he could cry. At the same time, I felt so bad for him. Like, I wanted to go back in time and hide in the bushes while he was on his date and then jump out and take him away.

The subject changed to work. Dennis told me about the graphic-design firm he owns, and I told him about my ad career, which was now freelance. I explained how advertising is what I do to make money, like waiting tables, to support my writing. And the best way to do it is freelance. *Sellevision* had just hit bookstores, and even though I was thrilled to have my first book published, I knew it wasn't going to earn me enough money to quit advertising altogether. *Maybe* it would earn me enough money to buy some shirts. At the Gap.

"But that is so exciting about your book," he said.

"Thanks," I said. I tried to sound casual, because it was the biggest thing that had ever happened to me, my small yellow paperback-original book. It was a novel that was fluffy and mean and funny, and I was extremely proud because writing a book was what I'd always felt I would do. And had never done. Had been a drunk instead.

"I can't wait to read it," he said. "Maybe I'll be able to read it over the weekend."

Here, Dennis was shouting. Other people glanced at our table, looking for the fight. He was speaking like a person who had been deaf for most of his life and then suddenly could hear but didn't have all those years practicing voice modulation. I didn't dare tell him to lower his voice. He was much too passionate and intense. I liked it. I would just ignore the curious glances from the other meat eaters.

"Aren't you going to have another glass of wine?" I asked.

"No, I'm fine," he said.

I didn't believe him. "You're just saying that because I don't drink."

He admitted this was true. "I don't want you to feel uncomfortable."

"I knew it. NO," I said. "It doesn't make me uncomfortable at all. Honestly." The more I insisted, the more uncomfortable I probably looked. But it was true. I wanted him to be himself and not refrain from anything because of me. Also, I felt this was an incredibly thoughtful act on his part that could easily have gone unnoticed.

Except I noticed. I motioned for the waiter to come to the table, and when he did I looked at Dennis.

Dennis smiled at me and ordered another glass of merlot.

"I don't know anything about wine," I said. "I could easily drink seven bottles at any given moment, and used to sometimes. And I can't tell you the brand or anything about it. I just know I paid thirty dollars a bottle and drank three bottles a night."

"Thirty dollars? Must have been good wine."

"I guess," I said with an air of disinterest. "It's all a blur."

After dinner we stepped outside, and a man walked past us. He was a shortish man with a balding head and a trimmed red beard. He was wearing neon-blue Lycra. We looked at him, his butt. It was not a good butt. It was not a butt that should ever be in Lycra. Dennis said without prompting, "I should be the one who decides who gets to wear Lycra. You know? That should be my job, I should be the director of Lycra for the United States or the ambassador or whatever it would be called."

Then he looked at my ass. It was a quick look, but I caught it. And from his face, I couldn't tell if he was pleased or upset.

To be honest, I don't have a great ass. It's on the skinny side. It's a skinny white-guy ass.

When it was time to part, I didn't want to. And, it seemed, neither did he. I got the feeling he was slightly afraid of me, wary. But also interested. Also sort of glued to me.

"Well," I said, in that tone of voice people use when they're finishing something, wrapping things up for the evening.

He said the same thing, in exactly the same way, at the same time.

I had the sensation one experiences of making all the green lights. I knew at that moment that if I were to play slot machines or bet on a horse at the Derby, I would win. It wasn't so much a feeling as it was certain knowledge. Like déjà vu, except instead of seen before, it was more certainty.

As I walked away, I looked back at him.

He was already looking back at me.

I smiled the whole way home. I was walking and smiling, and because of this, because of my Happy Face, I probably looked like a very simple person, unencumbered by complicated thoughts. Like somebody who was just happy because there was macaroni and cheese in the world. And socks! Maybe people looked at me and wished they were more simple and idiotic, *like that guy there*.

Normally when I come home from a date, I replay the entire evening in my head. I pulverize it and then examine the grains of dust. Sometimes I actually write it all out, capturing the dialogue while it's still fresh. I then examine what was said from every angle, trying to peer into the nuance and subtle meaning between the words. I project into the near and distant future. I make a sort of mental flowchart of how the date could lead to either a relationship or a disaster.

"What did he mean when he said . . ." or "Was he smiling because he was happy or uncomfortable?"

I obsess so thoroughly that after twenty-four hours of imagining various scenarios, I am sick of the other person and can't bear the thought of a second date with them, let alone a committed relationship.

But tonight, this night after my first date with Dennis, it's different. Something in the world feels supernaturally askew. As though something in space has shifted, creating a rare opening.

I come home and feel the distinct sensation of complete peace. I am exactly, absolutely, perfectly okay. At the same time, I know I could easily topple the feeling. It's like I am balancing a china plate on my head. One abrupt move, the plate will fall and shatter. It is not something I have ever felt before, yet it feels more comfortable than anything I can name. Instead of pondering any of this further, I climb into bed and open a book.

I am not going to rush this. I am not going to write this. I am not going to force this.

I am going to feel this plate on my head. It's nice. I like it.

It was a good date.

He is a good guy.

I am going to read a book.

I read forty pages. Then I turn off the light, which can be dangerous. But my mind is clear. I dream of disks. One red. One green.

Bring it on.

THE SCHNAUZER

In bed the Schnauzer lies on his back. His chest is muscular and tight with coarse hairs, which he clips short. His chest is like a bed in the military: you could bounce a quarter off it. When I first saw him without his shirt, as he reclined against the pillows, he laughed hard at something I said, and I happened to look at his stomach. There, I saw an extra bone. It ran horizontally just below his rib cage. At first this disturbed me. It was like seeing an extra toe. Could I love him despite this mutation? Then when he laughed harder, another bone appeared. And I realized they were not bones; they were abs.

I looked down at my own stomach which is not fat, which is sort of flat, but does not have defined abs.

I asked him, "What's the biggest disability you could overlook in a guy in order to date him?"

The Schnauzer turned to me, and his blue eyes sparkled. "What do you mean?"

I nestled up against him and placed my head on his chest. "You know, like a missing leg, no arms?"

"Oh," he said.

I sat up to watch him think.

With his left hand, he scratched behind his right ear. This caused the biceps in his arm to swell to the size of a ripe mango. He looked like a magazine centerfold, like he should have a line of staples right down the middle. "A limp I guess," he said with a smile.

I laughed at him. "A limp! I can't believe you said a limp." I pretended to be appalled by his shallowness, although I, myself, would have problems with even a limp. "You're certainly willing to cut people slack."

He hugged me closer. He was smiling, the full smile that I like most. The one that gives him dimples and lights up his eyes and makes him look like a movie star. The smile that makes me feel lucky when I see it because I know that he couldn't flash it all day. Not everyone gets to see it. In fact, I'm starting to consider it mine alone.

"Could you date somebody with Down's syndrome?" I ask.

Without thinking, he replied, "If he had a bubble butt, pecs, and a big dick."

He thinks he's being very clever, so I tell him my scary story. I say, "You remember I told you about my Australian friend, Hateful Harold?"

The Schnauzer nods because he does remember Hateful Harold; he remembers everything I tell him.

"Well, he got drunk one night and went to that awful Ty's bar on Christopher Street?"

The Schnauzer made a sour face. He knows the bar and can imagine exactly the sleazy clientele that goes there, a crowd that has already been to every other bar on the street and is now sweating and desperate. I continue, "So he was depressed and at this pit of a bar, and he was drunk and horny. And all of a sudden, some guy came up to him, and they started talking. But Hateful Harold wasn't in a talkative mood, so he suggested they just hop on the subway and go back to his Jersey City apartment. So that's what they did.

"Flash forward to the next morning, when Hateful Harold wakes up, completely hungover and next to a body. The guy's back is to him, and he can barely remember even going out the night before, let alone picking somebody up. So gently he turns the guy over, and—surprise—the guy had Down's syndrome."

The Schnauzer yelps with glee.

"It's true!" I say. "And so then he, the guy with Down's syndrome, wakes up with this big fat hard-on and Hateful Harold just recoils from the bed. He flies out of it and stumbles backward. And the Down's syndrome guy says to him, 'I love you.'" Here, I look directly into the Schnauzer's eyes. "So you better be careful what you wish for."

Later we order Chinese food. It arrives about forty-five seconds after we hang up the phone. We open the bag and fortune cookies wrapped in cellophane spill onto the counter. I take one, rip off the wrapper and break the cookie in two. I peel out the fortune and read it. "You are gifted in business matters."

"We must have the wrong order," Dennis says.

"I am good at business," I protest.

"Oh?" he says, raising just an eyebrow. With this look I know he is referring to my oven. The thing is, I live in a studio, so space is limited, and I never cook. So naturally, I keep all my tax crap in the oven.

"Ick, what is this?" I say, peeling the plastic lid off one of the containers.

"It doesn't matter," Dennis says. "It all comes from the same place." Then he explains Chinese food in Manhattan to me: "See the way it works is, there's one central location out on Long Island where all this stuff is made. Then it's piped into the city through a series of underground pipes that run parallel to the train and subway tracks. The restaurants then just pull a lever. One lever for General Tso's chicken, another for beef with broccoli sauce. It's like beer; it's on tap."

It's amazing how convincing he is when he says this. There's no pause in his description, nowhere for him to stop and think, to make this up as he goes along. It's as though he's simply repeating something he read in the *Times* yesterday.

This makes me love him more than I did just five minutes ago.

The Schnauzer is a responsible business owner who balances his checkbook down to the penny. Whereas I throw my bank statements into the trash unopened. He shops at Fairway market, where there is an entire aisle devoted to olives. I shop at the Korean market downstairs from my crummy apartment, where there is an entire aisle devoted to cream-flavored Japanese gummy worms.

There are other differences between us.

He washes and reuses Zip-Loc storage bags. And I have single-handedly destroyed many acres of rain forest through my extensive use of yellow Post-it notes and paper towels, which I use compulsively for everything.

He has no vices whereas I have had all of them at one point but now have only Nicorette gum, which I chew constantly, causing my jaw to snap and pop.

The Schnauzer listens to jazz. I listen to jazz because he likes it, and I have even gone to jazz concerts with him, but truthfully I would rather listen to retarded children pounding on pan lids with wooden spoons.

Our many differences have been cause for worry for the Schnauzer. And he has had many therapy sessions devoted exclusively to this topic.

"I'm just getting used to the fact that people have differences and that in a relationship, you make sacrifices and compromises," he tells me. "But sometimes I worry about our differences. I worry that we have too many."

I try to comfort him with the one fact that I believe and hold onto: we are nearly the same on a molecular level; on the soul level, where it truly matters, we are identical. Therefore, I never worry about our differences and in fact find many of them amusing if not outright hysterical.

For example, I am into furry arms and legs. While the Schnauzer has a thing for butts. Some people are into hair. Or hands. Or legs. Or chests. Or feet. Or genitals. The Schnauzer is a butt connoisseur. He likes a full, round muscular butt. Street name: bubble butt. It's a butt most commonly attached to muscular black men. Which could explain why Dennis has always had a thing for beefy black guys.

Which can make a tall white guy who is already neurotic to begin with even more insecure. But he reassures me that I have a fine butt, that it's not as flat as I believe it to be. He tells me this despite what I see in the mirror, which looks like an eleven-year-old's butt. So while I never much considered butts before, now I want one. And it's one of those things you can't really get.

So it occurs to me that the Schnauzer is accepting a handicap with me in a way. My lack of a bubble butt, his favorite body part, is worth giving up for more. Which is generous. Which seems shallow to talk about but actually, like so much that is shallow, is a quality that runs deep through his strata. The Schnauzer is a very generous man. It's his nature. He likes people because he likes to share in conversations. I like people when they have large checks for me.

Because of my questionable background Dennis has encouraged me to go to therapy. Perhaps "encouraged" isn't the right word. Perhaps "insisted" is more accurate. But I don't mind; I've had some very interesting experiences behind the closed doors of a psychiatrist's office.

My therapist is a slim, attractive man in his mid-forties. He's extremely intelligent and truly loves what he does. More important, he has impeccable taste. His office reflects a man with interests in the world, an understanding of fabric and financial success. If a therapist has a plain, white office with two chairs and a white noise machine, I won't come back. I require a therapist with a tasteful, well-decorated office. I tell my therapist, "I'm tired of living in the shallow end of the pool."

He says, "What do you mean?"

I reach into my backpack and hunt for my ChapStick. I am thinking as I do this, stalling for time.

"Do you need something?" he asks.

"I'm just looking for my ChapStick," I tell him.

He reaches into his front pocket and offers me his. First, I am surprised that he has ChapStick not only within reaching distance, but on his person. And second, that he would offer me this very intimate personal item.

I can't help it—I instantly imagine taking the ChapStick and then, when he turns his head, biting off the end before handing it back to him.

I am reeling from this. My therapist has offered me his Chap-Stick. It almost seems like something a therapist could be fined for.

I break into a fit of laughter.

"What is it?" he asks, grinning.

Then, when I can't control my laughter, can't slow it or stop it altogether, when I begin to get tears in my eyes, his smile fades.

"What?" he says.

I pull myself together slightly. "I'm sorry. It's just . . . it's nothing. I mean, I'm such an ass. I'm just laughing because I'm talking about how worried I am about being shallow, which in itself seems like such a vapid concern, being worried about being shallow. Worried, why? Because of what other people think? That's shallow. Worried that I'm not 'deep' enough for Dennis? He knows me. Knows I am."

My therapist nods and listens closely. He has completely forgotten about my eruption of laughter.

I have fooled him.

Later at home, I tell the Schnauzer. "Do you think that's weird or is it just me?"

"Oh no," he says. "It's definitely weird."

"I mean, what would you do if your therapist offered you his ChapStick?"

The Schnauzer thinks about this briefly before answering. "I'd probably try and forget it happened."

Then I call my friend Christopher, who referred me to my shrink in the first place. Christopher abandoned therapy last year, and he gave me Bruce. "You take him," he said. "I'm flying without a net for a while." I tell him what Bruce did, and Christopher sucks air in so sharply, I feel like my ear will be stuck to the phone.

"Is that weird?" I ask him.

"Oh my god, that is beyond weird. It's borderline creepy."

"I know!" I say. "I thought it was so disturbing. And then I thought, am I just overly sensitive? Is he just a normal guy, and I'm like some sort of unsocialized German shepherd? But it's true, he's weird."

Christopher stops laughing long enough to tell me, "You know what? Some people are just like that with ChapStick. I think that's all it is. I mean, I've known people, almost strangers, who have offered me theirs, too. So I think it's like some people have this very liberal relationship with their ChapStick."

The Schnauzer makes my favorite thing for dinner. He calls it

Lesbian Expander. It's a sort of chili, made from tempeh, cubed and browned on all sides in butter; brown rice, which he seasons in a mysterious and perfect way; shredded Cheddar cheese; onions; lentil chili; and jalapeño peppers. It's named Lesbian Expander because it's something only a lesbian would cook. And Expander because once you eat it, it swells in your stomach to six times its original mass, and you must lie on your side in bed and clutch your stomach.

So this is what we do, we lie in bed, clutching our stomachs and facing each other. I look at his eyes, then his mouth. And then his eyes do the same thing, and then we smile at each other.

"Do you want some ChapStick?" he asks.

"Okay," I say.

"I'll get up in a minute and get it for you."

"Okay," I say.

We move closer together until we are breathing the same air. And we fall asleep.

KEY WORST

The only Hemingway I've ever been remotely interested in is Mariel. Though I've tried to expand my mind by reading some of her grandfather's little stories. I read *The Old Man and the Sea* but my eyelids bled from the toothpicks that I used to keep them open. It amuses me that Hemingway is now a line of sofas, chairs, and bedroom dressers at Thomasville furniture. I wonder how long it will be before I can get a Joan Didion coffee table or perhaps a Philip Roth throw rug for in front of the washer.

I should have considered this before Dennis and I went to Key West, Florida, otherwise known as "Hemingway's Hideaway" or "the tropical residence of America's greatest writer."

I had to admit, even though I never cared much about Hemingway, the name alone lends a certain appeal, as Thomasville obviously knows through extensive consumer testing in shopping malls. "Hemingway" conjures images of thick-slat Venetian blinds, palm fronds, and quaint bungalows scattered on narrow, winding streets, paved with crushed white clamshells.

In no way did I expect a Ripley's Believe It or Not! museum or an entire street devoted to extra-extra-large T-shirts embossed with slogans such as "I like my woman like I like my dog, on all fours" and "Yes boys, they're real."

"God, this is absolutely hideous. It's worse than Fourteenth Street," I said the instant we stepped foot on Duval Street.

Dennis is an optimist. "Hold on, hold on," he said, dragging me by the arm. "We just got here five minutes ago. This is just a touristy part of town. Let's give it a chance, okay?"

On the one hand, Dennis is the reasonable one in the relationship. On the other, he's just the slower one.

"Fine," I said, turning away from the Hard Rock Café, "I'll give it a chance."

We crossed the street, and a man who weighed at least three hundred pounds turned to his larger wife and said, "I can't believe there ain't no fucking roller coaster in this town. Why the hell ain't they got one?"

His wife's hair had made unfortunate contact with a large amount of hydrogen peroxide, and the result was blinding in the noon sun.

Dennis gripped my arm tighter. "Okay, this place should be bombed," he said.

We immediately went back to our hotel room.

As it turned out, our hotel room was actually a private bungalow, something out of an actual Hemingway novel. There were two pools on the grounds, with brick walkways and wildflowers blooming in places that seemed to hold only shadows. Manly, yet expressive, like Papa himself. The hotel had been a splurge, four hundred dollars a night. We'd assumed that after spending nine or ten hours exploring Key West, it would be nice to come back to a luxurious room.

Now, we both checked to make sure the television worked.

"Look on the bright side," Dennis said. "At least we can lie by the pool and get a tan."

This was the bright side until later that afternoon when the rains came. We assumed this was a tropical shower sort of thing. But we began to worry by noon the following morning when the rains had only become harder and the streets began to flood.

"I sure am sorry about this weather, fellas," the friendly gentleman behind the front desk told us. "I'm sorry for you, but boy do we need this rain. We've had a drought down here. Haven't had a drop of rain for five months."

"Why don't we fly back to New York?" I suggested once we were back in our room under the covers.

"Because we've already paid for the room," Dennis said. "And I'm sure the rain won't last. Let's just try to enjoy it. You've been saying you haven't been able to read for ages. So read a novel."

But I couldn't read because I was so irritated. If I'd wanted to stay in bed and watch terrorist attacks and Amtrak train wrecks on CNN, we could have stayed home.

"Then let's just go out for a walk, anyway," Dennis said. "Who cares if we get wet, we're on an island."

So this is what we did. We decided that rain be damned, we'd explore the island, away from the tourist-infested streets. And to our delight, the rain had driven the fat Americans back to their motel rooms. And we were able to walk the streets in solitude.

And finally, finally, I was able to see what might have caused Hemingway to live here. The homes were quite charming, tucked away on narrow side streets and covered with flora. Grand porches, tall windows, wavy old glass. It was easy to imagine that several decades ago, this was a quaint island. Once, the wax museum was probably a corner hardware store. The Gap was probably a drugstore, complete with a soda fountain where you could buy an egg cream for thirty cents. And the restaurant owned by non-lesbian Kelly McGillis was probably once a dive bar with swordfish pinned to the walls and fifty-cent tumblers of malted whiskey.

I longed for the Key West that existed in my imagination. Where was the old man sitting on the steps of a diner named "Jack's Place," picking flecks of Lucky Strike tobacco off his lips? Where was the young French nanny who'd become a hooker and wore torn fishnet stockings and smelled like lye soap and lavender?

Instead, there was a sign that advertised glass-bottom boat rides. "Oh, fuck. We might as well," Dennis said.

So we followed the street to the southern tip, and here we were surprised to see that the fat Americans had not been driven inside to their rooms; they had been driven into a line for the glass-bottom boat rides.

"Oh, there's no way. I can't stand in that line," I said.

Dennis gave me the eye. "Like you have something better to do?"

I whispered, "But I don't like these people."

He said, "Well, you don't have to marry any of them."

Knowing I would never win, I sighed and jammed my hands into my pockets. It was going to be a long and painful vacation—also very wet and cold—but I'd suffered through worse. Like rehab when I was thirty. Twenty-eight days of hell. At least this would be a shorter period of time. So this is what I thought on my vacation: *I'm not in a rehab hospital. Yay!*

"God damn it, Hank. Hold that umbrella over me. The rain keeps puttin' out my cigarette."

"So chew your damn cigarette gum," the gigantic man—Hank, I assume—replied.

"I am chewing my cigarette gum, Einstein. And I got a patch on, too. But I'd like to enjoy my cigarette while we wait in line."

I have always loved eavesdropping. But even more, I love knowing that somebody is eavesdropping on my own conversation. My former art director, Greer, and I had a lot of fun playing games with people. We'd be traveling on business, off to L.A. to shoot a commercial, and we'd be sitting near the gate waiting for our flight and chatting. Then we would become aware that somebody else was listening, so I would say, "Honey, tell me you arranged for your parents to stay with the baby." And she would feign horror. "Oh my fucking God, I totally forgot. The baby is alone. Shit. Do you think she can last on her own for two days?" And I would reply, "Well, I guess. Babies are supposed to be pretty durable."

As the couple bickered about her smoking, his umbrella, and the line for the boat, I could not stop myself from staring at them. The woman's forehead was dented, as though she had bullet fragments in her skull that the surgeon had been unable to remove. She seemed like a woman who could become dangerous without warning, like one of the creatures I enjoyed watching on *Animal Planet*. Clearly, she already had enough nicotine in her system to kill a laboratory of rats.

"Why don't we just go back to the room," I whispered to Dennis.

He was enjoying this, my misery. "Oh come on . . . we're almost there." He winked. Dennis is the only person I have ever known who can wink and get away with it. When Dennis winks, the world is safe.

A child kicked me.

"What the fuck?" I said, looking down and seeing a young Chinese girl with a vinyl Hello Kitty knapsack.

She laughed, and then she kicked me again, harder.

I looked at her parents, but they both had dead, distant faces. The resigned expressions of older parents who had accidentally had a child, late in life. No doubt their little girl had kicked them both senseless, and now they were oblivious.

But I was not oblivious. And I was not amused.

"Stop that," I said, leaning down and speaking into the top of her head. "Don't kick."

She kicked again.

The little fucker. I bent down. "Do you speak English?" I asked, sweetly. I smiled. "Do you speak English, you little cutie pie?"

She nodded, gave a little giggle, and then stepped on my toes, which were exposed through the straps of my sandals.

I immediately stopped smiling and narrowed my eyes. I whispered, "You kick me one more time you little cocksucker, and once we get on the boat, I'll push your mother into the ocean, and she'll die. And then I'll hurt your daddy. And then I'll be your new daddy, and I'll take you home with me."

She moved quickly to the other side of her parents, where she kept a wary, silent eye on me.

"Next time people ask if we're ever going to have kids, I think I'll tell them this little story," Dennis said.

"What?" I said, indignant. "She's a horrible, spoiled little bitch."

"She's just a little girl," he said.

I laughed. "Little girl, my ass. She's a little Chinese dragon."

Dennis rolled his eyes, and we finally boarded the glass-bottom boat.

"Pepsi!" shouted a kid sitting near us. The kid pointed to the glass below us and sure enough, a Pepsi can.

"Maybe we'll see a body! What would you think of that?" the kid's dad said. "Maybe a swimmer who was attacked by a shark!"

"Doug, stop," the mother said, slapping her husband's meaty shoulder.

Dennis and I looked at each other. The true curiosities were not outside the glass bottom of the boat; they were sitting in the chairs next to us.

A guide's voice crackled through the speakers, explaining the various fish that swam past us. But by far, there were more license plates, plastic six-pack holders, and soda cans than fish.

"Maybe we won't have seafood tonight," Dennis said.

I watched as a mutton snapper glided over an old hubcap. "Yeah, burgers sound good."

I stood up to stretch my back and saw the little monster child glaring at me from the safety of the other side of the boat. I winked at her, and she turned away.

And then in a moment of sanity, I realized I probably really had terrified that little girl. And I'd certainly ruined Key West for her. In fact, I was fairly certain that she would never return to Florida at all.

So clearly, Hemingway would have been proud of me.

Ass Burger

The summer my big brother, John, turned fifteen, he read the *Encyclopedia Britannica* from A to Z. As he finished each volume, he would leave it on my bed, so that I could do likewise. But I did not do likewise. What little factual information I absorbed in my life was gleaned from lectures the Professor gave to Gilligan.

For Christmas that year, my brother was astounded that I did not know how to use the slide rule he had given me. "What the fuck?" he said in his deep monotone voice. "You must have read about how these things work."

I glanced up over the liner notes of my new Marlo Thomas *Free to Be You and Me* album and told him that of course I didn't know how it worked; I didn't read the encyclopedia like he did.

His mouth opened in disgust. He simply could not comprehend this. "You didn't read *any* of them?"

I told him I looked at some of the pictures. "Those transparent pages with naked people and their insides, that was neat," I said.

"Well, that's just unacceptable. I mean, you're reading at a third-grade level. Don't you find that alarming?" Considering I was in the third grade, no, I didn't.

And from this moment on my brother treated me as not just his younger brother, but his "borderline retarded" younger brother. In fact, this is exactly how he introduced me to his friends: "This is my younger brother. You can just ignore him; he's basically retarded. Our mother smoked while she was pregnant with him, and I guess there was brain damage."

But to me, it was my brother who seemed retarded. Either that or a genius, I couldn't decide. All I knew for sure was that he was a peculiar creature. While he could not fathom a younger brother who did not share his fascination with quantum mechanics, I likewise could not comprehend that my brother didn't own a single pair of platform shoes. As far as I was concerned, he was in training to become a creepy gas station attendant, while I was going to be a star.

So what, exactly, was he?

On the one hand, my brother knew how to create something called a circuit board, which, when attached with wires to a series of strobe lights and placed next to our sleeping mother, provided a shocking amount of fun. He could create an entire automobile engine Frankensteined together from parts he found at the dump. The floor of my brother's room was littered with transistors, tiny batteries, wires, bits of lead from his soldering iron, red-and-black rubber-capped clamps. Instead of a baseball glove, my brother had an oscilloscope on his dresser. And if you asked him, "Are platinum records really made of platinum?" you would get a thirty-minute discourse on the periodic table, including the half-life of each element.

But on the other hand my brother seemed like somebody best confined to a basement. Not only was he gruff and abrupt, but he spoke in a deadly monotone at all times. He never made eye contact. And he took no pride in his appearance, seeing nothing wrong with wearing pants that had been too short for years. When my parents had guests, my brother often asked shockingly rude questions: "Didn't you have an abortion last year?" he asked my mother's friend Nancy. When my mother shrieked, "John, that is absolutely none of your business. How dare you ask such a question," my brother simply grunted and then snorted, "Well, I thought you said she had an abortion. One of your friends did. I thought it was this 'Nancy' character." Nancy herself simply sat in mute horror on the sofa, her hands protectively folded across her chest.

Thankfully, my brother spent much of his time alone in his room, the walls of which were covered with images of trains: steam engines, cabooses, sometimes close-ups of the wheels themselves. Quite different from the walls of my room, which were decorated with pages torn from *Tiger Beat* and cigarette ads from old *Life* magazines.

Occasionally, we would do "activities" together. Once, we took an old pair of his jeans and an old shirt and stuffed them with bed sheets. Next we stapled the seams to create a "body." My brother then led me down a path a few miles from our house, and we tied a rope around the body and slung it up over one of the rails of the power-line scaffolding. Later at home my brother phoned the local police and informed them that there had been a ritual hanging in the neighborhood. As sirens streamed down our little dirt road my brother smirked and chuckled. "That should occupy them for a while."

My brother moved out of the house when he was seventeen

and began living with a rock band. He wasn't interested in playing an instrument; he was interested in building the various electronic components. Before long, he'd installed sound systems in many of the local bars and clubs. Then, thrillingly, he created disco dance floors at black nightclubs in Springfield. Word spread about a grubby, clever kid who was good with electronics. And this is how it happened that my strange and aloof brother built the rocket-shooting, fire-spitting, exploding guitars for the band Kiss. He built every special-effect guitar for the band's Dynasty World Tour in his bedroom. His name began to appear in magazines next to the word "brilliant."

This same year, his high-school classmates merely graduated.

Other kids say "My big brother can beat you up." I was able to say "My big brother is a genius like Einstein."

It's twenty-five years later, and I'm home at the computer, e-mailing my friend Suzanne in California. She is telling me she found the head of a rat in her driveway, and I'm writing her back saying it's a sign. "You're only half a rat away," I tell her, but away from what, I don't say.

My brother calls. "Woof," he says, his standard greeting for friends, family, the president, were he to call. "Hey," I say back to him.

My brother's rock-band days are over. He owns a very successful car dealership and service center where he sells previously owned Range Rovers, Rolls Royces, and other staggeringly expensive cars. He takes photographs—thousands of them—with his nine-thousand-dollar digital camera and then e-mails the images to me, which take hours to download. He is married now, and he has a son. We speak on the phone each day because he calls me on the way to work in the morning. If I am sleeping in and don't answer the phone, he will simply call again and again until I am forced to answer.

My brother never asks how I am or what I'm feeling. He simply begins speaking, as though we have already been on the phone for an hour. Often, he begins midthought. "So the kid," he says, meaning his son. "He's not very happy with me."

I ask why, what did he do now?

"Well, I told him about Santa Claus."

There is helium in his tone of voice, a lightness that means mischief.

"I said, 'You know kid, Santa can't earn a living working just one day a year.' And then I told him how on the off-season, Santa works at Europoort in Rotterdam, unloading container ships. Only he got fired for drinking on the job, and now he's depressed, so there might not even be a Christmas this year."

My brother laughs, and I smile at how awful he is to his ten-year-old son, who already takes his father with a grain of salt. "That's horrible. You shouldn't tell him things like that."

He laughs. When my brother laughs, there is something mechanical to the sound, like the noise a train would make if it could chuckle. "Yup. And he believed it."

My brother has been telling his son stories like this for years. Jack once believed that you can tell a nuclear-powered artificial horse from a regular horse in a field because the nuclear-powered horses have steam venting through their nostrils.

"Oh, and I went to a psychologist, and she said I have Asperger's syndrome."

I think I don't hear him. "What?"

"She said I've had it my whole life, and it explains why people think I'm weird."

I try to get him to slow down. "Wait a minute, what? Why did you see a psychologist? What is this thing called again?"

He tells me the name again and spells it (because I thought it was "Ass-Burger") and then says, "I gotta run." And he is gone.

I go online to read about this condition, which my brother

suddenly has, which sounds like a sandwich made from donkey flesh.

Asperger's syndrome was named for Hans Asperger, a Viennese physician who published a paper in 1944 describing autisticlike behavior in several young boys. But it wasn't until 1994 that Asperger's syndrome was added to the DSM IV, and only in the past few years has AS been recognized by professionals and parents. So for fifty years, these kids were driving their families insane, undiagnosed, and wanting to chase trains in the car. And now, suddenly, Asperger's syndrome is chic. Bill Gates is said to have Asperger's. It is also suspected that the condition afflicted Albert Einstein. It is associated with geniuses, and this is why Manhattan parents are often secretly thrilled to have their bratty, brainy, introverted children diagnosed with this condition. It is the first trendy thing ever to occur in the atmosphere surrounding my brother.

People with Asperger's tend to be obsessed with trains and cars. My brother's first word was "car." He owns a car dealership that fixes high-end automobiles. And all his life his walls (and now office) have been hung with pictures of trains. Check.

People with Asperger's tend to have "fanciful vocabularies." Immediately, I know exactly what this means. When my brother's dog is happy, he describes it as "tail up." As in, "Yup. Dog-o is tail up ninety percent of the time." He also speaks of Fire Lizards. These, he claims, are employed in shops by glass artisans. They sleep on the floor in the work area, and then the glass blower steps on the Fire Lizard's tail, and it exhales fire, which the artist uses to melt and shape the glass.

The more I read about this condition, the more I read about my brother, an individual unlike anybody I have ever met before. Clearly, not only does my brother have Asperger's syndrome, he is the poster boy for it. A lack of interest in other people. Avoidance of eye-to-eye contact. A lack of social skills. Check, check, check.

It was a list. But when you combine the elements on the list, the result is a person most kindly described as "extremely eccentric."

A weight has been lifted. And I understand why sometimes people speak in clichés because sometimes there is simply no other way to describe something. A weight has been lifted. It's not all my fault. I'm not retarded. Or slow. It's him. It's always been him. And nobody knew it.

My next emotion is one of protection. I will now beat the shit out of anybody who is mean to my big, lumbering brother with his unusual, one-in-a-trillion brain.

Animals gravitate toward my brother. All farm animals, including chickens, dogs, and cats, as well as zoo animals such as tigers and llamas. My brother photographs animals, and in every picture the animal's nose is pressed nearly to the lens, its eyes soft and loving. I see these pictures, and it is proof to me that my brother is wholly good.

Six months after I met Dennis, when I felt more serious about him than I'd ever felt about anybody, I brought him to Massachusctts to mcct my brother. I'd warned him beforehand. "He's very abrupt. He has no social skills, so don't take it personally. My brother's going to ask you too many personal questions and maybe not give you eye contact."

Dennis was nervous.

We took the train, and when we pulled into the station and walked down the stairs, I saw my brother's Rolls Royce (chosen not for its snob appeal but rather for its machinery, its finish, and its mechanical perfection). My brother climbed from the car and walked over to us.

I introduced them.

And my brother moved in, and he hugged Dennis.

I'd never seen anything like it. I was stunned. I could do nothing but stand there on the sidewalk next to the car and stare.

Then he got behind the wheel and started talking, nonstop, about the new hydraulic lifts he had installed in his garage.

This summer, Dennis and I bought a grill for the backyard of our house, and then we invited my brother, his wife, and son over for hamburgers.

But my brother just stared at his plate while the rest of us tucked into ours.

"Is something wrong, John?" Dennis asked.

"Well," my brother began, slouching down in his seat and furrowing his eyebrows. "The thing about ground meat is that you have no idea how many cows are in a given pound. So the opportunity for contamination is great."

Dennis said, "Oh, well. Shit. I'm sorry, I didn't realize you don't eat meat. Next time, we'll . . ."

Without missing a beat my brother interrupted and said, brightly, "Oh no. I'll still eat an animal. As long as it's local and hammer-killed."

Then my brother stood from the table and announced, "Oh, I got you a present." He stepped outside and returned a moment later with what looked like a lawnmower engine. He set it on the floor and it immediately began to leak oil into the floorboards.

"Get that fucking thing out of here," I said. "What is it?"

"What do you mean, 'What is it?' It's a gas-operated pump. What did you think it was?"

As always with my brother, I hadn't a clue. "But why?" I asked.

He looked at me as though I had just asked him to recite the first twelve lines of *Macbeth*.

"Why?" he said. "Because there may come a day when you need a gas-operated pump and now you'll have one."

Once again, my brother was unlikely and correct.

LIFE CYCLE OF THE NORTH AMERICAN OPOSSUM

Because Bentley is a city dog, he's accustomed to relieving himself on pavement. We've trained him to go in the gutter against the curb, and not on the sidewalk. So when we first started taking him to our weekend house in western Massachusetts, Bentley became constipated and confused.

"It's okay, boy!" I would coach enthusiastically while I pointed at the ratty grass behind the house. "Go ahead!"

And Bentley would continue to stare at me, a pained expression on his face. When Bentley is troubled, his French Bulldog forehead crinkles together and his gigantic bat ears twitch.

"But watch," I said as I crossed the backyard and stood next to the tree. "See?" I crouched down and pretended to take a dump. "Just like this."

Bentley simply ran back up the stairs and barked for Dennis to let him inside. So I was forced to put his collar and leash on him, then take him for a walk along our asphalt driveway. And here, he was able to go.

Just like in New York, I slipped my hand into a little plastic bag, and I picked up the turd, then slipped the bag off my hand, inside out. So now I had a nice pouch of poo.

In Manhattan, I just toss this into the trash can on the corner, but what to do out here? I decided to place the baggie on the floor of the small, falling-down barn next to our house until Dennis and I could figure out a proper "system." Even though it was a little gross to just lay this bag on the floor of the barn, how much trouble could it possibly cause?

It turned out, quite a bit.

The next morning, we walked Bentley on the driveway again, and once again, I had a plastic baggie to dispose of. I walked over to the barn, thinking I'd leave it right next to the other one. Later, I said to myself, we'd go to Home Depot and buy a container.

But the other bag was gone.

My first thought was, *Impossible.*

I was certain I'd placed the bag in here. It had been a big mental production to do so. But where was it?

Then I realized, of course. Dennis. Dennis probably saw the bag and was horrified by my sloppiness. He has probably solved our poo problem.

I walked inside. "So what'd you do with the shit?" I said, smiling. I was curious to see what he'd thought of. Dennis thinks of a lot of great things.

"What shit?" he said.

"The bag in the barn. His," I said, pointing to Bentley, who was looking at us, first one and then the other, exactly as a child would.

"I don't know what you're talking about," he said.

And I almost gave him a playful shove but then realized that he actually wouldn't joke about something like this. It was unworthy subject matter.

I explained the situation. "And then when I went out there just two seconds ago, it was gone."

"It was gone?" He stopped scooping coffee into the filter. He just paused, midair. He said, "Did it blow away?" But I could tell he didn't think it was the wind. And neither did I.

"Okay," I said in the same flat tone of voice you hear cops use on TV. "What kind of psycho would go into out barn at night and steal dog shit?"

He let the coffee fall into the filter, and then he hit the switch. We were silent for a moment.

"I don't like the idea of somebody walking around here at night," he said. "We may need to get a submachine gun from your brother."

That evening we were having dinner, sitting at our long table. The table is long because I had originally purchased it as a combination desk/writing table. But I never write at it, so it's only for the two of us. So each night we feel as though we are members of a large family, and they prefer not to dine with us.

Bentley sits on the floor between us, praying in his doggie way that a scrap will fall to the floor. Nothing ever falls, but he never gives up hope. I love this about him, his relentless optimism. This is a trait that we share.

He started barking, growling, actually, in a voice he never uses. He ran to the sliding-glass doors and pressed his already mashed-up nose against the glass. He sounded ferocious, like a pit bull. Although only thirty pounds, I could clearly see that if he wanted to, he was capable of causing harm.

"What the fuck?" Dennis said.

I instantly pushed back from the table and ran to the wall. I hit the light and looked out the door.

It was the shit-stealer; this much was clear. And it wasn't

human. This much was also clear. But what the hell it was? This part was entirely unclear. "Oh my God," I said, my default expression for everything from joy to horror. Inflection is the only difference. Here, it was shock, horror, and curiosity. "Oh my God, you have to see this . . . thing."

Dennis got up from the table and rushed to my side. He peered out the window and looked at the creature in our backyard.

It had a long nose, thin, like a Swedish man's penis. A water-balloon–shaped head and a full, hairy body. The tail was pink and at least a foot in length. It had rodent eyes, and it was nuzzling a plastic baggie of Bentley's shit.

Whatever it was, it was fearless. Because even though I pounded on the glass with my hands and shouted, "Die, motherfucker!" it refused to so much as glance in my direction. Very briefly, it made direct eye contact with Bentley, which caused Bentley to literally jump in surprise.

I went online immediately and did a Google search. Keywords: "snout, Massachusetts, horrid, tail, garbage, pest."

And to my amazement, I almost immediately located a photograph of the exact creature in our backyard. "It's a North American opossum," I called to Dennis.

Neither of us had been able to finish dinner. The creature had a powerful appetite-suppressant effect.

Dennis leaned over my shoulder and peered at the image on the computer screen. "That's it," he said, poking the screen with his index finger. Poke, poke, poke. "That's exactly what the hell it is." Then he said, "Scroll down and see if it says how to kill it."

I did this, but unfortunately, I was at a website created by some varmint-lover at a university. Instead of instructions on how to kill, it provided useless information such as life cycle, eating habits (where it didn't even mention French Bulldog shit), and mating rituals.

We both walked back to the sliding-glass doors and looked. It was still there, though now it was on the prowl. It moved slowly, but I was worried that if I opened the door and threw something at it—an egg, a spatula, a can of Pepsi—that it would suddenly display speed and charge me at my own door.

We'd finally calmed Bentley down with a rawhide chew, but every once in a while he would glance in the direction of the glass and growl.

I went back to my computer and saw that the Undertaker was online. The Undertaker is a friend of mine, an actual former undertaker who now works in website development.

I sent him an instant message. "Hey. There's a opossum loose in the yard. How do I kill it?"

He replied instantly. "Tylenol."

I wrote, "U sure?"

"Yup."

"How do u no?"

"Cause. Killed neighbor girl's kitten with it."

I said to Dennis, "I have to call the Undertaker, can you hand me the phone."

After rummaging though my sixteen-year-old Filofax, I found the Undertaker's phone number scrawled on an old, yellow Post-It note. I phoned him, and he answered on the first ring, as though expecting my call. "Yup?"

"Hey, it's me," I said.

"Yeah? So?" he said.

"So wait. You killed the neighbor girl's kitten?"

He chuckled. "The fucking thing would come to my basement window, and it would make all these little yowling sounds all night long. So I went online and found out that Tylenol is fatal to cats. So I gave it some crushed up and mixed into a can of tuna."

"That's horrible," I said. "You live in a basement?"

He said, "Yeah, well. The house has two floors, but I like the basement best."

"Oh, you would. You really would. You are such an undertaker."

Again, he laughed, pleased.

"And I can't believe you killed a little girl's kitten. That's something serial killers do. That's how it starts, with pets."

"Oh, stop," he said. "Cats are a dime a fucking dozen."

I couldn't argue with him. As much as I'm a dog person, I'm not a cat person. Still, I would never kill one. Shave it and paint it blue with food coloring? Okay, twist my arm. But I certainly wouldn't kill one. I killed a mouse that crawled in my tub once, and I still feel guilty about it, ten years later.

"I think you're a bad person," I told him. "But do you think the Tylenol trick would work on this creature?"

He said, "It's worth a try."

After I hung up, I thought about this some more. Did normal Americans kill everything that caused them trouble? Was this what normal people did? Dennis and I were not only new to the country, but I am not normal in any way. So it's very hard for me to know.

It was pretty clear that more mothers than you'd think routinely killed their kids with bathtubs and heavy rocks. My own mother was of this same strain. But that was appalling and certainly not representative.

But then I considered the statistics: each year four million dogs are "put down" in animal shelters. And twice as many cats. And even at our local supermarket, there is a glue trap designed especially for snakes.

There isn't a house in all of Connecticut that doesn't have a twelve-hundred-dollar "bug zapper" from Brookstone in the backyard. And these are often designed to emit a pleasing glow yet destroy everything that flies into them.

And, of course, in New York City there are entire committees of suit-wearing professionals devoted to the destruction of rats in Central Park.

So it did seem that the American way of dealing with a pest was to make a kill.

I was hoping for a less nefarious solution, so I called my friend Suzanne, who lives in California. Suzanne is one of these people who is always smiling and you can see her smile, even over the phone. She is quintessentially Californian in this way. "Set a trap," she said. "And then you can take it into a field and let it go."

But this required a bit more of a relationship with the opossum than I was willing to have. I just wanted it to go away from wherever it came from and leave me and my dog's shit alone. The idea of trapping the scavenger in some sort of contraption and then going on a little nature hike with it just so I could then let it go seemed like more than an act of kindness than I was capable. That, to me, was approaching an act of God.

Wasn't there some sort of giant mouse trap that would just clamp down on its head? And couldn't I place this deep in the woods, near the river? And just never, ever go for a walk back there again, so that I wouldn't have to see it?

But then Dennis, as he is prone to do, had a brilliant idea. "Why don't we just get a trash can with a lid."

Well . . . yeah? Why didn't we?

The next afternoon we bought a small canister designed to hold wood stove pellets. It was smaller than a typical trash can, but it was sturdy. The lid fit snuggly. It was perfect.

We set the can in the barn, tucked against the wall, right near the door. And for a while, this solution seemed to be perfect.

Each time Bentley relieved himself on the driveway, we simply collected the mess in a baggie and tossed it in the trash can.

The opossum, finding nothing of interest on the floor of the barn, did not make another appearance.

I felt really good, positive, and nature-friendly.

For a month.

As adults, Easter morning means little to us. In fact, I don't think we've exchanged baskets or hunted for eggs in all the years we've been together. For us, Easter is just another day. But on the Easter Sunday one month after we bought our poo can, we did wake up early. Because there was a little girl screaming in our backyard.

"Mommy!"

"What the fuck?" Dennis said.

I don't think either of us had ever heard a little girl scream, except on television. If you don't actually *have* a little girl, to suddenly hear one screaming in your own backyard is shocking.

"Mommy! Hurry!"

We both climbed out of bed and walked across the hall into the guest bedroom. Here, we peered like perverts out the window overlooking the backyard. We were crouched down low, so nobody would see us. And just beyond our yard, in the field that abuts the riverfront, we saw a little girl. She was dressed in a pretty blue dress, bordered in white ribbon. She wore a white hat. In one hand, she held a basket, overflowing with green, artificial Easter grass. In her other hand, she held a plastic bag of dog shit.

She screamed for her mother again. "I thought it was an egg!" she cried.

And then Dennis said, "Oh no, look at that. Look over to her left. And there," he pointed, "to her right, over by that tree."

The field was filled with plastic bags. Because it was morning, the sun hit the plastic at an angle and the bags actually appeared to sparkle, like treasures. What little girl wouldn't see one of the sparkly bags and then run toward it? Only to discover that it contained not candy or perhaps gems, but turds.

More bags littered our own backyard. And when I pressed my face against the window, I could just make out the front of the barn. And I could just see the trash can turned over on its side. There was no lid.

"We should have killed it," Dennis said that evening. We'd spent the afternoon on our own nasty little Easter Egg hunt.

"Yeah, we should have," I said. Because I felt pretty certain that sometimes, you really do have to kill. It's the American way.

CUNNILINGUSVILLE

Last weekend, Dennis and I drove to Lancaster County, in southeastern Pennsylvania, otherwise known as Amish country. Ironically, it turns out that the Amish happen to live in towns with names like Blue Ball and Intercourse.

And these people forbid zippers?

I thought Dennis was joking when he read the names from the map. "What?" I asked, "No Fist Fucking? Check the map again."

"Yes," he agreed. "There should be a Fist Fucking, Pennsylvania. And it should be in Gang Bang County."

Had the Amish moved to towns with these names, or had the Amish named the towns after they arrived? It seemed important to know.

The one thing we did know was that neither Blue Ball nor

Intercourse was anything like they were when the Amish first arrived. Because while there were still hints of nature—the occasional farm, a gently rolling pasture or two—most of these towns had been developed into strip malls and superstores. So at any given intersection, you might see Banana Republic and Adidas factory outlet stores. And just across the street, another store twice the size of the Best Buy: a Mishmash Amish Treasures and more!

The traffic on the narrow, two-lane road that led to Blue Ball was particularly dense. It was bumper-to-bumper from one Wendy's to the next.

"Oh my God," I said, pointing to a remarkable sight out the window.

"See," Dennis said. "I told you."

In the opposite lane, right behind a white BMW 5 Series sedan, was a small black buggy drawn by a single old horse. The driver appeared to be a man with a peculiar beard and a black hat with a wide brim. But perhaps it was only Kelly McGillis, who is rumored to have moved to this area? Then as we passed the buggy, I could see that it was not Kelly but in fact a real-life Amish man. He was smiling and waving and, to my utter shock, did not appear drunk. Behind him, a line of cars inched forward, the drivers rolling their eyes and slapping at the steering wheels. This peaceful old Amish man was unknowingly being willed cardiac arrest by every driver a mile behind him.

"Is he insane?" I asked. "I mean, how can he live here? This is like the most commercial area of the state. It's awful."

Dennis agreed. "Yeah, it does seem that strip malls are contrary to the Amish way of life."

We watched as the Amish man with the doubtfully clean beard aimed his buggy into the driveway of a small house, instantly freeing the cars behind him. The house was what a real estate agent would optimistically call a "starter home, a fixer-upper." With its peeling beige paint, its lack of shutters, and its bare dirt lawn, the house was in need of far more than a little TLC. The house needed to be leveled and replaced by an AutoZone, in keeping with the spirit of the neighborhood.

As we drove past, three little Amish girls were playing in the dirt alongside the house. They wore drab white smock dresses and scarves that resembled dishrags on their heads, covering their hair. They were playing with some sort of curious round wooden hoop. It appeared to be a cross between a toy and some sort of primitive tool for extracting roots or stones from the earth. The girls tossed the hoop to one another, and then one of the girls would bang the hoop on the ground, sending up a cloud of dust and pebbles. This appeared to be the point of the game: to watch the dust rise. I could not imagine my thirteen-year-old nephew trading in his Game Boy for this hoop.

A small garden was barely visible from the street. This "garden" would be completely unacceptable to Martha Stewart as even a compost area. Any vegetables that came from this plot of land would most certainly be contaminated with carbon monoxide and every other imaginable traffic carcinogen. Any woman eating a salad from this garden would certainly have a child born with flippers.

"It wasn't always like this," Dennis said, driving on. "It used to be all farms out here, and then the tourists came and ruined everything."

But from the look of it, the Amish didn't seem to mind that the natural beauty of their land had been destroyed. Quite the contrary. The Amish had become filthy rich.

The streets were lined with Amish souvenir shops, Amish furniture stores, even a corrugated metal warehouse that sold "authentic Amish children's clothing." Though I can't imagine a parent within two thousand miles of this area dressing their child in such a way. "Look, Megan! A burlap pinafore! And a matching bonnet!"

"So why the fuck," I wondered, "didn't they get the hell out of here? How can they live this monastic, Amish life in the midst of such horrid commercialism?"

It seemed like some mass pathological level of denial, or rabid persistence, a refusal to accept change. Maybe the Amish were not living in a simpler time, holding fast to a more wholesome way of life, but in fact they were mentally ill and in desperate need of power tools.

"Well, a lot of them have moved to the Midwest," Dennis said.

That's exactly what I would do if I were Amish. I've been through Kansas, Iowa, Wisconsin, and I can tell you, it's the perfect place to live off the land and avoid zippers.

"But why didn't they *all* move?" I asked as another buggy approached, infuriating the Lexus owner behind it.

We watched the buggy crawl ahead and the driver behind restrain himself from honking. Because I knew, on the one hand he wanted to honk, wanted badly to slide down the power window and shout "Get that fucking thing into the breakdown lane, you old cocksucker!" But on the other hand, the Amish in the buggy was the reason the driver in the Lexus was here in Blue Ball, so he really couldn't complain. He wanted quaint, and he got it, at seven miles per hour. Supersize those fries for you?

Eventually, we found the center of town, which was, actually, rather quaint. The town of Blue Ball itself was more country store than strip mall.

We parked and began strolling. These stores were not part of larger franchises but appeared to be owned by individuals. Many of the signs were made of wood, hand-carved and leafed with gold. The lure was so powerful that we were sucked into nearly every store. One sold candles that had such an unusual, rustic charm, I bought all seventeen of them. "Do you have a website?" I asked, and the woman behind the counter simply smiled and shook her head, no. I was thrilled with these candles, which smelled of nutmeg, cinnamon, and paraffin. And I felt certain they wouldn't explode, like the last candles I bought at Pottery

Barn had. But then again, this store didn't have a website and a toll-free customer service number I could call. And if something were to happen with these candles, I don't believe this little store would send me a five-hundred-dollar gift certificate, and a customer service follow-up phone call the way Pottery Barn had. So in this way, we—the materialistic, commercialized, ruined modern peoples—take good care of ourselves.

Another store sold quilts. I'm not interested in crafts, as a general rule, but these quilts were very impressive. Just as impressive was the price.

"Look at this," I whispered to Dennis, holding up the tag for him to see.

His reply was a startled intake of air. "Five thousand dollars? That can't be right."

I'd stitched a pair of moccasins when I was fifteen and locked in a mental hospital, so I knew firsthand how difficult it would be to stitch something as large as this quilt. "Oh no," I said. "I'm sure that's the right price."

"Well, that just proves my point. These Amish are rich, rich, rich," he said. "It's easy to look at their houses and their ratty clothes and think they're poor. But they're not. They own all this land out here. And what land they don't own, they sold to the Gap and Walmart for millions."

That may be true, I thought. *But they don't have digital cable or Internet access, so really what's the point of being alive?* Civilized life, with all its threats and potential dooms, is too much to bear without the respite of three hundred channels. True, Osama bin Laden may very well send nuclear-bomb–filled suitcases on Amtrak trains into Penn Station, but until then: *I Love the 80s* on VH1.

We ambled down the street and into a furniture store. Here, we encountered an amazing solid cherry chest of drawers that was handmade without hardware—it featured tongue-and-groove construction. The wood was so glossy it looked plastic, and the finish smelled faintly of beeswax. When I pulled the drawer out, it slid with solid confidence. It was an excellent piece of furniture. The perfect size to tuck into a small corner of a room, perhaps a place to hold a few sweaters. Nine thousand dollars.

"It's tomorrow's antique . . . today," Dennis said. And this was true. This isn't the kind of thing you find at Hold Everything. This is the kind of thing your grandfather might have made, if you had that sort of grandfather, which I didn't. My grandfather was a Nyquil salesman, and while he did make millions of dollars selling the sticky green cough suppressant, the closest he came to building furniture was specifying red leather for his Cadillac Fleetwood.

Being in the store surrounded by such fine items activated the intense need section of my brain, and I deeply wanted the hand-carved bed, the chest of drawers, the dining room table and matching chairs. The modern furniture in our apartment suddenly seemed incompatible with long life and mental health. Ray and Charles Eames were, in retrospect, total hacks having a little fun with some plywood.

We crossed the street, and an old lady in the passenger seat of a buggy waved at us. She was a happy, nice-looking lady, and her wave contained no sexual innuendo, no sarcastic irony as one might expect in Manhattan. Her warmth was so genuine and pure, I was taken aback. I managed to smile back at her and even wave. But suddenly, I wanted to chase after her and make her my mother. I wanted to scream, "Take me with you! Make me a dresser!"

The fact is, you can't fake that kind of warmth. You just can't. I've tried. And it seems to me, you just don't encounter such warmth from strangers that often, unless they're drunk or have a hard-on.

So maybe, I thought, these Amish aren't in denial or mentally ill. Maybe they really are living better, richer, more wholesome lives, even if they are surrounded by Gap outlet stores and tourists. Maybe they have found some sort of excellent secret and are living with it, letting the world accelerate and brake and scream and crash and blow up around them. By day they offer us their Amishness, then at night they go home and experience a level of humanity and connection we've traded for Chronic Fatigue Syndrome and *The 700 Club*.

While the name Blue Ball does bring to mind an image of a horny testicular cancer survivor, these Amish seem oblivious to the tawdry innuendo of their town's name. And somehow, this made me feel mentally ill and in denial.

As she passed by, the buggy lady did not break eye contact, and she did not lower her hand. She continued to wave, like a queen. And I did the same, waving back, like her subject.

So what if she didn't go online and look at porn or use zippers? What have zippers ever really done for me?

They are, after all, just something for a dick to hang out of.

I Kid You Not

Now that gay people are allowed to adopt children, the new gay thing in Manhattan is to be a parent. Just ten years ago, this was unheard of. Then it was all about having a shar-pei puppy, the more wrinkles the better.

You never see shar-peis anymore. Like in-line skates, they're all gone now. And where did they go? I think the gay guys dropped off their shar-peis at animal shelters on the way to JFK to pick up their new, adopted third-world babies.

These days, it's all about Baby Gap and Abercrombie Kids. It's about play dates and hunky pediatricians with tattooed forearms.

But Dennis and I will have none of this madness.

Neither of us wants to accept the special challenges presented by a severely handicapped Romanian child or a baby who was born addicted to crack and has only half a head.

As Dennis says, "That's what they give us. The day-old-bread kids, the dented-can kids."

And we don't want them.

"So, are you guys going to have kids?" people ask us, as though this is the single defining proof of our commitment to each other.

"God, no," I say. I make a face, as though asked if I would ever consider having my intestines surgically moved to the outside of my body.

"But you'd make such great parents!"

Yes and no. Dennis would make a good parent. He loves to cook, and he does it extremely well. He listens. He nurtures. He flosses.

But this relationship contains two people, and the other one is unfit.

Whenever I see a baby-slapper on CNN, I think, *There but for the grace of God.*

I'm terrified of what sort of parent I would make. First, because I am startlingly self-centered. I require hours alone each day to write about myself. It takes no leap of imagination to know that in our home, there would be a Sony Playstation in every room. "Leave daddy alone and go make it to level four. And Daddy will give you ten bucks if you put it on mute."

Another problem is that I was raised without proper parenting myself. So I really have no wisdom to impart. If a bully so much as touched him at school, my kid would be armed with a stun gun the next day.

And I have a wide, deep cruel streak. This is not something I am proud of. But it's a fact I've come to accept about myself. Maybe I'll bring it up in therapy, after I have addressed my other issues (fear of intimacy, sexual dysfunction, obsessive-compulsive behavior, social anxiety disorder, and mania).

Last week Dennis and I were browsing in a store in Northampton, Massachusetts, that sells a selection of incongruous though carefully chosen items. For example, they sell dishwashing detergent with retro, nineteen-fifties packaging alongside greeting cards handmade from fibrous paper and flowers picked from a lesbian's garden. I happened to be looking at a beautiful book of magic spells and incantations when I stepped just a few inches to my left and shifted my weight onto that leg.

I felt something under my foot, an unevenness. It hardly registered, it was so subtle. Almost like a floorboard beneath the carpeting was warped. Just the same, I glanced down and was surprised to see the hand of a little girl, almost a little baby girl.

She couldn't have been more than two, because she didn't have any teeth. I saw this now because her mouth was all the way open, and her eyes—both of them—mirrored her mouth. Her whole face was all the way open. She was about to scream; I was certain. The wonderful thing about children is that they do not yet have complex emotions. They have the starter set of factory-standard emotions. And they cannot hide them. She was feeling the shock of pain in her little fingers, and she was going to scream.

I quickly slid away. I walked a good twelve feet to my right and began fingering the display of colorful wool pillows.

And that little girl screamed. It was shrill and passionate, and her mother came immediately to the rescue.

The mother had been standing just a few feet to the left of the little girl, inspecting some soy-based gift-wrapping paper. Now, the mother was crouched down to be face to face with her little screaming girl thing.

"What is the matter?" she asked in that musical tone of voice parents use.

The girl would only wail. She was too young to form thoughts, let alone sentences. She only looked vaguely in my direction and then back at her mother, screaming and streaming tears.

The store had thoughtfully placed items for small children at floor level, near the register where I had been standing next to (or actually on top of) the little girl. These were cute toys, colorful and soft. There were tiny stuffed lambs with black collars, blocky wood cars and trucks, a number of squishy plastic things that had bubbles trapped inside neon liquid.

The girl reached her damaged hand out toward her mother, but because her sense of direction was not yet fully formed, the hand landed on the shelf, among the toys.

"No, you are not getting one of those," the mother said. "And I want you to stop crying this instant. You may not have those."

The girl cried harder.

The mother picked her up and scolded. "What's gotten in to you?" she said. "Why are you acting like this all of a sudden? Do you need a nap? Well, we're going to leave right now and I'm going to set you down for a nap."

So now the girl would be punished after having had her hand stepped on by a gay guy from New York.

Horribly, I laughed.

This poor little girl had been crawling along the floor next to her mother. When suddenly, perhaps, she did see the pretty little blocks with letters printed on the sides in bright, primary colors. Perhaps she wormed her way over just a foot, and then I crushed her little fingers flat into the carpet.

Now a scolding, and soon a nap.

I, like an especially clever and devious shoplifter, was entirely off the hook. It was sheer luck that some other mother hadn't seen me and come to the rescue. "No, that bad man there stepped on your daughter's fingers!"

The fact is, life is hideous, and it's a good thing this girl learned it now. I convinced myself of this later.

Because later I was feeling remorse. I was feeling awful that I hadn't rushed over and explained what had happened. Then the little baby girl would have been scooped up and kissed. Her mother would have soothed her and made her feel better.

Instead, she learned that life is stunningly, painfully unfair. That guys always get off. And that your mother can turn on you.

With my left shoe, I had sealed the little girl's fate: a life on the therapist's couch and tens of thousands of dollars to explore a paralyzing obsession with men's feet.

Still, I do sometimes fantasize about what it would be like to have a child. Perhaps a little girl like the one whose hand I accidentally crushed. I already know what her name would be: Malibu.

Malibu evokes a kinder era, the seventies. It conjures images of a customized van, painted white but with glowing orange-and-yellow graphics airbrushed along the side and a small wet bar inside between the captain's seats. It's a blond hair, green eyes, ponytail-worn-to-one-side kind of name.

In an age of Mayas, Karas, and Naomis, Malibu is refreshingly sunny.

"Sure, sweetie. You can wear makeup. Just make sure the other second-graders don't steal it," I would say, sticking a Nars mascara into the zipper pocket of her Powerpuff Girls plastic knapsack.

My daughter Malibu would understand that she was certainly smart enough to become president, if that is what she desired. But no matter what, she was going to wear heels, and she was going to have good haircuts. For her fifteenth birthday, I would get her a set of breast implants or a nose job: her choice.

Of course, Malibu would, in the end, hate men because of me. She would gain weight, not shave her legs, cut all her hair off, and work in a bookstore named Womynfire. She would drop the first and last letters of her name to become simply Ali. I would be forced to literally tear the Chastity Bono and Jodie Foster posters down from her bedroom walls.

But as a rule, gay guys do not make bad parents; they make excellent parents. Because unlike straight people, gay people can't have kids by accident. Only by power of attorney. I would be a questionable parent not because I'm gay, but because I was raised by lunatics.

So maybe seeing gay guys with kids isn't really about being trendy. Maybe it's about progress.

And maybe the reason I never see shar-peis on the street anymore is because they're all inside, curled up on the sofa with the kid, while dad number one is making dinner and dad number two is cleaning some sort of stain off the carpet.

Let the people who want to have kids, have them. And let the rest of us spend the extra money on ourselves. Being gay doesn't make you a bad person. Not wanting kids doesn't make you a bad person. Perhaps crushing the bones in one little girl's hand makes you a bad person, but that was an accident.

Thus, feeling okay about the fact that I don't want kids, feeling good for applying my energies to my career, I embarked on the last leg of my book tour. Only to then find myself on an ill-fated Delta flight from L.A. to New York.

The flight was totally full, but I was happy. My first book tour had gone well: nobody threw anything at me, and booksellers didn't make me strip the covers off my own books so they could send them back for a refund. I walked down the aisle searching for my seat, and there, I saw, impossibly, the only remaining seat. A woman sat in the window seat and a man sat in the aisle seat, and the center seat was for me. But there was a live BABY standing on my seat. Standing and grinning while what appeared to be mashed potato bubbled from its lips. The mother plucked the baby thing up and said, "Here you go." She smiled at me like, "No harm done!"

But still it did not sink in. I thought, *Not possible. I, THE BABY HATER, COULD NOT POSSIBLY END UP IN THIS SEAT.* I checked my ticket again, looked at the number above the seat, which of course matched my ticket, but it could not be true. After a brief confrontation with the flight attendant, I took my seat. The middle seat. Next to the mom holding the only baby on the plane.

It tried to grab my hands as I read my Donna Tartt galley, ironically titled *The Little Friend*. It tried to coo at me and get my attention, and I ignored it, as though it were not there. Then, when the mother nodded off to sleep, I turned to the baby thing and made a monster face, wild-eyed with my fangs showing, which caused it to clap and laugh hysterically and wake up the mother. I pretended I had done nothing and turned another page. But the baby wanted me more now and kept poking me, so I made a claw hand and tried to snap, snap, snap at it. I was trying to be very mean to the baby, but it thought I was playing with it.

It had a rash around its mouth, and when it dropped its apple juice feeder-bottle thing on me, the nipple brushed against my arm, and I immediately had to take my beta-blocker stage-fright pill to slow my heart down.

As I sat in my seat, checking my watch every four minutes, I thought, *This is just horrible:* a tiny little single-aisle plane (an airbus, known to fall from the sky because of faulty composite materials). What an awful, rashy, clappy baby.

Eventually, the mother fell asleep again, and shortly after, the baby followed suit. But the baby's cool, alive little feet kept brushing up against my knee. Gradually, over two hours and many hundreds of air miles, the baby slid off the mother's lap and partially onto my legs. Both of its feet and legs up to the knees were now resting completely on my right leg. I was outraged and wanted to press the flight attendant call button over and over until one of them came. But then what? They certainly wouldn't pick the baby up and place it in some sort of container in the rear of the plane. And I knew they wouldn't give me a Valium. So it was useless. I was trapped.

I looked over at the mother. She was young, but her body now was destroyed. It was doughy from the baby, and I knew she would never lose this weight. Her breasts sagged into one soft fat pillow for her baby's head. And her long hair was pulled back into a permanent ponytail. Of course, she wore no makeup, and the front of her shirt was covered with crumbs and stains.

I pitied her.

The baby, somehow, sensed that I was staring at its mother and thinking mean thoughts. It stirred and opened its eyes. It realized it was sliding off its mother's lap, so it fidgeted and started gripping its mother's breasts/neck/face. The mother automatically, in her sleep, hoisted the baby up higher onto her body, and she then relaxed her arms protectively around it.

Then the baby again drifted off to sleep.

After many hours, the plane was ready to land. Mother and baby sat upright. "I hope you weren't too uncomfortable," the mother said to me. "I know it must be really kind of awful to sit in the middle seat next to some mom and baby, but she's a pretty good traveler. She really doesn't cry."

I had to admit, although I detested admitting it, the baby thing had been well behaved. Mostly.

In fact, if one wanted to be entirely technical about it, I was the only one who really misbehaved on the flight.

I'M GONNA LIVE FOREVER

As a teenager in the eighties, the most appealing career options presented to me were featured in *Fame* and *Flashdance*. Pat Benatar was right, Love *is* a battlefield. I knew this from my relationship with a mentally ill pedophile, so I was in no hurry to fall into the love pit again. Better, I thought, to focus on my career. And what better career than celebrity?

I would move to New York City and become famous. I hadn't thought of exactly *what* I would become famous for. I just felt certain that it would happen. And I hoped it would not be for the slaughter of another person. Then again, perhaps I didn't have to be famous "for" anything. In the seventies, there were plenty of people who were known only for being semifamous, like Charo and Pia Zadora.

But then, in my twenties, I decided I didn't want to be famous. I wanted to live in a log cabin in the woods, entirely removed from society. I wanted to have wolves as pets and not pay taxes. And while I hadn't yet reached the point of sticking bombs in manila envelopes and mailing them, I was getting close.

In the end, I wound up somewhere in the middle.

While not famous on the same level as Gwyneth Paltrow or even Monica Lewinsky, I am more known than I would have been had I chosen a more Ted Kaczynski life (unless, of course, I had mailed the exploding envelopes).

I wrote a novel called *Sellevision*. It was published and reviewed by a few newspapers and magazines, and then slid quietly from the shelf, as though it had been a particularly vivid delusion instead of an actual publication.

But then two years later I wrote a memoir, and suddenly my face was on the masthead of *USA Today*. My embarrassing past made news in papers and magazines here and in Europe.

But while all of this was happening, I was still home in my apartment with Dennis and our dog, Bentley, sitting at my computer and writing, like always. Nothing had changed except that I now gave interviews and posed for pictures which I hoped looked better than the actual me. I still didn't go to literary parties or art gallery openings. I didn't suddenly have a posse of fashionable friends with famous last names. I continued to wear the same dog-hair–covered sweatpants around the house for two weeks at a time.

Of course, writer famous isn't like movie famous. Movies are consumed in public, along with hundreds of other people, and the actor's face is enlarged to the size of a minivan. And watching movies is the only thing besides sleeping and having sex that we do in the dark, so there's that intimacy. On screen, each breath is magnified, so it feels like it's on our own neck. Then we leave the theater and talk about the movie, obsess over the stars. We see their pictures on TV and in magazines and online. And as a result of this saturation, we would recognize Brad Pitt in a bathing suit before we would recognize our own aunt in one.

Books, on the other hand, are read by individuals in bathtubs, beds, on toilets. Always in solitude. And the author's face is only seen if the reader turns to the back of the book and looks at the jacket picture. Or, if a newspaper or magazine happens to print the author's photo. This happened to me a few times, and when I left the apartment, sometimes I was recognized.

Because my memoir was extremely confessional and contained scenes that were both mortifying and humiliating, people automatically feel comfortable approaching me in public and confessing their innermost secrets.

"Aren't you Augusten Burroughs?" one grandmother asked me outside Fairway Market.

She was a nice-looking old lady, dressed well in a tailored brown suit. She had a good haircut. Her makeup was of a modern palate. She was exactly the sort of grandmother I would like to have had. "Uh, yeah," I said. "That would be me."

She smiled and crossed her arms. The handle of her little black purse fell into the crook of her elbow. "Well, I just loved your book," she said.

Somebody's grandmother read my book! Not just some gay guy from West Orange, New Jersey, "Thank you so much," I said. "I really appreciate that." I needed to get inside the store because Dennis was at home waiting for his goat cheese. But I couldn't rush the old lady, especially when she was lavishing me with praise.

"You know," she said, leaning forward and lowering her voice to a conspirational whisper. "When I was a little girl my mother used to give me enemas with Dr Pepper. And then make me drink the liquid when it came out!"

Although I was able to maintain a pleasant expression, I was mentally throwing up in her face. This is the sort of detail you don't reveal to anybody, even a therapist. You simply avoid

Dr Pepper and take your dirty little secret to the grave with you. I said, "Did she?"

"Oh yes," said the old lady. "She was a wicked woman. And let me tell you, to this day I cannot drink Dr Pepper. If I even catch a whiff of it, my sphincter tightens up into a little knot."

It was such a visual set of words.

"Well, that's just an incredible story. And it was so nice to meet you. But I'm running late and need to pick something up inside the store."

Now, whenever I see an old lady on the street, my mind involuntarily plays the old jingle from Dr Pepper. *"I'm a Pepper, she's a Pepper, wouldn't you like to be a Pepper, too?"* A gigantic sphincter lip-synchs the words.

The trouble with writing a book is that you don't get to choose who reads it. Sometimes I wish I did get to choose. I wish people had to fill out an application and provide a brief biographical summary.

If I'd been allowed to personally select my readers, I wouldn't have had the confrontation with the Crosswalk Lady.

I was simply crossing the street to go to the shoe store when I was grabbed on the arm. "Hey, I know you."

I tried to escape with a smile. "Hi," I said and continued walking. But she followed.

"You wrote *Running with Scissors*. I just read that. Oh my God."

I made it to the other side of the street, and now she was standing next to me.

"You know, your book really helped me. Because I am in the middle of, well, actually let me take that back. I am at the *end* of a horrible, horrible divorce. You know, I caught my husband fucking our building super up the ass, right in our living room. Can you imagine? Well, of course you can, being gay and all. And by the way, I thought those scenes of you having sex when you were such a little boy were so alarming and beautifully written. But anyway, like I was saying, my husband, whom I had been married to for seventeen years, was fucking the super up against my Stein-way piano. I mean, I have nothing against gay people, but I honest to God do not want to be married to one, no offense."

It was impossible to escape her. She provided no natural break in the conversation, and she spoke with such intensity that I would have had to abruptly shout "SHUT THE FUCK UP," punch her, and then run away in order to be free. But I couldn't do that. It would be rude. So I listened to her, hoping that she would come to her senses and stop talking and leave me alone. *No wonder your husband left you*, I was thinking, *You would never shut up.*

Eventually, she did stop talking but only because she happened to glance at the building across the street and see the digital clock. "Oh my God, I'm going to be late to the lawyer's office. Well, it was so nice talking with you, and I'm going to read everything you write from now on."

It was very nice that she liked my book so much and felt comfortable telling me the details of her crisis. But at the same time, I wouldn't have been sad if she'd slipped under the wheels of a garbage truck.

Would I have done this if the tables had been turned? Would I stop and approach Donna Tartt on the street and tell her that when I was a little kid, I was fucked up the ass by some guy who used hair conditioner as lubricant? Oh, and your little bob is adorable, by the way.

I know for certain that I would never send an author a picture of my dick.

It's amazing to me how many gay guys send me photographs of their penises as if it's the most normal thing in the world. Frankly, I find it odd when somebody who's read my book e-mails me a picture of their face. Why do I need to see what they look like? As a result, I am often tempted to objectively comment: "Thanks for the picture. You have a bulbous nasal tip and should get that surgically repaired." Or perhaps: "Please don't write me again until you have had a chin implant."

But to send a picture of your dick reveals an entirely different pathology.

"Hey. Loved the book, man. And you're cute. Here's my pic," one e-mail read. "Here's my pic." As though this was simply a snapshot taken by his mom.

One man from Italy sent me a photograph of his penis with a glass eyeball tucked into the folds of his foreskin, so that it appeared his penis was looking at the camera. He wrote, "As he say in the movies, here looking at your kid."

In addition to their penises, gay guys also send me pictures of their arms. This, because in my memoir, out of three hundred pages, there are a couple of tiny sentences about how as a child I was entranced by Tony Orlando's arm hair.

"You like furry arms, and I got 'em!" one man wrote. He included a picture of his two fat arms crossed over his barrel chest.

Not all gay men send me penis pictures. But no straight men do. And to date, no woman has sent me a picture of her vaginal canal. "I know it's a little stretched out, but I've had four kids. What do you expect? LOL."

What is sometimes more shocking than a photograph is an extremely long letter. One man, who wrote from Massachusetts and claimed to be somehow acquainted with the crazy psychiatrist in my memoir, wrote me an e-mail that was thirty-five pages long. I was so stunned by the length, the way I just kept scrolling and scrolling endlessly, that I printed it and counted the pages. And you might think such an insanely long letter is uncommon, a freak event. But no. Many people feel the need to send me long letters saying things like "I know you're busy but . . ." and going on for ten pages about their dreams of being a famous author and do I know a good literary agent who would be able to sell their work and turn it into the blockbuster international publishing phenomenon that it most certainly is.

My editor had warned me about this when my book first started getting attention. "Just wait," she said. "Fans get this crazed look in their eyes when they get near you. There's something about a writer that makes people act really weird."

I see this look she speaks of when I do readings and signings. While the majority of the people who come to my readings are nice, normal people I would like to know and be friends with, a few are people who should probably be locked inside hospitals.

One man in Brooklyn came to my reading smelling like a gangrenous foot. He had the most disgusting breath, which was made all the more revolting by his lack of teeth. When he spoke, he gummed the words out. "I wuved wur book."

But then, look at me. My brain is incorrectly formed, and I'm shaped like a tube. Plus, I'm an alcoholic, a "survivor" of childhood sexual abuse, was raised in a cult and have no education. So, really, if you think about it, the only thing that separates me from the guy with the stinky foot and no teeth is a book deal and some cologne.

But even with my minimal amount of fame, there are certain perks. Recently, I was at a movie premier, and at the party after the movie, Meryl Streep was loose, walking around the room like a normal person. Absolutely nothing was preventing me from lunging toward her and shrieking "Dingoes ate my baby! Dingoes ate my baby!"

When you think about it, there are not only different tiers of fame but genres. The "classic" famous person is a movie star, and even here there are different grades, like eggs. There are grade-B actors, like Susan Anton, has-beens such as Ann Archer or the star of *Flashdance* herself, Jennifer Beals. Then, of course, there are top-tier movie stars like Ms. Streep. But there are other routes to fame. America always loves a good serial killer. And it's tough to beat John Wayne Gacy, also known as Pogo the Killer Clown. The clown paintings he did while on death row have sold at auction for thousands of dollars. I know, because I spent many a drunk hour online looking to buy one on Ebay.

Then there are those who become famous because they are in

the center of a scandal. Of course, one instantly thinks of Monica Lewinsky. Monica is now superfamous worldwide. Italians still call her Portly Pepper Pot.

The fame of a writer is altogether different. For the most part, Americans don't read. Statistically, virtually nobody reads; everybody watches TV and movies instead. Alice Sebold's debut novel, *The Lovely Bones*, was an enormous blockbuster, the likes of which had been unseen for years. In hardcover, it sold nearly two million copies. But if an issue of *Time* magazine sold two million copies, the editor would be fired. And yet most people wouldn't recognize Alice Sebold if she passed them on the street.

I didn't sell two million copies of my first memoir. So I am even less famous. But still, I am famous enough now for old ladies to stop me in front of grocery stores and tell me about their Dr Pepper enemas.

TOTAL TURNAROUND

Yesterday I went to Saks and bought Clinique Total Turnaround lotion. The label claims that it "instantly, continuously helps skin feel and look its best by getting new cell turnover performing optimally." I bought this for Dennis because he is in his mid-forties and uses a moisturizer on his face that was invented eighteen years ago. The technology has improved, was my thinking.

"But I like what I have," he said when I handed him the sleek gray bag. I'd bought not one bottle but three.

I laughed. "I know you do." I said this in the exact same tone I might use to speak to a baby or a retarded person. "But it's old. There are newer and better things on the market." I then explained, as simply as possible, about alpha-hydroxy compounds and how they are like dermabrasion you can do at home: a sort of chemical peel without the harsh chemicals.

He was not persuaded.

So I took his lotion of inferior, pore-clogging technology, and I hid it at the top of the closet, where he is too short to reach without the stepladder, which is in the front closet and very difficult to get out. Dennis is not a short man; he's five-nine-and-a-half. But that "and-a-half" tells you something. Short(er) guys always add the "and a half." Tall people never do this. So I hid his lotion and smiled at my mental image of him jumping up and reaching, jumping and reaching, with his old, prehistoric lotion just slightly out of reach.

When he went into the bathroom, he noticed his lotion was gone and in its place, my new improved lotion gift. "What'd you do with my stuff?" he shouted.

I was now sitting at the computer, which is on the dining room table, e-mailing my friend Suzanne in California. "I hid it," I said.

"You better not have," he said with surprising anger. Actually, it was so surprising that I assumed it to be mock.

"Yes I did. All gone. I threw it away." There was glee in my voice. Glee mixed with triumph.

He scampered back into the bathroom, skidding on the highly polished wood floor like a cartoon dog. I heard him rummaging through the trash can. This made me smile because it's just sort of cute.

He returned, indignant. "I mean it. Where is it?"

I sighed. "Okay, fine," I said. I padded across the floor and went to the closet where I barely reached—certainly no stretching—to the top shelf and produced his favorite pale green bottle. I handed it to him and became serious. "But will you at least try the new one?"

"I'll try it," he said, but I knew he wouldn't.

I explained the situation to him, doctor to patient. "Look. This will be better for your skin because it will remove more dead epithelial cells. I mean, I know it's just lotion, but there have been advances." I emphasized the word "advances," knowing that Dennis is wary of advances.

"Fine," he said. "I'll try it."

I was somewhat annoyed by his resistance to change, and I also felt like he was still angry with me for hiding his oily lotion, so when we crawled into bed that evening I said, "Are you pissed at me for hiding it?"

"Yes," he said, like a child who was very mad at having his blocks taken away.

I smiled and nestled against him. He kissed my shoulder. I'd never felt closer to him because I did know that he was mad and yet it didn't matter. He loved me enough to be mad at me and not then have to reconsider the entire relationship.

I took this as a sign that things were good between us.

But the next morning, he seemed off. He seemed distant. Dennis wakes up half an hour before I do, and when he's finished showering, kisses me between my eyes to wake me up. But this morning, there was a preoccupied tone to his voice, and his kiss seemed hurried, almost professional, as though he were paid to kiss me and was contemplating another line of employment.

After I took my own shower I said, "Is everything okay?"

He told me he was worried about a meeting he had that morning. It was with his new client, and things had not been going smoothly.

I felt a rush of hatred toward the client and fantasized about cornering said client in the parking lot after the meeting and producing a Henckels knife, which I would use to circumcise him.

But later that day at the horrible Japanese ad agency where I was working, I got an e-mail from Dennis. The subject line read

"Confession," and it went on to say that he was actually still mad about the lotion and felt I was being controlling and manipulative and that it really hit a nerve because he can't stand to be controlled.

I was furious and wanted to leave him immediately, find myself a much younger boyfriend who did not have fine lines and wrinkles but, more important, wasn't so averse to change. I'd read somewhere that one of the signs of aging is a resistance to new things. I have worried myself by losing my interest in contemporary music. Whereas when I was in my twenties, I bought twenty new CDs a week, now I buy maybe five a year. I don't listen to music on the radio, only NPR. So when Dennis expressed his own lack of willingness to embrace the new technology, I felt very strongly that maybe it was time to leave him and open myself up to the possibility of dating a twenty-year-old.

Instead, I wrote back a confident I Will Make You Seem Crazy e-mail that read: "Wow. I didn't realize you were so upset over the lotion. I never intended that. I actually thought it was kind of funny to hide your lotion and get you all ruffled. But I never imagined that you were truly upset. It's almost like I bought you a new color television but you like your black-and-white because you've never seen color. So all I wanted to do was turn you onto the new and better color."

He wrote back five minutes later saying "I am embarrassed now and feel like a fool."

I was immediately distressed; I'd gone too far. I never wanted him to feel embarrassed, because I wanted him always to feel he could tell me anything, no matter how seemingly small. So I wrote him back and said just this, adding "I felt so close to you when you told me you were still mad at me. I smiled, fell asleep instantly."

He wrote back and said he knew what I meant, he felt it, too.

Then, on the way home, I thought about taking the new lotion and throwing it into the trash, all three bottles. I thought maybe he would finally acquiesce and look for it to at least try it. And it would be gone and he would be puzzled, and I would say glibly "I threw it out," and this would build into a fight.

Or perhaps I would stop at Saks on the way home and buy two thousand dollars' worth. I would fill the medicine cabinet with these lotion bottles as a statement: "Not only do I embrace change, but I finance it."

I was mad walking home, making myself even madder by thinking of possible scenarios involving Dennis, myself, and bottles of lotion. What if I emptied his own lotion bottle and then replaced it with the new, technologically superior lotion. And then when he commented "See? My face looks great, my lotion is fantastic," I would reveal the ruse.

Who, but two gay men, could possibly have a fight over moisturizing lotion?

But as I passed Lincoln Center, I decided that it wasn't as shallow as it seemed. There was the very real issue that ten years come between us. That Dennis is much more conservative in many ways than I. He is averse to change and slow to make decisions. By the time I made it to the Tower Records a few blocks from our apartment, these seemed like insurmountable obstacles.

Until I imagined him being hit by a Honda Accord while he crossed the street, distracted and feeling bad about my manipulative e-mail. I saw him lying on the sidewalk, sliding into unconsciousness. And here, I nearly heaved a sob. I was overcome with a powerful feeling of utter devastation and loss. A door opened a crack, and I was able to see that I was now far beyond the point of merely being able to throw in any towel. Clearly, I was no longer dating somebody or living with somebody or in a relationship with somebody. I was married to somebody. I was merged with somebody.

Truthfully, if Dennis wanted to moisturize his face with mayonnaise, I would be in the kitchen cracking jumbo eggs and separating the yolks.

Tonight we saw the film *Iris,* with Judy Dench as Iris Murdoch, the acclaimed British author who descended into Alzheimer's. As we watched Iris Murdoch watch *Teletubbies* and pee in the living room, I had to breathe deeply to avoid making incredibly loud, humiliating heaving sobs in the theater.

"I'll take care of you when you get like that next year," I said, as we left the theater. Although realistically, I felt it was *I* who would be the one to lose his mind and probably not even when I'm old and have lived a rich, full life. Possibly as early as next spring.

It's ten-thirty on a Monday night, and Dennis is in the kitchen, lean cuts of pork splayed out on plastic wrap on the floor. He is wearing his suit, and in his left hand he is holding a silver meat-hammer thing. He places a sheet of plastic wrap on top of one of the cutlets, and he begins to smack it with the hammer. And it's surprisingly loud. I mean, you would really be amazed by how much sound a filet of pork can make when you place it on the floor and hit it with a hammer.

Before I moved in, Dennis had problems with his downstairs neighbor. The way I understand it is, the neighbor used to slam his door—at all hours. And the sound came straight up through the floor and into Dennis's eardrums. So he actually had to go downstairs and tell the man, don't slam your door. And ever since then, they've been like two wheaten terriers who see each other on the sidewalk and snarl.

So I was thinking about this as I watched him pound the meat. I was thinking, *Any minute, our neighbor is going to come upstairs and tell us to stop hammering into the floor. And I would then have to explain, we're not hammering. We're cooking. We're tenderizing. We're just doing it on the floor.*

Of course, the fact that this is Monday night at ten-thirty and Dennis is still in his suit and now in the kitchen pounding pork on the floor to make me dinner from a recipe in *COOK'S Illustrated* magazine is testament to his character. I truly, truly feel guilty that I am the only one who gets to have him as my mate.

"I love doing this," Dennis says when I tell him how sweet it is of him and how guilty I feel that he's going to so much trouble after working all day. And I believe him, I think he really does love to cook.

I bought him a set of French copper pots and pans, and he enjoys these. The saucepan weighs like seventeen pounds. The endorphins released just from picking the thing up make you drunk enough to think, *Snails are great! Bring on the stomach lining!*

At midnight, we eat. Our beastly French bulldog watches us for a few minutes, but he is too tired to stare with his typically penetrating gaze, and he goes under the table to become flat. When he is exhausted, he lies down on his belly, all his little arms and legs sticking out straight.

And it was incredible, the dinner. It was one of his best, and this is saying quite a lot because Dennis is an incredible cook.

I washed the dishes, and while I was washing, Dennis went into the other room to lie on the bed. Or so I assumed.

A moment later, Bentley was barking, and I could hear his nails scratching along the floor, like he's chasing. Or being chased. Then, more barking. It was his play bark, the bark he makes in the mornings when Dennis chases him around nude after his shower.

I said, "No, don't do that. Don't get him all excited before bed. We need to wind him down."

Bentley is the first dog Dennis has ever lived with. We got him together. But I was raised with dogs. So I am our resident dog expert. "Really," I shouted over the running water, "just put him on the bed and stroke his back, make him calm."

Dennis called back to me, but I couldn't understand him. I heard only the one word "he."

So I said, "What?" The dog's barking was getting more intense. I was now positive our neighbor was going to knock on the door. First the pounding, now the crazed animal. "Dennis," I shouted, "don't get him all excited."

And Dennis shouted right back, "I didn't start it. *He* started it."

I turned off the water and walked out of the kitchen. They were together on the bed, Dennis attempting to turn down the covers and Bentley standing on the covers. Dennis was fluffing the pillows, panting. Bentley's eyes were crazed, like he'd just swallowed a package of bacon, wrapper and all. Dennis, also, looked slightly crazed. He was smirking, and I could tell he was hot. His face was red, and he was beginning to sweat. Dennis sweats at the first sign of physical exertion.

"Let me get this straight," I said. And I said this still wearing the yellow rubber dish-washing gloves. "What you're saying to me is, 'It's not my fault. He started it'?"

Dennis choked out an absurd half laugh, but then his face registered indignation. "Well, yes. I suppose that is what I said, but it's true. He started it. I didn't. I was making the bed, and he thought it was a game."

"So in other words," I continued, "this master/dog stuff is just bullshit, because HE STARTED IT."

Dennis said, "Well. Yes. He started it. It's his fault, not mine."

Another reason why I am lucky to have Dennis.

So clearly, we are not this dog's owners. We are not his masters. We are his peers.

And I wonder if this is because we let him sleep with us. Not only in bed, but under the covers, between us in bed.

It seems impossible not to. It seems like maybe we tried to sleep normally a long time ago, when Bentley was a puppy. But then he gradually moved from his little bed to the floor next to our bed. And then from the floor to the foot of the bed. And then from the foot to next to me. And now from next to me to between us, under the covers, with his head on a pillow next to ours.

And at this point, I do not know if I could sleep any other way. Even though this is probably horribly unhealthy and is creating all sorts of terrible canine-dependency issues for the dog. Or us.

But it works. At night, we all crawl into bed and watch a little TV, or we read our books and Bentley falls asleep between us, and then when we turn off the light, of course we don't ask him to move. He snores softly and like a Glade plug-in, his puppy scenter becomes activated, and the smell makes my mouth water. And how could I move him?

So we don't. I turn on my side, Dennis turns on his side, facing my back, and Bentley lies between us. Then Dennis reaches his arm across Bentley and hooks it under my arm, so that his forearm rests against my chest. Which is exactly, exactly as it should be.

I watch him in the kitchen, and I think of how much it hurts to love somebody. How deep the hurt is, how almost unbearable. It's not the love that hurts; it's the possibility of anything happening to the object of your love. Like, I would not want Dennis to lose his mind. But I'd be much more fearful of me losing my mind, because then he'd be the one left alone.

Just like I want him to die first, so that he doesn't have to lose me and then be alone. Or if I do have to die first, I want to find him another boyfriend beforehand, I want to hand-pick somebody and then get to know this person and make sure he's up to the task. I imagine there would be paperwork involved, with serious consequences if he breached the contract in any way. Love, unconditional. Or else you will lose your 401(k) plan, and your credit report will be forever destroyed, and there will be prison time.

So then I stop myself from thinking these thoughts because it's like tearing at a wound, opening it wider when it's trying to heal. Or actually, it's more like inflicting the wound yourself with a paring knife.

What's painful and wonderful about loving somebody is loving their small things, like the way he is able to smile when he sips his wine, the way his hands fall down at his sides, fingers slightly cupped, or the way he is conducting the orchestra on the radio. Or now, the way he is lighting candles, just now this one in front of me. This is the one he lit first, actually. The one in front of me. Even though there was one on the way, he passed that one, lit it next.

The truth is, Dennis has no bad qualities and no faults. When he's working late and I'm alone, or sometimes when we're in bed together, the lights off, I try and make even a small list in my mind of his faults: Things I Put Up With Out of Love. But I haven't been able to think of a single thing that I am not able to first overlook and then come to cherish. Even the fact that he sometimes loses things has led to a treasured nickname: Mittenclips.

Because sometimes, he misplaces things: keys, his wallet, our car once. But his face, when he sees that he's done this— where are my keys?—it's the most precious crestfallen face, and I tell him, "Have you checked the pockets on that jacket you wore last night?" And I check the bathroom and the floor under the sofa and all the unlikely but possible places for lost things to be. And we always, always manage to find whatever was missing.

Unconditional love. That's what this is. I love him, as is, fully. I've had to stop arm wrestling with the facts. Why me? Didn't I already have a big love once? And lost it? So why should I get it again? I've had to stop trying to look for cracks and flaws to prove that it's not as good as it seems. Because it's as good as it seems. Even when we fight, we fight inside the container of *good*.

Somehow, through a flip of the coin, I ended up here. Feeling like somebody at the top of the heart-lung transplant recipient list. Damaged but invigorated and fucking lucky.

ROID RAGE

Not long after I met Dennis, I started seeing a doctor who was willing to regularly inject heavy doses of steroids into my body so I could gain muscle mass, strictly for cosmetic reasons. During a routine physical examination, I asked him, "Is there anything I can do to get bigger? I feel like I work out constantly, and it doesn't show. I'm trapped in this awful ectomorph body."

My doctor, whom I found on referral from my cocaine-snorting, Xanax-popping friend Sean, cleared his throat and leaned forward. He spoke in a low, blackjack dealer voice. "What are you asking?"

I don't know why I thought to press it. Call it the addict's instinct. "I was just wondering if there's any way I can, you know, go on steroids."

It turned out, there was a way. Eighty-five dollars in cash and a zipped lip.

"I believe in hormone-enhancement therapy," he told me. "A lot of doctors just dismiss it entirely, without thinking about it. Look, I've done a lot of research in this area, published a lot of papers. And I've found that many patients experience enormous benefits from a very moderate dose."

I liked the idea of *enormous* benefits, especially if I could stretch a T-shirt over them.

He then went on to explain that there were many different varieties of steroids and that he would give me what was considered one of the safer ones, and in a small dose. He would also give me an injection made from cow uterus lining, which would prevent my balls from shrinking. In addition, I would have to endure his finger up my ass occasionally to check my prostate, and also monthly blood work. All in all, a small price to pay to get the body I've always wanted.

Dennis disliked that I was taking steroids. But, as I frequently pointed out to him, he enjoyed the results. And the results were dramatic. Almost immediately, I noticed that I was able to lift more weight at the gym, without more effort. So I pushed myself harder. And I started lifting far more weight than I ever had before. My body fat started to melt away. And my arms became hairier. Zits spread across my shoulders and along my forehead. I had so much energy, I felt twenty-five. Except that when I was twenty-five, I was a total mess, in a constant blackout. So twenty-five was a new feeling.

I had tits now, for the first time in my life. I had bulges in all places. So when Dennis complained, I reminded him that my doctor was administering these drugs; I wasn't buying them online. I got regular blood tests. I said, "I'm doing it for medical reasons." Dennis always replied, "Your vanity is not a medical reason." But I disagreed. First, because a doctor was involved, that made it medical. Second, because having a body I don't like makes me panic. That's a reason. *Medical reasons*.

So Dennis didn't press the issue often. But he didn't like it. Especially the bad moods.

Usually, I felt irritable on the second day following my testosterone injection. So once every ten days I was grumpy and hostile for no apparent reason, and the next morning it passed and I would be apologizing with toothpaste foam in my mouth.

But when I was in one of my foul moods, the tiniest thing could enrage me. Something Dennis said, for example. Such as, "How's my sweetie?"

He would have no idea that my testosterone level was approximately that of a Neanderthal chasing a wild boar.

"I'm having one my moods," I would tell him through clenched teeth, our code for *This is fucking not a motherfucking good time*.

He would take this opportunity to go out for coffee or a run or see a movie. I would be left alone in his apartment and often, I would clean.

One Saturday, I decided to channel my fury into vacuuming. Because we live near the West Side Highway, a thin coating of dust settles over everything, every day. On typical days, it's simply irritating. On Roid Rage days, it made me want to stomp down to the highway, pull drivers out of their cars, and bash their faces into the pavement. *Suck up that dirt like a good little Electrolux, Jersey boy bitch*.

Dennis had decided he'd go for a run. He was gone for a few hours, and when he returned, I was still going at the walls with the brush attachment. "What the FUCK are these little specks?" I was shouting as he set his keys and wallet down on the table.

He maintained a distance between us of at least ten feet. "Um, those are . . . cracks in the plaster."

His logical reply infuriated me, and I suddenly felt extremely homicidal. "Fuck those motherfucking cracks," I hollered, stabbing at them with the brush, mashing the bristles into the wall. "Those fucking fifties architects didn't know shit about walls. Mies van der Rohe can kiss my ass." Steroids induce a primal feeling of *me against the world*. Picture 1,000 Helen Reddys.

Dennis took the wand of the vacuum cleaner out of my hand like it was a hatchet and suggested I watch some television. "Why don't you just relax. You've done so much cleaning already. Maybe there's a nice complicated pregnancy on The Discovery Channel. You'd like that, wouldn't you? A breach birth or maybe a preemie?"

Even in my wild animal mood, Dennis knew how to soothe me. I nodded my head and flopped on the bed, remote control in hand.

Dennis is suspicious of this man, my primary-care physician. "Ask your Dr. Unscrupulous if there's anything he can do for your horrible moods."

So I did ask him, and he was surprised I had such moods. He asked me to describe them. I said, "It's weird. The day after I get the shot, I'm usually fine. It's the day *after* this where I turn into somebody capable of committing a triple homicide, then going to a Ben Stiller movie."

Unfortunately, there wasn't anything he could give me to nice me down. He suggested yoga.

So of course, Dennis talked to his therapist about it, and his therapist was: (a) alarmed that I was taking steroids, (b) disgusted that a physician was prescribing them, (c) concerned about me in general as long-term relationship material.

Actually, Dennis's therapist annoyed me. A therapist is an extremely influential person. And the fact that this guy sat in his plush office and formed opinions about me and then passed them onto my boyfriend infuriated me and caused me to behave in ways that made me live up to his warnings about me.

Still, I couldn't argue my way around those moods. The only good thing was that they didn't always happen and they never lasted for more than a day and I hadn't used a box-cutter on any-body. Yet.

To nobody's surprise, steroid use is common among gay men. When you combine a love for men with a love for drama, you end up with a guy on steroids.

As a result, it's easier than ever to spot a gay man in a room full of men. He's the one with the superhero chest and the arms that look like breasts, when flexed. And because of the severe acne that steroids create, he undoubtedly smells like Stridex.

Though it's only a matter of time before straight guys start taking steroids. Because while it annoys many straight guys to be the object of a gay guy's affection, it's far more alarming to find that no gay guy in the room would sleep with your flat-chested straight-guy ass.

Another reason gay guys take steroids is because many were nelly, femmy little sissies when they were kids, and now they have the chance to transgender into masculine men. They get everything they never got as kids: aggression, respect, and bulk. Of course, the illusion is shattered once the mouth is opened and the sibilant *s*'s leak out, but when your body is that good, who's listening to you yammer on about something you saw in *French Vogue* anyway?

Then there are the guys like me: the fat-girl guys. The nerd guys who were never attracted to bodybuilders, who didn't feel particularly swishy but who felt like they were cheated: too thin and bitter about it.

As a teenager I ate ice cream by the half-gallon in the hope of adding a few pounds to my tall, lanky frame. I spent hours look-ing at my flat, non-ass in the mirror and wondering if the padded underwear I saw advertised in the back of *GQ* would really work. I endured comments from large women like, "I would give my right arm to be as skinny as you" and "If you were a woman, you could be a fashion model."

Really, there is no difference between being fat and being skinny. They are two sides of the same Oreo. This is why I have always had a special affection for overweight people. Because while I may not look like it, I am every bit as miserable as the woman who wakes up in the morning with dried frosting in her hair, clutching a spoon.

By the time I was twenty, I was able to disguise my scrawny frame by wearing the baggy, fashionable clothes of the era. But I would always feel deep shame when I had to undress in front of somebody. Out of my Willi Wear suit, I had the body of a twelve-year-old.

So when I was twenty-four, I joined a gym and hired a personal trainer. He was a hunky, bulging Italian who pitied me but also saw my determination. Three times a week I met him at six in the morning, and he worked me through a grueling hour-and-a-half routine to develop my chest, arms, legs, and back.

After six months, I did see a difference. After a year, my body was transformed. But only from Auschwitz into lean.

I was still tall and thin, and this made me depressed. No amount of bench pressing could give me the large, round chest I desired. The chest where your nipples point down, that's what I wanted and what I could never have. I could do squats until I couldn't walk anymore, but I still had praying mantis legs.

I'd reached my genetic potential, it seemed. Until my best friend, Pighead the AIDS Baby, gave me his testosterone patches. His doctor had prescribed them so he could gain muscle mass and stop wasting away. But Pighead didn't want to take yet another drug, so he gave me the patches. "You want these? They seem like something you'd be into."

I placed the man patches all over my body so that I resembled a fish. I wore a scale suit of patches. But I only had enough of them to last a month.

Pighead offered to go back to his doctor and ask for more man patches, but then thoughtlessly died before he got the chance.

A number of years later, I started to notice that every gay man in the city seemed to be getting larger. At the gym where I'd gone for years, guys who had previously been as skinny as me had ballooned into Mayflower moving men. There were now men walking the streets of New York with breasts that Pam Anderson would envy. Overnight, it seemed, biceps were in. But where had they come from?

At the same time, I noticed every gay man suddenly had acne. Not a blemish here, a pimple there. But a rash of angry zits spreading across both shoulders and up the back of the neck. Fifty-year-old men suddenly appeared on the sidewalk shirtless, their ripped abs glistening in the sun. I wanted to corner one of them, grab his shoulders, and shout, "What the hell is happening? And why isn't it happening to me?"

This is when I learned of steroids. "Deca" was the name I heard most often. I began spending hours at my computer, scanning newsgroups, reading message boards, visiting websites.

Steroids were the new goatee. They were the new black. Steroids were in, and I had to find a way to get them.

I considered ordering them from websites in Thailand but worried I would be caught by drug enforcement officials and taken to Riker's Island, where my thin frame would be the death of me.

So when I found out my own doctor would give them to me, I didn't hesitate. There could be side effects, he said. But I was willing to accept the risk. If I was going to die of prostate cancer, at least I'd look hunky as they turned the ventilator off and gave me my last sponge bath. Besides, didn't cell phones cause brain cancer? Considering I'd been using a cell phone since the days when they cost $1,000, what difference would a little testosterone make to my longevity?

If my problem had been being fat, you can bet I would have been sitting right there in the waiting room next to Carnie Wilson, an extra box of staples in my coat pocket.

Had I been fat, nobody would have told me that I shouldn't go under general anesthesia and have liposuction. They would have offered to drive me home. Everybody wants fat people to get their fat sucked out. So why don't they want skinny people to get pumped up?

Is this really so different from the other things people do to make themselves happier with their bodies? Breast implants, chin augmentation, rhinoplasty—at least steroids don't require the use of a scalpel. Until, I suppose, they remove your cancerous parts.

MAGICAL THINKING

My friend Jill is the type of person who will cross the street at a crosswalk, keeping her eyes on the WALK light. She thinks, *If I make it to the other side before it starts flashing* DON'T WALK, *I'll have a good day.* Conversely, she believes that if the light changes while she's still crossing, something "vague but definitely bad" may occur.

This is the adult version of the superstitious game children play: "Step on a crack and break your mother's back" is a saying Jesus himself probably heard on the playground. And with each generation, kids can be seen walking together, automatically stepping over cracks to spare their mothers from a life spent in a wheelchair.

I, on the other hand, can recall stomping on sidewalk cracks, pretending the line dividing the pavement from the sidewalk itself was my crazy mother's spine. Whether because of this or for reasons unrelated, she's now in a wheelchair, partially paralyzed.

Technically, both are examples of something psychologists call "magical thinking," which is the belief that one exerts more influence over events than one actually has.

My friend Suzanne is another example. She is a fearful flier who sits bolt upright in her seat, concentrating hard on keeping the plane aloft. Who refuses to read a magazine or take a nap for fear that if she stops thinking about the plane soaring high above the clouds, it may indeed nose-dive straight down through them and into the earth. "I just sit there clenching the armrests with my hands and thinking, *fly, fly, fly*." She understands, of course, that the plane will either continue to fly, or it will crash, regardless of whether she continues to concentrate or not. It's between God and the terrorists.

I have never been one of these people who believes that some micron of the universe will shift if I concentrate hard enough or make it to the other side of the street before the light changes. Rather, I believe I control the world with my mind.

Take, for example, Charlotte.

In the mid-nineties I was courted by an advertising agency in Chicago. At the time, I was working in New York City on the Burger King account, and I was extremely miserable. My life consisted of nothing but shooting commercials for Whopper Value Meals. Leather, as I discovered, absorbs odors, so my shoes smelled like Whopper meat during this period of my life. After six months on the account, even my wallet smelled like dead cow.

I was ready for a change, and the Chicago agency offered just that. I would have an office that overlooked the lake. I would work on a variety of products, not just one. And I would work for Charlotte.

When I met her, the first thing Charlotte did was say, "Oh, my

God. You're here! Let's go have tea and finger sandwiches across the street at the Fairmont."

So we crossed the street through an underground strip mall, and we ended up in the lobby of the Fairmont Hotel. Here, we enjoyed Earl Grey tea and cucumber sandwiches with the crusts already trimmed off.

Charlotte was tall, with short blonde hair, which she wore in a trendy "bed-head" fashion. She wore primary colors and earrings in bold, geometric forms leftover from the eighties. She was charming and a little scatterbrained. She changed subjects quickly and without warning, jumping from beautiful Chicago summers to "how can I get rid of the flesh wings under my arms?" She was funny and she was smart, and I loved her completely.

I accepted the job, after spending that single day in Chicago. The following week, I flew back and met with a broker to look at apartments. I found one near the lake for almost no money and wondered, *Why didn't I move here years ago?*

My first week was bliss. Charlotte frequently stopped by my office just to chat. She loved all my ideas. And she told me to leave every day at five so I didn't burn out.

But by the fifth week, another version of Charlotte began to emerge. One not so primary colored.

I was in a studio on Wacker Drive doing color correction on a cheesecake spot when I got a call from Charlotte.

"What's the idea behind this teaser campaign I see on my desk?" she snapped.

The teaser campaign was something she'd asked me to do for another client. She hadn't been around, and I was due at the editing studio, so I left the storyboards on her desk with a sticky note.

"What do you mean?" I asked.

"I mean, why the fuck isn't the client's name in these storyboards, you arrogant cocksucker? You think you can come out here from New York City and start doing commercials that don't even have the client's name mentioned? You think we are fucking stupid out here in the Midwest? Because let me tell you, buddy. We invented the motherfucking Dough Boy and the Green Giant."

I was horrified and shocked, exactly like when I watched *The Exorcist* for the first time. A teaser ad typically does *not* have the client's brand name mentioned. That's why it's called a "teaser." It's supposed to be intriguing enough to make you wonder, "Hm-mmmm. . . . What interesting brand is that?" So this is what I told Charlotte.

"Oh, you condescending fuck. I know what the hell a teaser is." She was screaming now. "You get the fuck back here now, you son of a bitch, and you come see me."

I said, "Charlotte, you don't know what you're talking about. And I will not be spoken to like this." I hung up.

I'd been in advertising for fifteen years, and nobody had ever yelled at me. I'm just not one of those people other people scream at. I'm easygoing. I'm nice. People considered me a swell guy: a drunk but not one you'd call an arrogant cocksucker.

I went back to the office, furious. My inner serial killer had been activated. Charlotte was going to pay.

I stepped into her office, and I said, "Screw you. You have serious brain-chemistry issues. I'm quitting and I'm going to tell the president of the agency that I'm quitting because you're not fit to be a creative director."

Charlotte raged at me, her neck bright red and bulging with veins. "You get your ass back in here right this minute."

I turned to her and spoke matter-of-factly. "Listen you crazy old snake. Just because your husband is screwing your daughter at home is no reason to take it out on people at the office."

Her eyes bulged from her face, and when she opened her mouth, a string of saliva joined her two lips together. I'd shocked her.

"Put two and two together, Ms. Oblivious," I continued. "Your daughter's having trouble at school, your husband is a stay-at-home dad. Everybody in the office knows. We talk about it. Your slut daughter even flirts with some of the older male art directors. It's pathetic. She's totally fucking her father, and it's obvious to everyone here."

Of course, I'd made this all up in a moment of inspiration, but she recoiled against the back of her chair.

I went downstairs to the president's office, and I explained that Chicago wasn't going to work for me after all. I detailed what happened with Charlotte, revising everything I said.

His eyes slid to the floor, and he admitted, "Charlotte can be difficult. We've had some problems."

Back in New York, I spent the rest of the year loathing Charlotte and then moving past loathing to simply wishing her dead. I decided an emotionally abusive nightmare like Charlotte does not deserve to live. So I willed her under the wheels of a bus.

The following month I got a phone call from one of the account executives at the Chicago agency. "Did you hear?" she said. "Are you coming?"

"Coming where?" I asked.

"To Charlotte's funeral."

What do you know? Charlotte was waiting for an elevator, had an aneurism, and dropped dead, holding an armful of storyboards.

I hung up the phone smiling and marveled, "That's even better than a bus."

I have also used my powers of magical thinking for good, if you consider tricking Dennis into being my boyfriend "good."

Dennis is attracted to muscular black guys, and I am unfortunately not an African American man with large, full buttocks. I am a lanky WASP, the product of centuries of inbreeding. I have almost no butt. I am as pale as the moon.

And yet I was able to cause Dennis to see me as a homeboy. I sent my thoughts into his eyes, where they rearranged the neural rods and cones of vision and instead of seeing me for what I am, he saw me for what I wanted him to see me as: a bro.

"And I can't even get a tan," I joke to him now, shaking my head at the wonder of it all and sticking my butt out in a pathetic, teasing fashion.

Once or twice, and a person could easily chalk it all up to coincidence, but coincidence implies a lack of control, a random occurrence. With me, I can manipulate the external influences in my life as surely as I can make a baby cry just by grinning.

I can give countless examples. I feel certain that conjoined twins are born so that they can later be profiled on the Discovery Channel and watched by me. My hunger for conjoined-twin stories is so powerful that I believe it actually rearranges molecules in the universe that affect the very cells in the womb. So that when I need it most—when I'm feeling depressed or anxious and turn on the television to distract myself—there's a two-headed girl in a one-piece bathing suit!

Skeptics might say "Yes, but who doesn't enjoy a good conjoined-twin profile on the Discovery Channel? Surely, you can't think you're the only one? You didn't cause them to be born . . . it was a simple matter of an egg not dividing correctly."

Fine, another example: I obsess endlessly over wanting a French bulldog puppy. I check websites and call Dennis over to the computer. "Look!" I say. And each time he says, "No way. Absolutely not. We're not getting a dog."

One evening, we find ourselves downtown shopping for halogen light bulbs next door to a place with puppies in the window. "Oh, let's just go inside and look," I whine. Dennis agrees. "But just to look. We're absolutely not getting a dog, Augusten. I'm serious."

They have a French bulldog puppy in a cage. He's skinny and

shaking, sickly. He looks more like a lab rat injected with sham-poo than a puppy. I ask to see the puppy, and they take him out of the cage and hand him to me. He trembles in my hands, terrified, undoglike.

At this moment, he becomes mine.

Dennis says, "Oh, that's so sad. The poor thing."

We put the puppy on the floor, and he trembles, unsteady. The salesman informs us that the dog is from Russia, that he had recently had an operation to treat his "cherry eye." The salesman says he's nine weeks old.

After fifteen minutes, the damaged puppy is slightly less timid. It is able to walk from me to Dennis. When it reaches Dennis's lap, it tries to climb into it.

This was on a Friday.

That Saturday, Dennis, mysteriously, inexplicably intoxicated without the consumption of alcohol, enters the pet store in a supernatural blackout and comes home with the French bulldog puppy.

The puppy grows into a strong, healthy dog that shrieks and levitates each time Dennis enters the room. The dog is so strong we call it The Beast.

Dennis cannot imagine life without him. It seems now, we never existed without Bentley, that he has been ours all along, since before he was born.

Perhaps my supernatural abilities come from my solid spiri-tual beliefs. I believe in the baby Jesus. And I believe he is hand-some and lives in the sky with his pet cow. I believe that it is essential the cow like you. And if you pet the cow with your mind, it will lick your hand and give you cash. But if you make the cow angry, it will turn away from you, forget you exist, and your life will fall into shambles. I believe that as long as the cow likes you, you can get what you want.

In order to keep in the cow's favor, you need to "let go and let God," meaning, you can't obsess about controlling every little thing. You have to let things unfold naturally and not try to change things you cannot change. On the other hand, I believe that if you've made the cow happy by living this way, you're allowed to ask for favors.

I tell people my theory, and they think I am either kidding or insane. But think this as they may, I have cow saliva on my hands, and many of them do not.

My friend Larry complains constantly about his career. And it's true that he has suffered a series of career setbacks that are stunning in their coincidence. Larry has had a string of such unfortunate luck it can be only one of two things.

"Either you've made the baby Jesus mad or his pet cow hates you," I tell him. "You need to conjure images of a cow in a field of green, munching on grass. Then you need to reach out and scratch between his ears."

Larry tells me to go away.

But I believe that he does exactly what I say because a month later, he has a new job, and he's begun using the phrase "the baby Jesus."

When I was thirty-four, I decided to stop being an alcoholic and become a *New York Times* bestselling author. The gap between active alcoholic advertising copywriter living in squalor and literary sensation with a scrapbook of rave reviews seemed large. A virtual canyon. Yet one day, I decided that's exactly what I would do. And I began writing my first novel, *Sellevision*.

Fourteen days later, *Sellevision* was written, and I had my first manuscript. But I needed an agent, and I didn't have any idea how to get one. So I bought a book on literary agents that provided me with names and e-mail addresses. Still, how to tell them apart from each other? I decided to send my query letter to literary agents whose names I liked. This seemed as good a method as any. Within a week, seven agents had requested the manuscript. Two weeks later, I began to hear feedback. One agent wrote: "No, this isn't something I'd be interested in at all. Satire is over." But another agent was more optimistic: "Well, I liked it. It needs work, but I wouldn't know what to tell you to revise. I could send it to a couple of publishers, but I wouldn't accept you as a regular client. It would be a situation where I send the manuscript as is to two or three publishers, and that's it." At the end of his note he explained that his office charges for photocopies and postage.

I immediately opened a new e-mail document and wrote to my friend Suzanne. "Should I go with him? He sounds like he's willing to lift a finger—a pinkie—but that's all. And he doesn't LOVE the manuscript. And who the hell is he? For all I know, he's some old pervert who's into taxidermy and lives in a studio apartment in Hell's Kitchen. What if some other better real agent comes along? One without a drinking problem and a history of sexually abusing children? But then again, what if no other agent wants me? What should I do? Should I go with this creep?"

I hit SEND.

In my excitement, I'd accidentally typed my note to my friend Suzanne in the wrong document. I'd just sent the letter to the agent.

Instantly, I wrote the agent another e-mail: "As you can see, I am mentally unstable and unfit for representation. I am truly sorry for my horrible comments. I deserve to be electrocuted, I know."

I never heard back from him.

But I did hear back from another agent, who loved the manuscript. He was a very enthusiastic man who laughed at all my mean jokes and he thought the book needed a lot of work, but he was willing to go through it with a red pen and mark up the pages.

He became my agent, and a couple of months after he helped me revise the manuscript, he sold it.

I never expected *Sellevision* to be a bestseller. I called it "my cheese popcorn book." What I did expect was that *Sellevision* would be published. Which is exactly what happened.

Then I wrote a memoir about my childhood. And this, I decided, needed to be a *New York Times* bestseller, high on the list. It needed to be translated into a dozen languages and optioned for film.

"You need to tone down your ambitions," my agent said. "Because you're only setting yourself up for disappointment."

I understood his point of view. I also understood that the book would be huge, not because it was exceptionally well written—in fact, the book felt like a sloppy mess—but nonetheless I knew it would be a bestseller because it had to be a bestseller, so I could quit my loathsome advertising job and write full time. I didn't have to become rich. I just had to be able to publish another book and then another.

I needed the book to be a *New York Times* bestseller because I needed those words "*New York Times* bestseller" to accompany my name for the rest of my life, even if I never wrote another book that sold more than two copies. It was like "M.D." I felt I needed those letters to be complete.

My therapist expressed concern. "Why do you feel you require this event outside yourself to make you happy? It's something that is not only highly unlikely, but something you have absolutely no control over whatsoever."

I merely smiled and said, "You'll just have to watch and see."

After *Running with Scissors* was published, I was sad to see that the Barnes & Noble at Lincoln Center didn't have it displayed on the front table, like other new books. Instead, they had it tucked away where nobody would see it. I willed the chain to have a corporate scandal and fall into financial ruin. KABOOM: the next day, the free-standing shelf units were removed and my book placed on a large new table.

A month later, the book reached number five on the *Times* list. A few months after this, it was sold in nine countries and optioned for film. I quit my advertising job.

Luck? The greedy wishes of a desperate man randomly fulfilled? No. There are no accidents.

My editor phones me and says, "Augusten. You need to concentrate hard on *DRY*. You need to make it another bestseller. I know you can do it. You did it with *Running with Scissors*, and you need to do it again with *DRY*."

"Okay," I tell her, as though she has asked me to turn her brother into a toad and I am able to do this. "I will think hard. But first, I'm focused on something else."

"What? What are you working on now?" Jennifer believes completely in magical thinking. She says she can do it, too, and I know she can. She is the only other person I know who shares my mental powers.

"Well, right now I'm obsessed with Elizabeth Smart."

"That little girl who went missing from her bedroom?"

"Yes, exactly. It's making me crazy that they can't find her. I need them to find her. Either she has to come home, or they have to find her head on a stick in the woods."

"God, I certainly hope she comes home."

"I can't control that. There are limits," I say.

"Wow," Jen says. "Okay, I'll think of Elizabeth Smart, too. And then we'll work together on *DRY*."

"Okay, Jen."

We hang up.

Three days later, Elizabeth Smart is found, returned to her parents. No longer a virgin, of course, but at least her head was still attached to her body.

PUFF DERBY

Know this: the Kentucky Derby is not about the horses. It's about the hats. These creations are wider than a professional linebacker's shoulders and cost about as much as his annual salary. They come in all colors, from that pale blue in sanitary napkin commercials to unapologetic red. Profusions of flowers or feathers or both extend at least a foot in every possible eye-poking direction. Know this also: it is apparently a Kentucky State law that the hat and dress must be a coordinated twinset. Therefore, if the dress has violet leopard-print spots, so, too, must the hat. The dress itself must hug the body like a second layer of cells, and if it is above a size four, the wearer of the dress must stay within one hundred yards of the parking lot. Said hat and dress are always, *always* worn with strappy, open-toed high heels in a complimentary hue.

This is Easter with gigantic, leaking breast implants.

I know these things because last week, Dennis and I drove from Manhattan to Louisville for Derby Day. But as mesmerizing as these hats are, my eyes were involuntarily drawn to the faces of the ladies who wore them. Though many were in their early twenties, they'd already racked up multiple face-lifts, evidenced by their unnaturally uniform skin and a nearly identical facial expression: "Southern cordial." These Dixie chicks wear so much makeup that if you touched one of their cheeks, your finger would look as though you'd just dipped it into a jar of Skippy.

These ladies have one final accoutrement: a man's arm hooked territorially—predatorily, even—around their waists. The arm is clad in a flawless Hickey-Freeman seersucker suit. At the wrist: a heavy, shiny Rolex. On the hand: a wedding band, sized slightly up for easy removal in airport lounges.

The men don't have hats, but they do have thick, penis-width cigars protruding from the smug corners of their mouths. Their mere presence say "old money/young wife."

Yet for all their composure and utter self-confidence, not one of these ladies or gentlemen passed by our seats without giving us a look of mild curiosity tinged with jealousy.

Dennis and I were dressed in shorts from Abercrombie, oxford-cloth shirts, and loud striped ties. We both wore linen navy blazers and baseball caps. Dennis wore Nikes; I wore New Balance. The security guard at the front gate remarked, "This is the best outfit I've seen today," as she scanned Dennis's camouflage cargo pockets with her wand. Apparently she'd already had her fill of plastic women in dangerous headgear.

But our outfits were not the source of Derby envy. Quite simply, we had the best seats at Churchill Downs. Private box seats, right on the track, at the finish line. The box seats belong to Dennis's friend Sheila or, more accurately, to Sheila's grandfather, Doc Twining.

Doc Twining was a doctor in the day when being a doctor meant something grand, like a Cadillac Eldorado convertible, a large home without a mortgage, and a lake house for the summer. He was a surgeon, saved lives in World War Two, and became best friends with the governor of Kentucky. Thus, the box seats. He probably paid for them with a round of drinks and a hand-shake. Or perhaps a free appendectomy. These days, a typical doctor who worked for an HMO might not even be able to afford digital cable to watch the Derby on TV.

When Doc Twining dies, the box reverts to the Derby, where it will be auctioned yearly to the highest bidder. Sadly, a corporation will probably be the highest bidder, and uncouth middle managers at a snack-chip company will occupy the box. I imagine they will wave flags of some sort. Perhaps they will brandish sticks.

But last weekend, the box belonged to six of us: Dennis, me, Sheila, Sheila's husband, mother, and brother. The brother was fresh out of prison, having served time for an unnamed crime. He wore gray polyester slacks and a Hawaiian shirt and ate beef jerky. He seemed like a really cool guy and for a moment I thought, *Maybe I should commit a petty crime just to see what jail is really like*.

At the start of the third race, a young black man approached our box with a tray of mint juleps. They were in *glass* glasses, with tall sprigs of mint sticking up higher than the straws. Just like one of the Hats. I ordered a round for everybody except myself, because I don't drink. As each julep was pulled from the tray, I saw that the glasses were encrusted with ice. Such civility.

As I sat in the box watching the glossy and ultramuscular horses blur past me, I thought about how unlikely it was that I was at the Derby in the first place. In one sense I am a highly likely candidate, since it would be difficult to find a person whose blood was a more perfect shade of blue than mine. On my father's side I am a descendant of the original Jamestown colonists, who arrived in America in 1620, a few years before the Mayflower. My mother's people owned enormous pecan orchards and Taralike plantation houses in southern Georgia. My ancestors were judges, doctors, lawyers, mayors, governors, and land owners.

Unfortunately, a wide streak of mental illness, alcoholism, and irresponsibility runs through my family tree like a sort of gypsy-moth rot. So while I may, indeed, be a blue-blooded, purebred American with roots in the Great South, I no longer have my papers.

So I sat there in the Derby box feeling a bit like an imposter. "Got any more of those?" I asked the former inmate. He handed me a greasy stick of jerky.

During the seventh race, a man in a blindingly white suit approached our box and, seeing that it was full, stood at the opening of the box next to ours, the one just slightly ahead of the finish line. A murmur rippled through the box, and I heard the word "Daddy," a word that for various reasons always gets my attention.

His diamond earrings flashed in the sun. Of course: P. Diddy (formerly Sean "Puffy" Combs), rap star, music producer, recently acquitted gun-out-the-window-thrower. A small entourage of impeccably dressed and very handsome black men huddled behind him.

A crowd materialized, and there seemed to be less oxygen in the air. The dozens of photographers in front of us on the track now turned around to face Puffy. Auto-focus lenses whirred into action. Flashes fired.

"Puffy!" yelped one of the debutantes. "A picture? Pretty please, Daddy?"

Puffy extended his arm, and the girl parted the crowd and slid right in. Flashes exploded on their faces. The light around us popped.

The crowd seemed to close in on our little box. Puffy signed autographs, signed anything passed to him. He held a cigar between his teeth. There was not a single smudge on his white suit. His Rolex shone. When he spoke, he sounded like a senator.

Even without his white, white suit, Puff Daddy would have been the whitest man at the Derby. And yet I couldn't help but think: all these Hats, swooning over him, their faces melting into smiles, their bodies leaning into him, their eyes trained on his every gesture—these ladies wouldn't give him a quarter to save his life if he were wearing sweat pants, a Fubu jersey, and a backward baseball cap. Yet now, I was certain, any of them would have been proud to bear his children. The men, too. Any one of them would happily shrug, "What the hell?" and be his bitch.

People sneer at "new money." Until, that is, they are actually face-to-sneer with it. Puffy single-handedly stole the show from the Hats, who had themselves stolen it from the horses.

"Nice outfits, guys," he said to Dennis and me, leaning over the railing that separated our box from his. He nodded and made an effort to reach over and shake our hands. He had the sincerity of JFK and certainly as much charm.

"Thanks," I said.

We were dressed for comfort, with a nod to tradition. Puffy was dressed for tradition, with a nod to world domination. The ladies were dressed to impress and found themselves hopelessly in awe of a black man who had reinvented himself as the richest, whitest man at the Derby.

I didn't feel so out of place then.

MEANWHILE, BACK
AT THE RANCH

Dennis and I live in Manhattan, on the Upper West Side, in a large studio apartment that overlooks the new Trump development along the river. From our living room, we can peer into the two-million-dollar apartments across the street and admire the popcorn ceilings and overhead fluorescent lights that apparently come standard in every kitchen. We used to have a view of the Hudson River, but this is no longer the case. We now get a sliver of sky and a chunk of New Jersey, and that is all, which is clearly not enough for anyone. So we've decided that this summer, we need "a place in the country." A place where we can go to decompress and look at trees in their natural habitat. As opposed to trees that have been reformed into particle board and placed into a Trump window frame.

So we began looking at houses in western Massachusetts. And we recently found a farmhouse from the seventeen-eighties that has been fully restored by its current owner, a New Yorker. This means all the molding has been stripped and left tastefully bare, the wide pine floors polished with European wax. In the kitchen there is a sink made of slate and the faucet is from Paris, but it's not fancy; it's blissfully plain in a way that only the French could manage to pull off. I'm dead certain this faucet has added twelve thousand dollars to the price of the house.

In the living room is an enormous beehive fireplace complete with Dutch oven. This fireplace is what made us want the house. This is a fireplace a person of six feet can nearly stand in. The bricks are, of course, handmade.

There is a huge apple tree in front and just below this, an old stone wall that has mostly melted into the earth. The house is on eighty acres of pastures and woodlands. At the western edge of the yard there is even a post-and-beam barn with a bright red door, like an Elizabeth Arden spa. This barn has plumbing, a soapstone woodstove, and two bedrooms.

In other words, this is a perfect house. The ultimate escape hatch from the stress of the city, yes?

Actually, no.

This house would, in fact, triple your stress. Because you would feel the need to be accountable to it. It would be like dating royalty: a fine idea in the abstract but draining financially and emotionally.

When you shopped for furniture, you would find yourself thinking words like "honest" and "authentic," and then nothing would ever be good enough and the one small thing that was good enough would cost you seven thousand dollars and would be fragile. No way could you ever go to Target, ever again. You would shop in places where you ran into Martha Stewart and Barbra Streisand, and they would both outbid you for everything.

In a normal house, if you have a clogged drain you call a

plumber. But in this antique New England Cape, a clogged drain would require a certified specialist and possibly even approval from the registry of historic homes.

And this, I understand now, is why the New Yorkers must sell it. It is too flawless a house to actually live in. It is a house to sit in and be photographed, not a house to sit in and eat eggs. You could absolutely never fart in this house.

In desperation I phoned a real estate agent on Nantucket. I said, "I'm just looking for a little summer shack. A writer's shack, really, very sort of simple and crude. Doesn't have to be on the water but close enough to walk."

She chuckled and said, "Let me think." And for a moment, there was silence, and then I heard her tapping on her keyboard. "Okay, okay," she said. "I think I have something here. It's like you want, very Hemingway-ish, very rustic, and sort of iconoclastic: one bedroom, kitchen, living room, bath, eighth of an acre. Eight hundred thousand."

It was beginning to seem that Dennis and I would be trapped in Manhattan forever, unless one of us won the Powerball lottery.

But then I got an idea. What about a log cabin? What if we bought a piece of land in the Berkshires and then bought one of those log cabins, from a kit?

The truth is, I've always fantasized about living in a log cabin. Maybe because I had such an unstable childhood, I deeply crave a house made of solid, ten-inch timbers. A house without dry-wall. A house made of solid trees that has a great, two-story field-stone fireplace dividing the living room and the kitchen.

As it turned out, Dennis had a similar fantasy. "I'd live in a log cabin," he said. "As long as it didn't have animal heads on the wall."

So I went online and discovered that one of the log-home man-ufacturers had a model home in Massachusetts, right in the general area where we would want to buy land and build our own home. The following Saturday, we drove there to inspect the house.

The model log home was located on a busy street, filled with fast-food restaurants and industrial park buildings. Not exactly what we'd envisioned for our dream home, but the house was there, strong and woody, and it was easy to picture it in a field or nestled in a clutch of pine trees.

"Good afternoon, gentlemen," said the warm, blonde-haired woman who was standing in the center of the Great Room when we stepped inside. "My name is Joanne. How can I make your log-home dreams come true?" She was wearing a patchwork vest and a rust-colored cotton turtleneck. Around her neck was a thin gold chain with a cross.

We smiled. Dennis said, "Hi. We're just sort of, you know, just looking. Just starting to look. This is the first time we've seen a log cabin."

"Well," she said, as she approached us, "this isn't a log *cabin*; it's a two-thousand-four-hundred-square-foot log home. This particular model is called the Timberdream, and it's perfect for families who like to entertain or who have a lot of children. Feel free to take a look around," she said, making a general sweeping gesture with her arm. "You'll find the bedrooms upstairs, along with a loft that overlooks this Great Room. On this floor you'll find the kitchen just over there on the other side of the fireplace. Down the hall over there is where the laundry room and pantry are located. And at the other end is a den, which is easily converted into a fourth bedroom." Then her eyes got wider. "And downstairs," she said, "is a finished basement."

Was it my imagination, or did she look at my crotch when she said this? Did she look at both of our crotches? Was she thinking, *Gay guys ... basement ... leather straps suspended from the ceiling ...*

"Thanks," I said and moved away from her, heading to the kitchen.

"Wow," Dennis said. "This is amazing."

And it was amazing. The kitchen gleamed with what I can

only imagine must have been a hundred thousand dollars' worth of the finest appliances. A Wolf range, a Subzero refrigerator with glass doors, a hammered-copper hood over the range.

"I think this kitchen costs more than what we could spend on a whole house," Dennis said.

Joanne appeared behind us. "With our kits, you have options. You have flexibility. You can choose to create a dream kitchen, like this one. Or you can opt for a more moderate arrangement. Standard with each of our kits are solid hardwood cabinets, an electric range, refrigerator, and microwave oven. But as you can see, you are free to customize your home any way you like."

We explored the rest of the house, feeling most intoxicated when we reached the mud room. "Imagine having our own washer and dryer and not having to give our laundry to the laundry wench," I said. The laundry wench worked in the lobby of our building. She had her own room where she collected everybody's laundry, sent it off to be washed and damaged, then gave it back to you, folded, at the end of the day. Years of handling Upper West Siders' eighty-five-dollar bras had made her bitter.

"I like the fireplace," Dennis said, admiring the two-story field-stone fireplace exactly as we'd imagined it.

"That," Joanne said, "is an amazing fireplace. But you should keep in mind that a fireplace such as this one will add about sixty thousand dollars to the price of the home."

Here, I paused. If the fireplace added sixty thousand dollars, how much more would my special features add?

Because there was no way I was living in a log cabin in the woods unless the entire basement was a large panic room. I would have to have two-foot-thick concrete walls throughout. Broadband Internet access. A vault door that was both blast and chemical agent proof. I would need a basement that could sustain us for at least a month. In addition, whatever house we built in the woods would need to be secured by a fourteen-foot-high chain-link fence surrounding the property. The fence would need to be electrified.

I voiced some of my concerns to Joanne, but she only absently fondled the cross around her neck and said, "I'm not sure I even understand what sort of house you're talking about. Because that doesn't seem like a house. That seems like some sort of military compound, and we certainly do not sell military compounds."

Back in the car Dennis said, "Where did that come from?"

"What?" I said.

"That panic room and electrified-fence stuff."

"Oh. Well, you know. If we're gonna live in the country, we have to be safe."

"I'll tell you what," Dennis said. "You can have a little pen in the backyard with an electrified fence around it."

This made me happy. Dennis always looked after me, indulged me, spoiled me rotten, like meat in the sun.

"Okay," I said and leaned over the seat to kiss him.

Back home in New York, we went through the book that Joanne gave us. The book contained two hundred log-home plans, along with prices. I thought it was fantastic that you could just pick a house out of this catalogue and then . . . have it built! Like ordering a sandwich from Subway.

Dennis, ever practical, suggested that we order more catalogues from more log-home companies. This is smart, as I would have simply picked a floor plan out of this book and then placed my order. But Dennis is not a take-what-you-can-get-and-be-glad-you-got-it sort of guy.

I went online and visited the websites for as many log-home companies as I could find. Then I sent away for their brochures.

And for the next week, we spent our free time looking at floor plans, an activity that proved to be entirely overwhelming. To make matters even worse, all the floor plans could be combined, mixed, and matched. So you could have the master bedroom you like from the Eagle's Nest together with that great in-law suite from the Montana. Then, if you wanted, you could steal the loft from the Pine Crest but use the loft railings from the Dusty Rose.

The process made me increasingly more anxious, and my obsessive-compulsive disorder went into overdrive. I began to twitch frequently, wash my hands every half hour, and adjust my glasses constantly. I took an extra ten milligrams of Lexapro to keep my symptoms in check.

Clearly, it will be years before we step foot inside our own log cabin. It will take at least five years to choose a plan. Then another three or four to decide on the finishing options. And of course before we can do any of this, we must first choose a piece of property. And I can't even imagine how this will happen. Once you find your property, you have to have it checked for radon, leveled, electric and water brought in. Honestly, I don't know how anybody builds anything. If I had been in charge of developing the modern world, we would all still be living in caves. We wouldn't even have fire yet.

So for now, we make do with our own view of the Trump apartments. When I get a craving for Nature, I turn on the Discovery Channel and watch bear-attack survivors recount their horror and show us the results of their reconstructive surgery.

My friend Suzanne in California gave me some advice that her own therapist gave to her: "Tend to your inner garden," he said.

This seems wise to me. I will stop obsessing over log cabins and weekend houses. I will instead focus on my inner garden. Around which is my own personal electrified fence.

Up the Escalator

I'm through the revolving door, and instantly, profoundly, the air is different. Washed with chemicals and mercury
vapor light, scented in such a specific way that I would know the
name of this store if blindfolded, hog-tied, and instructed to sniff
the air. I'm in Kmart in Manhattan's East Village. It's a new store,
their first in New York City. Yet it smells exactly like the Kmart
in Hadley, Massachusetts, that I remember from childhood. I
glance around and see, am comforted to see, that this Kmart looks
identical to every other. There has been no concession made to
Manhattan's refined tastes. The floor is not raw concrete, stainless steel, or anything remotely groovy. It is pale beige tile.

The only difference between this Kmart and every other is that
this one is vertical. Three stories. And the escalator is broken, so

I have to walk up. I climb three of these tall, steel steps and feel tired and heavy. I look up and see that I am still very far from the top. Why is this so much harder than climbing a normal flight of stairs? It's like each foot is a frozen Butterball turkey.

I think it's because of *expectations*.

Your brain sees the escalator and tells your body it can relax, make progress while leaning. It's like a little vacation from walking. But then you get there, and the escalator is broken, and the disappointment starts sinking from your chest, gathering mass along the way until it hits your feet, where it congeals and leaves you with twenty-pound heels.

And it seems pathetic that the escalator is out of order, a sign of failure. How hard can it be to keep an escalator working? All it has to do is go around and around, like a hamster on a wheel. It's not a ventilator in Lenox Hill hospital. People have to hire attorneys and appear before judges just to get one of those turned off.

I wouldn't even have to walk up this broken escalator if I were wheelchair-bound. I could have rung a bell on the ground floor, and an elevator would have come, along with a minimum-wage employee with averted eyes. I would be an excellent quadriplegic, not at all like those awful, independent cripples who are always talking about how *abled* they are. I would sit in my wheelchair, and I would moan and shake my head "no" as though in excruciating pain, until somebody came to assist me, possibly even carrying a beverage. I believe a person must use whatever it is they have. I, myself, am an emotional cripple, certainly. Raised without school or normal parents, I do not know how to mix with others. In a way, I am a psychological transsexual, always trying to "pass" for a normal person but being clocked every time.

I do not belong in Kmart.

Or, if I am here, I should be here ironically. "I'm in Kmart. Wink, wink. Where are the Toughskin jeans?" But I am not here ironically; I am here sincerely.

I need an iron.

I am thinking about my need for an iron as I climb the escalator stairs. I am halfway to the top and briefly I consider turning around and walking back down the steps and going to another store. But this cannot happen. I am being pressed forward by doughy shoppers holding family-sized boxes of Rice Chex and flimsy Kathy Ireland coordinates, which are impossible to imagine on any person with a full set of chromosomes. These grim, fleshy shoppers stomping up, on, forward into their Kmart futures. They add weight to my feet. And they confuse me, because these are not people I normally see on the streets of Manhattan, certainly not the East Village. Where are the pierced eyebrows? The tattoos? Where are the buff gay guys with manicured facial hair and neatly trimmed chests? These people are like ordinary people one might find in Idaho or Kentucky. And while there's certainly nothing wrong with this, it's odd to see them here. It is as if Kmart has bussed in their own shoppers along with their own air.

Finally, at the top I am greeted by gigantic posters of Martha Stewart, sneering at me. I must admit that the posters comfort me and inspire me to shop for bed shams and stemware. I was raised by a mother similar to Martha Stewart in that she was self-consumed and incredibly successful and famous. Except my mother was only incredibly successful and famous in her brain, which was diseased. So I am drawn to women like Martha, Martha most specifically. More than once I have had fantasies of working for her and then having her fall in love with and adopt me. The thing is, I have always craved a home. I was raised in a makeshift mental institution, so this doesn't count as a home. I've always craved both the concept of home—security, comfort, safety—as well as the physical qualities of home—sheets, picture frames, door knobs. This is why Martha Stewart has the same effect on me that hardcore pornography has on Andrea Dworkin: intense interest.

I pass by a mirror and catch a glimpse of my arms. I think, *I*

really need to work on my shoulders more at the gym. I should have
a separate shoulder day as opposed to lumping shoulders together
with arms. If I really work on my shoulders, the deltoid will cut into
the part of my arm that separates my triceps from my biceps. And I
need this. And this strikes me immediately as the difference
between a gay man and everybody else. A straight man or woman
might think, I can relax a little once my 401(k) reaches a certain
level. A gay man thinks, I'll be happy once I've added another two
inches to my chest.

Near the stacking plastic trash cans, a pack of children is
standing in a confused mass, adult-less. They are looking in
different directions, little heads turning, arms down at their
sides, fingers gripping and releasing air. I can see spittle in the
corners of their pink mouths. A pedophile could walk into the
group and take over. He could clap his hands and say, "Time to
get some lunch," and I bet at least two of them would follow. It'd
be easy. People don't get how easy.

I walk past the pyramid display of plastic Martha Stewart soap
dishes and head into the housewares section in search of my iron.

My pulse is thrumming at my wrists, and I can feel that my
face has flushed. It's the same feeling I had the first time I went to
Las Vegas and put a silver dollar in one of the slot machines. And
won five hundred dollars. I am deeply excited by this environ-
ment and thrilled to consider what might happen.

Every day, millions of people come to stores like this, and they
buy small appliances without so much as a second thought. Perhaps for most, it's even a chore. But I have waited my entire life
to buy an iron. In a sense, I might as well be walking up the steps
to accept my Grammy.

The iron is not for me. It's for Dennis. I haven't ironed anything since I stuck crayons between two sheets of wax paper in
third grade. But Dennis irons frequently and well.

At first, without ever actually watching him iron, I suggested
he just "give it to the Dragon Lady." By which I meant he could

simply bring it downstairs to the coy Chinese lady who runs the dry-cleaner place. Dennis smiled, as if with secret knowledge. He said, "I like to iron."

But this didn't make any sense to me. Ironing was just something you gave up when you lived in Manhattan. You either dropped your clothes off at the cleaners or, like me, let gravity take care of the wrinkles.

Dennis sauntered over to the closet and pulled his ironing board off its hook on the wall. He carried it back under his arm and then made a display of opening it. He winked at me, flirting. Then he walked into the kitchen and pulled his old iron out from one of the kitchen cabinets that I never open.

And he went at it.

When Dennis irons, it is a slow, soothing, and careful thing. Creases are blended away, smoothed into soft flat plains. Wrinkles melt. He works very gently, with the tip. He edges around buttons as if he is driving an exquisite car, handmade in Italy. Gliding along the stitching on the cuff, then the cuff itself.

I watched him iron and experienced what my friend Christopher, a science-fiction reader, describes as a "time slip." This is when you become so absorbed in something that either one minute or one hour can pass, and you honestly couldn't say which it was. And when you snap out of it, things have shifted, sometimes in alarmingly perceptible ways.

Was it twenty minutes later? I was wearing the shirt, and it felt warm and smooth and loved. How had this happened?

So now I am pro-ironing and to show my support am buying him a new Rowenta.

Because an interesting metamorphosis has occurred. Against all odds, I am becoming domesticated.

The other day while I was at the doctor's office waiting for my suspicious mole appointment, I was paging through *Redbook* magazine. I was reading about how crumpled newspapers are actually better than paper towels for cleaning windows because they don't leave behind lint. And I was thinking, *I've got to try this!* I was so absorbed in the article that the receptionist had to call my name twice.

Our routine involves Dennis cooking dinner and me washing the dishes. And I love washing dishes by hand and even bought myself a stainless-steel dish rack from Williams-Sonoma. I was so excited in the cab with the box next to me that I went home and ate some gluey vanilla yogurt just so I could wash the bowl and place it in the new dish rack to dry.

Now I understand packaged-goods advertising. Softens hands *while* you do dishes. Before, when I had a loathsome job in advertising, I created lines like this without ever truly considering their meaning. I've gone from duping the public to being a target audience. I used to sit on the other side of the one-way mirror in focus groups and sneer at homemakers. "How pathetic," I would comment. "She's actually been brainwashed to believe in Tide with Bleach." But now, I see that all along, she was right. And I was the smug fool. The fact is, Tide with Bleach *does* remove more stains than regular detergent and bleach. I've spent hours downstairs in the basement laundry room experimenting.

My domestication was not a spontaneous event, like the collapse of a star. It has occurred as a direct result of living with Dennis.

I moved into Dennis's apartment one year, three months, and seventeen days after we met. It's on the Upper West Side of Manhattan, five minutes from Central Park and close to the Hudson River. It is large, with an entire wall of windows facing north. It has tall ceilings, art on the walls, a sofa with boiled wool, down-filled cushions from Wales.

The water pressure in the shower could strip the paint off a car. There is a doorman. And an elevator. And a garbage chute. These are not uncommon amenities in New York City, the city I have made my home for fifteen years. But they are new for me.

My previous apartment was a filthy three-hundred-square-foot studio on the third floor of a five-story building in the East Village. When it rained, water poured from the center of the single overhead light fixture. During a heavy storm, I would have to empty the twenty-gallon plastic tub I kept beneath it several times. The ceiling was permanently damp, moldy, and falling away in whole sections.

There was no heat because of a wiring problem in the wall, somewhere between the thermostat and the furnace downstairs. But I didn't care. I just opened the oven door in the winter and removed the smoke alarm so it wouldn't beep at the carbon monoxide.

Friends suggested that at the very least I fix the leak. "Call the super for God sakes. There are laws about things like that, even in New York."

But I didn't mind. The constant sound of falling water was like living in a hut in the rain forest. It was very *Gorillas in the Mist* and made me feel somewhat exotic and adventurous.

"You're like a serial killer," my friend Suzanne commented. "You live in exactly the sort of apartment that ends up in a photograph on the cover of the *Post*. With a big fat headline over it: PSYCHO'S DEN OF SQUALOR."

But I've always been comfortable in squalor. Because I was raised in chaos and filth, because the psychiatrist's house was so messy and disgusting, this has become my default. What may horrify other people is mundane to me. "That's just old chow fun, don't worry. It's dry. It doesn't stink anymore, so no rats will smell it."

While it's true that I spent five thousand dollars on a shabby chic sofa, it is also true that the white slipcover eventually became beige, and the sofa itself vanished beneath a mound of clothing. I was in the habit of wearing a pair of khaki slacks twice, and then instead of taking them across the street to the cleaners, I would simply buy another pair. As a result, I owned seventy pairs of the exact same khaki slacks. The same was true of shirts, underwear, and socks.

I never used the stove and during the warm months filled the oven with paperback novels. At any given moment, the refrigerator contained twenty bottles of seltzer water; my watch, keys, and wallet (so I wouldn't misplace them); and a hundred rolls of Fuji Velvia slide film.

The kitchen cabinets themselves were filled with more books, empty seltzer bottles, and unread mail.

The sink in the bathroom was crusted with five years' worth of dried toothpaste. And the dozens of magazines that covered the bathroom floor were all crinkly from water because I never used a shower curtain.

It wasn't because I was poor that I lived this way. I made decent money at my advertising job. It was just that I really didn't know how to live any other way. I'd even begun to feel *above* all things domestic. Anybody could clean, after all. But not just anybody can create the next global advertising campaign for UPS. So I spent all my time at the computer, either working or writing in my journal. "I live in my head," was my own justification.

Dennis didn't see my apartment until we'd been dating for nearly two months. In one way, this wasn't odd because we were taking it very slow. We weren't sleeping together; we were getting to know each other in jazz clubs on the Bowery, at restaurants, on park benches in Central Park at midnight. We were courting each other like people did in the forties.

When Dennis took a trip south to Kentucky to visit his business partner's family, I took the opportunity to clean my apartment. He was going to be gone for four days. I calculated that if I worked twelve hours a day, I might have the apartment presentable by the time he returned. While I understood that I would not be able to have the apartment "clean" by this time, I could at least remove the majority of the debris and make it appear as though a bachelor lived here and not a psychopath.

By the end of day four, I had slept a total of nine hours, removed fifty-one garbage bags, and torn a ligament in my back.

Yet the apartment still looked terrible. I felt like an unattractive girl who must wear a ton of makeup in order to get all the way up to "plain."

But at least the sofa was free of clothing, the wood floors bare. I'd collected all the books that were previously strewn around the apartment and stacked them into two skyscrapers next to the bed. I went across the street to the store where the NYU college students get their dorm room furniture and purchased three metal Metro shelving units. I assembled these and lined them up against one wall. Then I stacked my clothing on the shelves. In between two piles of white T-shirts, I placed my Bang & Olufsen stereo. I bought a twenty-dollar area rug to cover the dark stain of unknown origin in the center of the floor. And I bought a shower curtain.

When Dennis finally saw the apartment, he was surprised by the tiny size. But he was pleased with my bed, which was now fitted with three thousand dollars' worth of sheets, down pillows, and down comforter from ABC Home.

I was relieved that Dennis thought me eccentric for being able to live in such a tiny apartment. "It's like the dorm room of some rich kid," he said. While certainly not impressive, at least the apartment was no longer a deal breaker.

And now, one year, three months, and seventeen days later, I am in Kmart selecting an iron.

I choose the top-of-the-line. There will be absolutely no compromise here.

Back at the escalator, I see that the "down" side is working. Of course, this would be the case. The "down" side always works. You can always slide down with ease. It's going up that sometimes takes extra effort.

The symbolism is not lost on me as I drift down to the main floor.

I take the subway uptown. I think, *Have I given up anything by living with another person? Has there been a trade-off?* Always, there is a trade-off. And the answer comes to me instantly. I have given up a certain degree of freedom. The ability to plow through my life with utter disregard for the thoughts and feelings of other people. I can no longer read a magazine and throw it on the floor.

In exchange, I get unlimited access to the one person I have met in my life whom I automatically felt was out of my league. My favorite human being, the single person I cherish above all others. This is the person I get to share the oxygen in the room with.

And for this, I will happily scrub the toilet. And I won't make fun of anybody who drives an SUV. Unless, of course, they really deserve it. And I'll try to let things *happen*. Not always feel like I have to control everything.

With the exception of those things I can control, that is, with my mind.

**Read an excerpt from *Possible Side Effects*
by Augusten Burroughs, now available.**

Unclear Sailing

Marblehead, Massachusetts, is known as a "coastal town," which means "the narrow streets are cut through the rock so you are always in danger of falling onto jagged shards and being swept away by Poseidon." Curiously, this increases the property values. Expansive, cedar-shingled homes dot the landscape. Sailboats outnumber seagulls, especially in the summer.

It would appear there's a law that allows only Saabs, Volvos, and BMWs. And in the winter, the owners must fix Christmas wreaths to their grilles. Anybody who dares present a Star of David on their lawn will certainly have their home burned to the ground.

Need I mention that not one black person lives in Marblehead?

At least, not when I lived there, at the age of eighteen. I had just graduated from a computer programming trade school but had decided two weeks before graduation to "get into advertising."

So far, I hadn't had any luck.

I'd thought of a few ads, typed them up, and stuck them into a three-ring binder. Then I'd phoned ad agencies in Boston and asked to show my portfolio.

Four agencies had agreed, and all four told me to go away within ten minutes of staring in horror at my mistyped, messy pages.

So I decided to hone my entrepreneurial skills and secure my own accounts. At eighteen, I could pass for twenty-four, which seemed more than old enough to start my own ad agency. Right here in Marblehead.

And I'd start with Hood Sailmaker, a company that made sails for sailboats and the seventy-five million yachts crowding the Marblehead bay. They occupied an impressive loft building, so surely they'd offer me a fortune.

I walked to Hood and presented my sweaty self to the receptionist. "I'd like to speak with the owner, please."

She said, "I'm sorry, the owner is unavailable. I'll get a manager for you, if you like."

This was as good a time as any to get familiar with corporate bureaucracy. I nodded.

She waved me toward a sofa. "Have a seat."

A moment later, a startlingly blond man in his early thirties appeared. His hair was streaked almost white from the sun; even the hair on his arms was bleached beyond color.

"Hi. I'm Cliff. What can I do for ya?"

I told him that I was starting an ad agency and that I would be honored if he would consider giving me his account, as my first. And that if he did, I would service it for just two hundred dollars a month, which I was positive was many hundreds of thousands less than his current ad agency in Boston charged. And then, somewhat embarrassed, I told him my name.

Cliff smiled. He said, "Wow, you sure talk fast! Why don't you come back to my office."

So I followed him down a long hallway of polished wood. The walls were lined with artful yet repetitive photographs of yachts cutting through ocean.

Cliff sat at the chair behind his desk and said, "So you're going to start your own ad agency, huh?"

His face was so open and friendly, I was tempted to tell him my entire life story, including my recent failure to get a job in advertising. But instead I swallowed and said, "Yes."

He looked apologetic, shrugged his shoulders, and said, "To tell you the truth, we're pretty happy with our existing ad agency."

I deflated. Of course he was happy with his current ad agency. I was an idiot to even try this stunt. I shrank back against my chair.

"But if you're looking for work . . ."

Well. Maybe just for a *few* months. Until I could save enough money to start my own empire. I asked, "What kind of work?" Knowing he would say, "Janitorial."

"We could use a new sail cutter," he said.

And because he hadn't said the word "toilet" I was puzzled. "What's that?"

Chip explained. "Sail cutters take the canvas and use a pattern to cut the shapes that then get sewn together into the finished product. The sail. To be honest with you, it's hard work. But there's a lot of opportunity to advance within Hood."

I'd never in my life been offered a position so quickly. The usual process involved filling out an application, waiting two weeks, then being rejected. And unlike any other position I'd applied for, this one did not involve a deep-fry bin.

"Yeah?" I said. I was doubtful. "Does it not pay any money or anything? Do you have to, like, volunteer for a while?"

Cliff laughed. "Of course it pays. Seven-fifty an hour."

More than three times what McDonald's offered. And *they* didn't even want me.

But I did have a small amount of pride. "Well, I really want to start my own ad agency. Eventually, at least. But I guess I could do that on the side and cut some sails."

"Yeah!" he said. "You could!"

"So. When would I start?"

He clapped his hands together. "How about right now?"

And now I was even more suspicious. I'd never heard of a job that you started the day you applied. Without even applying in the first place.

But maybe this was how things were done here in Marblehead. After all, for all he knew, I was a local boy whose dad owned a brokerage firm in Boston. Maybe I was raised in Marblehead and our fathers were in the same French lit class at Harvard.

I said, "Okay. I'll do it."

Cliff stood. His striped cotton oxford shirt was crisp, even at three in the afternoon. And his khakis were pressed. I noticed, too, that he wore no socks. Just bare tan feet slipped into white-soled Top-Siders.

No mustard stains on him, that was for sure. How hard could this job be?

All the managers I'd known—Ground Round, Woolworth's—had sweated profusely and smelled strongly of alcohol.

I followed Cliff as he gave me a tour of Hood. Here are the restrooms. The time clock, please punch in. This is the vending machine. These are the corporate offices. That over there is a client showroom.

"And here's where you'll be," he said, opening the wide door of a freight elevator we were on to reveal an enormous room, empty except for walls of windows, overhead lights, and fabric on the floor.

"This is where we do the actual cutting," he said.

On the floor, men leaned over gigantic panels of white canvas. These were twenty-, thirty-foot-tall sheets of the brightest white fabric, made brighter by the sunlight that flooded the place.

The room was so huge that many sails could be spread out like this on the floor at once. And then dozens of people could busy themselves around them.

There was an almost holy quality to the room. The respect the men felt for the sailcloth could be felt in the air.

I followed Cliff to the far corner of the room where he introduced me to three guys. These were Cliffs in miniature—all blond, all handsome. The oldest was probably twenty-two. We were peers. But grade school was as far as I'd made it academically, so I was uncomfortable around them and unsure how to behave.

I was fine around people who were much older than me because I wanted to please them. But I didn't know what to do around these three guys my own age.

"Hey," they each said, nodding.

I said "Hey" back to them. Like a monkey staring in a mirror. I said "Hey" instead of the more formal "Hello." Or worse, "It's just wonderful to meet you," which was actually the first phrase that came to mind.

Then Cliff began speaking in tongues. "Start him off with a tri-radial spinnaker for a thirty-footer. If that goes okay, get him on a vertical batten mainsail for in-mast furling."

"Will do," one of the guys said, whose name had simply bounced off my forehead.

Cliff grabbed my upper arm and gave it a squeeze. "So, great. This is really exciting. You'll do a fine job and I think you'll have a terrific time here with the guys. And don't sweat if it's a little confusing at first. It'll take you a couple days to get the hang. But, like I said, I think you'll do a fantastic job. And if you have any problems or if you need anything, you know where to find me." He smiled, revealing flawless white teeth, and walked away.

I watched him as he strode toward the elevator. *Is that it?*

"So it's pretty easy," the guy said to the back of my head.

I jerked around to look at him. "I'm sorry, what's your name again?"

"*Chip.* Anyway, it's pretty easy. Here, why don't you just watch me for a few and then I'll let you loose. But to be honest, I think I'm gonna start you out on a simple jib."

I didn't know what a jib was, but I liked that he described it as *simple.* And I also liked that all I had to do was watch. Maybe I could stretch this *watching* thing out all week, then quit and collect my week's pay.

"Come with me," Chip said. And I followed him across the floor of the loft and into a storage room filled with bolts of cloth. The bolts were huge—over ten feet long—and stored on shelves, ceiling high. Cliff removed one of the bolts and told me to grab the other end. I did, but just barely. It was heavy and I was weak. Which instantly made me feel ashamed. Because I struggled so obviously to keep my end of the fabric bolt off the floor, I felt the words "Pansy Cake" etching into my forehead with an electric knife.

Now I was not only overwhelmed but horribly self-conscious. This combination had the effect of generating static electricity in my mind. At that moment, I couldn't have named the color of the sky.

"Bring this out here," he said, and I had no choice but to run, struggling under the weight of the canvas, to keep up.

After we got back to the main floor, Chip unfurled the bolt of fabric, allowing a good twenty-five feet. He used an industrial blade to cut the fabric from the bolt, stepping on the back of the roll so that he kept the face of the fabric clean.

"Never," he said firmly, "step on the fabric. Always, *always* step on the opposite side of the roll, here. You don't want sneaker marks all over it. Ever."

And at that moment, I was cursed to a career, however brief, of sails covered with a tango of my footprints.

Then, to my utter horror, he removed a calculator from his pocket and set it on the floor. The only use for a calculator that I'd ever had in my entire life was to use it to spell the words "Shell Oil" upside down.

"Basically, it works like this," he said. "We make custom sails. So, you gotta know about the boat before you can make a sail. I'm gonna have you work on a sail for the same boat we're working on right now. So here's the deal." He turned to face me. "Shapes for different types of sails might look the same, but there are small, important differences for every boat. You know, like the sheeting angle, spreader length, and spreader locations. These are added so that we can develop the proper twist distribution for the sail to make sure it'll sheet correctly around the individual rig."

I noticed that while his teeth were just as white as Cliff's, they weren't as straight. My teeth, I knew, were neither white nor straight. And this is all I was thinking as he continued to speak ancient Greek.

"So basically, we're looking at four different steps: two-dimensional measurements, three-dimensional shapes, panel layout and calculation, and nesting for cutting."

He squatted and removed a small pad of paper and pencil from his back pocket. Then he began to sketch some terrifying figures.

"First thing to do is input the two-dimensional numbers. The luff, leech, and then foot for what we call *mainsails*. Okay? And luff, leech, and foot," he scratched the side of his nose with the eraser of his pencil, "or luff and clew positions for the headsails.

"Then we just fill in the specifics for head width, roach, leech hollow, and the foot round. See what I mean?"

I did not see what he meant, but I nodded, which meant, "I see that you have a large Adam's apple and I am very tempted to reach over and touch it."

"So now we need a three-dimensional profile for the sail. We apply the mast bend for our mainsails. The headstay sag for headsails? This calculation we get based on the size and the geometry of our sail, along with wind force for the range of the sail, and the headstay tension."

He'd filled the page with sketches and numbers. Abstract lines and angles. A horror of mathematics.

"We define the sail shape for a few different cross sections of the sail. You know, in some ways this is a lot like certain aspects of automotive design or, probably, aviation engineering. But anyway, so these cross sections. At each of them we figure camber, which is the depth of the sail taken as a percent of its width, right? Then the distance from the leading edge right here"—he tapped his drawing— "to the point of maximum depth. The rate of the curve at any given point in the cross section. Entry angle and exit angle, then twist. This is the way to get a smooth, organic flow to the sail."

A tune was beginning to form in my head, but I couldn't quite place it. It was from a movie I'd seen recently. And the name would come to me at any moment.

"So, you got that?"

I said, "Um. I don't know."

He stood, smiling: "Yeah, I know. It might sound a little confusing at first. But believe me, you'll get it. So why don't we do this. I've sort of sketched out a simple pattern for you here. It's a jib. Just follow what I've got down here, it's just cutting, I did all the figuring out. And then call me over so I can take a look. Okay?" He smiled.

At least he was friendly.

"Okay!" I said. By raising my voice, I figured I might pass for a confident person.

He slapped me on the back and then walked away. I had the crushing urge to pee. *What just happened?*

I had no idea what to do. Was this a situation where one should walk away? Or just run?

Or, or. *Or,* should I just take a look at what he drew and see if I could figure it out?

So I glanced down at the paper he'd given me. And there, among the numbers and the lines and the strange mathematical symbols that I vaguely recognized as geometry—about which I knew not one thing, including the names of basic shapes—I saw what resembled a sail.

It was pointy on top, with two long lines going down. And then a flat base. At the heart of all his gibberish was the same little sail I'd drawn myself with crayons a hundred times as a preschooler.

So. Yeah. I could do that.

I looked at his drawing one more time. And then I looked at the cloth on the floor of the loft. And then I looked at my hand, which was somehow holding the cutting blade.

And I shrugged. And I began to cut.

Because there was a fixed amount of canvas on the floor, I assumed that this was the height he wanted the sail to be. So I started at the flat end where he had trimmed the fabric from the bolt, and then worked my way up from there, cutting away the sides of the fabric, and then tapering to create a point. I had to hack some extra fabric away at the top. But in the end, it was pretty much a point.

And yeah! It was a sail. It looked just like his picture.

Just as I had long suspected, a person didn't really need math for anything, anyway. Maybe some people did. Some *limited* people. But I was smart and resourceful, and I was able to take a sketch and turn it into reality because I understood his vision.

I decided it was time to show him my work, so I walked across the floor to where he was working on a sail of his own. I felt much more confident now. Almost a little cocky. Because I'd accomplished something.

Chip was on his knees and looked up. He said, "What's up? Got a problem?"

I smiled and said, "Nah. I finished that one. Do you have another one you want me to work on?"

He stood. "What do you mean, *you finished it?* That's impossible."

"No," I said, slightly less confident now. "I finished cutting it out. Your drawing, it was really good. It was very clear. So I finished it. I used to cut people's hair and stuff sometimes. So I'm pretty good with, you know, cutting. Pretty much."

Chip said, "I need to see what you did. How could you have finished that jib in less than," he glanced at his watch, "in less than nine minutes?"

I walked toward my sail with Chip just behind me. But before we even reached it, I began to worry. Because from this angle, approaching it from this other direction, it didn't look quite so much like what he had drawn. In fact, I could see clearly that my two cuts along the sides weren't exactly straight. But then I remembered, these things get sewn. So it's okay. Somebody can fix it.

"Holy Christ," he said. "You've just ruined a ton of fabric. What the fuck do you think you're doing? What the FUCK?"

"I had to eyeball it," I said.

"You *WHAT*?"

I said, "I had to eyeball it. You know. Look at your picture and then just try and copy it."

"I do NOT understand this. Why did you do this? How could you do such a thing? All you had to do was use some basic geometry. *Jesus.* This doesn't make any sense."

I shoved my hands in my pockets and looked down at the floor. "I don't *know* geometry," I said, now defeated. Seeing clearly how stupid I was. How delusional. "I don't know any math at all. I can't even add."

I glanced up at him and he was staring at me in disbelief. "Are you for real?"

"I tried to make it look like the picture. I guess I don't belong here."

"No, I don't suppose you do belong here, you retard. Why don't you get the hell out of here. You stupid little faggot. Go. NOW."

So I didn't have to say good-bye to the other guys or even him. I just walked across the floor.

Because Chip had been shouting, other guys had stopped working and were standing to watch me.

To save face, I walked across the floor, making sure to step across every sail in my way. I tried to hold my head high, as though I had just been promoted and would, within weeks, own the entire company.

I imagined firing all of the Chips and Cliffs and Biffs, one blond head at a time.

UNDER NEW MANAGEMENT, a sign out front would read. I would then hire all the losers and winos and misfits. And we would make a new kind of sail. The kind that maybe doesn't work as well, but was built by hand with great, white hope.